MYSTICS
OF OUR TIMES

MYSTICS
OF OUR TIMES

Hilda Graef

NOS·NE·CESSES
THOMA·TVERI

LONDON

BURNS & OATES

ORDER OF THE HOLY CROSS
WEST PARK, NEW YORK

Nihil obstat: Gall Higgins, O. F. M. Cap.
              Censor Librorum

Imprimatur: ✠ Francis Cardinal Spellman
              Archbishop of New York

              December 12, 1961

PRINTED IN HOLLAND BY N.V. GRAFISCHE INDUSTRIE HAARLEM

CONTENTS

PREFACE

It is comparatively easy to make a selection of mystics if one wishes to present those of the past; because they are generally acknowledged as such and there exists much informative literature on them. But if it comes to those of our own time, one is on very much less firm ground; it is more difficult to decide whether they can really be classed as mystics, and there are far fewer data available. It is, therefore, now my pleasant duty to thank all those who have helped me in various ways to choose and assemble the material that has gone to the making of this book, particularly Dom J. M. Beaurin, O.S.B., for his most valuable information on Père Hermann; Father A. Moynihan, O.P., for advising and supplying me with books on Edel Quinn; Father Magnus Beck, O.P., Father H. Jaeger, S.J., Father H. Nota, S.J., and Father John B. Sheerin, C.S.P., for detailed advice on several of the mystics included in this book; and last but not least, my publishers for supplying me with books on Isaac Hecker as well as for their unfailing encouragement.

Hilda Graef.

Oxford,
Trinity Sunday, 1961.

INTRODUCTION

What is a mystic? There seem many answers to this question. Some of us may think at once of a Buddhist, sitting immovable on the ground, his legs crossed under his body, his closed eyes staring, as it were, at the mysteries of his own interior. Others may think of one of the Desert Fathers, living on a few roots and berries, contemplating the divine Trinity, and fighting against demons. Or again, we may have in mind a nun of our own time, kneeling behind a Carmelite grille, rapt in prayer, or, perhaps, a lay woman lying motionless on her bed, bleeding from those strange wounds commonly called stigmata. Of such people most of us would probably think, when we hear the word "mystics."

They all have one thing in common: they are somehow taken out of our everyday world, set apart in a sphere of their own, where neither science nor technology, neither politics nor printing presses have any place, where all is silence and separation from earthly concerns. And in this mysterious sphere which they inhabit strange things may happen: there are ecstasies and visions, wonderful states to which many of our contemporaries are so irresistibly attracted that they try to procure them for themselves even by taking drugs and eating "magic mushrooms." For by such means their normal consciousness is enlarged: they are aware of things their eyes cannot see nor their ears hear in their ordinary state, and thus they think they experience what the mystics see and hear in their ecstasies.

Now we are here not concerned with these extraordinary states brought about by artificial means. Nor do we intend to discuss the mysticism of non-Christians, though we would not deny that they, too, can have genuinely mystical experiences. Here we only have in view Christian mystics. Having just briefly described the type of man or woman generally believed to be a "mystic," we would ask whether this instinctive exclusion from the mystical life of those living in the midst of our contemporary turmoil is justified. Are there mystics only in the desert or the convent—can they not be found also in offices and laboratories, in universities and factories?

If we assume that mystics must necessarily live in all but complete solitude, that most of their time must be given to prayer, and that their mystical experiences will ordinarily take the form of prolonged ecstasies making them unfit for normal work, then we must, indeed, say that in the world as it is at present the mystical life is an impossibility. But is such a view true? Does being a mystic necessitate such a separation?

In order to answer this question we must define what we mean by a "mystic." Christian theologians consider that a mystic is a man who is united to God in an experimental fashion. That is to say, he does not only know by faith that God dwells in him through His grace and through the sacraments, but he "experiences" this divine Presence within him in such a way that he is really aware of it, not, of course, through his bodily senses, as he is aware of the world around him, but through some interior faculty, if we may so call it. This divine Presence may make itself felt by a deep peace absorbing all his faculties, or it may suddenly invade him so forcefully that he is unable even to move, it may communicate quite new insights or it may give superhuman strength —but always the man in contact with this divine Presence will realize that it is not himself who produces this new life in him. Naturally, this realization is subject to error: there have been many men and women who thought they were in contact with God while their experiences were due only to their own conscious or subconscious imaginings. Therefore mystical theologians have worked out a number of tests by which to distinguish between genuine supernatural experiences and their counterfeits.

First of all, there is Christ's own axiom: by their fruits you shall know them. If someone is supposed to be a mystic, but does not lead a particularly holy life; if he seeks fame, if he is more concerned with his own reputation than with the Kingdom of God, if he is lacking in charity and humility, then, whatever strange experiences may be ascribed to him, he is certainly not a mystic. Nevertheless, there may be very holy people, and yet their visions may frequently be due to their own—conscious or subconscious—imagination. Here the second principle applies, which has been worked out especially by the Doctor of mystical theology, St. John of the Cross: the less the imagination comes into play, the higher the mystical experience. To give an example: one person has a very detailed vision of the Passion, seeing Our Lord, the soldiers crucifying, the Pharisees insulting Him, being able to describe even the colour of their clothes and the movements of their bodies. According to St. John of the Cross, such a vision would be of very little value, and we know that many visionaries have given mutually contradictory descriptions of such biblical events. On the other hand, if a man has what is called an "intellectual" vision, in which a profound insight into the meaning and value of Christ's sufferings is directly impressed on his mind without any imaginary details, then this vision will have a far greater worth, because human fancies cannot falsify it.

To be a mystic it is, therefore, not necessary to have many varied "experiences"; indeed, the fewer colourful visions and spectacular ecstasies or other phenomena, the less the danger of becoming a victim of illusions. For the mystical union is, above all, the spiritual awareness of being intimately united to God. This is the effect of an intense love between God and man, which in its turn expresses itself in a very delicate conscience, constant fight against even the slightest faults and great charity and apostolic zeal.

But, it may be objected, does not this description fit any

Christian saint? Does it not make "mystic" and "saint" inter-changeable terms? I should certainly say that in order to be a mystic, a Christian must already have acquired a high degree of virtue, but that this need not be sufficient for canonization. Without a great love of God it is impossible to be a mystic —for the centre of the mystical life is precisely the intimate, loving union with God, and Christ Himself has said: "If you love me, keep my commandments"; there is no other way to love Him but through obedience to His laws. But what about the reverse: must every saint be a mystic? This does not follow necessarily either, just as a mystic need not be a canonizable saint. A man may practise all the virtues to an heroic degree and perform the prescribed miracles after his death, yet God may withhold from him, for reasons of His own, the *experienced* union with Himself, which He may nevertheless accord to another person of lesser virtue. Yet, I should think, most saints will have experienced the mys-tical union with God. Why then do so many people not think of, say, St. Ignatius of Loyola as a mystic? This is due to the fact that he and many other saints like him are more noted for their active works. These were, indeed, the out-come of their intense mystical life, but this was, quite natu-rally, unknown to a wider public. We know of the mystics mostly through their own or their disciples' writings. Where these do not exist, we simply have not the material from which to judge whether they were mystics or not, unless we can get some glimpse here and there, from some unguarded remarks or notable incidents, which may convince us that they were, indeed, mystics.

And now we can perhaps approach with greater confi-dence the question whether it is really possible that there should be mystics in our own time who are interested in the modern world, concerned with our own problems, using modern inventions and being "contemporary" in the best sense of the word.

If the essence of the mystical life is the intimate union with God there is nothing to prevent it from being lived also in the circumstances of our times. True, intense prayer may be easier behind the grille of a convent; but as the felt union with Him is a gift of God there is no reason why He should not give it also to those who seek to please Him in the bustle of the "world" which, after all, was made by Him. ("World" is here, of course, taken as the divinely made cosmos, not in the pejorative sense of "the world, the flesh and the devil.") Indeed, it would seem that precisely because our world is so distracting and, at the same time, so desperately in need of God, He will give very special graces to those who, whether as priests or laymen, have been called to work for Him in this world and who must use those means contemporary society has placed at their disposal.

It is the purpose of the present book to prove the truth of this statement. We have therefore selected a number of men and women from various walks of life whose activities in the "world" have not prevented them from being true mystics. We have deliberately left out those living behind convent grilles, such as, for example, St. Thérèse of Lisieux or Elisabeth of the Trinity, because their mode of life has not changed since the Middle Ages. And we have confined our selection to the last century and a half, from the beginnings of the machine age to our own "atomic" days. We have further refrained from laying too much stress on mystical phenomena—not only because in some cases, such as that of Edel Quinn, for example, the evidence is extremely scanty—but also because these phenomena are, as we have seen, not the most important facts in the mystical life, and, further, because this book is more concerned to show that the mystical life is possible also in our own everyday world.

In this way we shall see that the problems with which we are faced are also the problems of our mystics. In fact, their way of tackling them may very often be an inspiration to ourselves. To take just a few examples: Africa is very much in the news today, and our politicians are wrestling with great difficulties; native aspirations on the one hand, "white" prejudices on the other. Francis Libermann, Charles de Foucauld, Edel Quinn were each one of them deeply concerned with these vital questions, the integration of these world-wide preoccupations with their own personal spiritual life should be of paramount interest today. To take another problem: the combination of a professional life with mystical experience. A brilliant university professor and a bank manager show how these two can be combined in a world where the layman is no longer a theological and spiritual "minor" but takes his active place in the Church of today which encourages the lay apostolate.

Again, in our time the institution of marriage is under fire: divorce is more and more taken for granted: a married woman has found that not only the vows of religion, but also the marriage vows can be a foundation on which to build the mystical life.

The press, too, so often an instrument of pandering to materialism and even atheism, can become a means of sanctification in the hands of a mystic. Father Hecker in the nineteenth century, and the Polish martyr Maximilian Kolbe in the twentieth, saw the tremendous possibilities of the printed word in the service of God, not only for spreading the Truth among those who did not know it, but also for sanctifying those engaged in this work.

Finally science, this much maligned subject. Can a scientist be a mystic—can he subscribe to the hypothesis of evolution and yet be united to God in the same way as the great contemplatives of the past? Our last chapter on Teilhard de Chardin will give the answer to that. For God, the Father of Christ, is also the Creator of the universe, and through the divine Word which was to become incarnate in Jesus of Nazareth He made heaven and earth.

Since the Renaissance this world and man in it have played an ever increasing part in our thought. In the sixteenth, seventeenth, and eighteenth centuries the mystics tended to shut themselves away from this world, which seemed to encroach so much on the prerogatives of its Creator. Even a man like St. Francis of Sales could not swim against the stream and, contrary to his own wishes, had to enclose his contemplative nuns of the Visitation behind the customary walls and grilles. Christians needed a long time to accustom themselves to the changing world—and the process of adaptation is not completed even now. They could not realize at once that the "new" universe—so different from the neat little world of the Middle Ages with the earth in the centre and sun, moon, and stars moving round it—was still the world that God had made. It also took time to get used to the disappearance of the feudal order and the fact that Europe had ceased to be synonymous with Christendom.

But all these changes, so often seen only in their negative aspects, held also tremendous promises. And it was the mystics, whose intimate union with God gave them a clearer insight, who first realized these positive sides of modern developments. While the Roman Curia still thought of America as a den of dangerous revolutionaries and materialists, Father Hecker recognized its great spiritual possibilities; while his Franciscan brethren wanted to confine their apostolate to the old-established means of preaching and hearing confessions, Father Kolbe saw the need for popular magazines; while evolution was still widely regarded as directly opposed to Christian doctrine, Teilhard de Chardin sought ways to integrate it with the Catholic view of the world.

And so the following chapters will present men and women whose lives will seem very different from those of earlier mystics—though we should remember that a Francis of Assisi, a Catherine of Siena, were also intensely concerned with the needs of their time. A mystic, like any other human being, is a child of his time, and he will normally be a "realist," because he is more intensely aware of the presence of God in the world than other Christians. Because of this awareness, he will often see Him also where his fellowmen can only see frustration or even sin—just as Christ Himself saw the good in men despised by the Pharisees.

Time and again new inventions have been regarded by devout Christians as the "work of the devil"—from printing to the splitting of the atom. And this negative attitude of her less enlightened children has often caused great damage to the Church. We hope that, among other things, the following pages will also show that just the most spiritual Christians are often those most widely open to all that is good in science, in scholarship, in technology, in social reforms—in short, in what is generally called "progress." For, in the Christian view, history moves from an irretrievable state of innocence through the Redemption forward to the final consummation of the "new heaven and the new earth." It is, therefore, a "progressive" religion in the best sense, just as the individual Christian can never rest content with past achievements but has to press forward to higher goals.

It is the great evil of our time that our tremendous material progress has not been accompanied by equal spiritual progress; on the contrary, that through a wrong use of our material achievements our spiritual standards have been lowered. The proper balance can only be restored through a great spiritual revival which, while fully appreciating all the positive gains of our age, will call attention to the basic principle pronounced by Christ Himself when He told the Tempter—and us—that man does not live by bread, that is to say by material things, alone. The mystics of our times have acknowledged this and have, in their own lives, set us an example how to reconcile the claims of God with those of our age, more, how to use all our opportunities, so much greater than those our ancestors had, in the service not of "mammon," as we are so often tempted to do, but of God.

MYSTICS
OF OUR TIMES

CHAPTER ONE

Father Francis Libermann

(1802–1852)

The life of the first of the mystics to be discussed here already sounds some of the themes that will occur again and again during the century and a half in which the subjects of this book lived their union with God. Africa, the continent that has become so problematical today, and the psychology of the black man loomed large in Father Libermann's thought. More, he himself was a nervous subject who had to husband his strength—not for him the hair shirts and severe scourgings that had played such an important role in the lives of earlier mystics. And, thirdly, he was a Jew, one of the first of the race of Christ to play a highly significant role in the modern Church.

Jacob Libermann was the son of a rabbi at Saverne, in Alsace and grew up in an atmosphere of strictest orthodoxy. Centuries of ghetto life had narrowed the conception of the Jewish religion to such an extent that the Jews were not only forbidden the study of Latin and Greek but even the use of Latin characters. Though Jacob could speak both German and French, he only knew the Hebrew alphabet, and his literary knowledge was confined to the Old Testament, the Talmud, and the other Jewish books.

The shadow of his father, Lazarus, loomed large over Jacob's childhood. He lost his mother, Lea, when he was only eleven, and a year later his father married again; but his step-mother, Sarah, could not take Lea's place in the boy's heart. He became all the more closely united to his five brothers, especially the eldest, Samson, twelve years his senior. In April 1815 Jacob was the centre of a great religious celebration: the Bar Mitzvah, his confirmation, when he was allowed for the first time to intone in public Old Testament readings and when he was given the tephillin, that is to say the leather straps which, at the time of prayer, every pious Jew affixes to his left wrist and his forehead. They contain the so-called Shema (Deuteronomy 6:4f) and some other Scriptural passages, in literal obedience to the text of Deuteronomy 6:8: "And thou shalt bind them as a sign on thy hand, and they shall be and shall move between thy eyes."

The religious ceremony was followed by a festive meal in the house of Rabbi Libermann, who pinned great hopes on his favourite son. For his eldest, Samson, who had been meant to follow in his father's footsteps had abandoned the rabbinic career and decided to study medicine, and his third son, Henoch, had become a soldier in the French army, careers little to the liking of their pious father. Jacob showed great promise, and so the rabbi instructed him carefully in the Talmud and, in 1822, sent him to Metz, to continue his studies at the famous rabbinic schools of that city.

Rabbi Libermann did not doubt that Jacob would receive the full benefit from the education he had provided for him and return from Metz a pious and learned rabbi, ready to make a name for himself among the Jews of France and Germany. He had been given two introductions, one to Rabbi Scholom, in whose house he was supposed to stay, another to a Hebrew scholar, Abraham Lubinowitz, who was to super-vise his studies. Jacob had scarcely arrived in Metz when he met with his first great disappointment. Rabbi Scholom, a selfish old man who disliked having his routine upset, refused point-blank to receive him into his house, and Lubinowitz had to find him lodgings. Jacob, who had hardly any money, chose the cheapest room in the boarding house recommended by his mentor and embarked with great zeal on his studies. His fellow lodgers were both orthodox and liberal Jews; against the latter he had been warned emphatically by Lubinowitz, who was fanatical in his rejection of anything that smacked, however slightly, of the culture of the *goiim* (Gentiles). Jacob had no intention of letting himself be contaminated by them; nevertheless, living in the same house with students of very different opinions, it was not easy to avoid all contact with them. One of them, Joseph Titescher, a man much older than himself, had a decisive influence on him. He informed Jacob that all those old-fashioned restrictions which denied the orthodox Jews any share in the learning of the Gentiles were both silly and detrimental to their own cause, and he read him some passages from Latin and Greek authors whose very names Jacob had never heard before.

The young rabbi in the making was deeply disturbed, and unburdened his heart to his brother Samson, by then married and practising medicine at Strasbourg. To his utter surprise, Samson agreed entirely with Titescher, and so in 1824 Jacob, who was becoming increasingly bored with his Talmudic studies, began to learn Latin and Greek and to read the classical authors. The unknown world that opened before him held him spellbound; the Talmud and his commentators were abandoned, and Jacob immersed himself with growing ardour in the dangerous heritage of the *goiim*.

When, by an unfortunate accident, his tutor Lubinowitz found out that his pupil had exchanged the Talmud for the classical authors he flew into a violent rage, forbade Jacob his house, and threatened to inform his father. For weeks the young man was living in constant fear that Lubinowitz might carry out his threat; but nothing happened. In the meantime he made friends with another liberal Jew, this time of his own age, Lazarus Libmann. Libmann was studying law, for which, of course, he had to read Latin and French. He encouraged Jacob to forget all about Lubinowitz and continue his classical studies. One day he brought home a New Testament in Hebrew, and the two friends read it together. It made, however, little impression on them, though they thought much of its teaching very beautiful.

For some time Jacob had felt unable to accept the miracles as well as much else in the Old Testament. By 1824 he had begun to lose his Jewish faith. There was as yet nothing that could take its place, and so he fell into a deep melancholy. Later in the year he received a letter from Samson which left him speechless: his brother with his wife and children had been baptized into the Catholic Church. Rabbi Libermann was completely broken by the defection of his eldest son from the faith of his forefathers; Jacob himself was badly upset and had one of the worst of his headaches, to which he had been subject ever since his boyhood. There ensued a long correspondence between the two brothers, in which Samson replied carefully to all Jacob's objections. For the latter now did not only study the classics, but also the works of French unbelievers like Voltaire. Strangely enough it was one of these unbelievers, Rousseau, who first drew his attention to the possibility that Christ might be what the Christians said He was; in the fourth book of his *Emile* (in "La profession de foi du Vicaire Savoyard") Rousseau discusses the reasons for and against the Divinity of Christ and concludes: "I have not so far been in a position to know what a rabbi of Amsterdam would reply to this." Jacob found that he had no answer either.

At Easter 1826 two more of his brothers, Felkel, who took the name of Felix, and Samuel, who became Alphonse, were baptized in Paris. This time he was even more shaken than at the conversion of Samson. For he loved his brothers dearly and felt that he would soon be completely isolated—only he and his father and his sisters would remain Jews. He became more and more depressed. When he confided his difficulties to his friend Lazarus Libmann, he advised Jacob to go to Paris to discuss matters with David Drach, a convert rabbi who had been baptized in 1823 and was at that moment professor of Hebrew at the Collège Stanislas. Jacob went back to Saverne to ask his father's permission. The rabbi, who knew nothing of Jacob's doubts, was delighted with the plan, for he hoped that Jacob would bring his two brothers back into the Jewish fold. He gave him a letter of introduction to Monsieur Deutz, the chief rabbi of Paris, and sent him on his way with his blessing.

Jacob stopped at Strasbourg to visit his brother Samson, whom he had not seen since Samson left their home at Saverne, and his wife Babette with their children. They received him with great warmth, though he was a little disconcerted when Babette told him that they were all praying very hard for his conversion. He was even more staggered when, before his departure for Paris, Babette suddenly told him: "In Paris everything will become quite clear. You will not only become a Christian, you will become a priest."

Nevertheless, Jacob was determined to see Rabbi Deutz, but to avoid Monsieur Drach. He simply could not disappoint his father, who trusted him so completely and who had already been so cruelly hit by the defection of three of his sons. In Paris he stayed with his brother Felkel, who had become a bookbinder and was supporting himself, as he had been cut off from his inheritance like his two convert brothers. The first long conversation with Felkel brought about another of Jacob's severe headaches. When he awoke next morning, rather than going to Rabbi Deutz as he had intended, he called instead on Monsieur Drach at the Collège Stanislas. The convert rabbi received him with great enthusiasm: he had been expected, a room was ready for him—when would he come to make a retreat to find out what God wanted him to do? Before Jacob quite knew what he had done he had agreed that he would come the following Friday. The next day he paid Rabbi Deutz a short visit, delivering his father's letter but already determined not to see him again. Then he went to the college to make his retreat.

Monsieur Drach provided several books, the New Testament, of course, as well as a history of Christian doctrine, showed him the garden and the refectory, and then left him severely alone. His complete solitude, the silence of the seminary, the absence of any occupation except reading and prayer, and, above all, his terrible uncertainty of what he was going to do produced at first a state of profound depression and anxiety. He prayed desperately that the God of his fathers should enlighten him, that He should make it clear to him whether the faith of the Christians was the true faith; that, if it were not, God should prevent him from embracing it.

After several weeks of uncertainty his prayer was suddenly answered with overwhelming certainty: "I saw the truth; the faith penetrated my spirit and my heart." He read the History of Christian Doctrine and found that none of the teachings of the Church presented any difficulty to him; he believed everything and had only the one desire to become a Christian. He was baptized on Christmas Eve, 1826, taking the names François-Marie-Paul. When the water was running over his forehead he saw an immense ball of fire and felt that he was no longer living only by his natural life: "Things impossible to describe were taking place within me. . . . All my uncertainties and fears vanished instantly . . . I felt a courage and an invincible power to practise the Christian Law . . . at that moment I loved Mary, whom I had hated before."

Francis Libermann, as he now was, had indeed need of these mystical graces to sustain the trials that were to come. As soon as he had been baptized he also knew that he must become a priest. Monsieur Drach arranged for him to enter the seminary of the Collège Stanislas and raised the necessary funds. He also advised him to delay informing his father of the step he had taken, so as to spare both of them the profound distress this announcement was bound to cause.

At Stanislas Francis threw himself into his studies with great zest. He was liked by most of his fellòw-seminarians, though one of them, Bernard Tellier, started a minor persecution of his own: how could Francis, who had hardly been baptized, aspire to the priesthood? Did his Jewish relatives know what he was doing? No? Was it not then terribly imprudent, indeed presumptuous, to embrace a vocation on which even cradle Catholics only decided after years of preparation and mature reflection? One night, after some particularly bitter remarks from Tellier, Francis had not only a very bad attack of his headaches, but also lost consciousness for a few moments. When he reported this to his brother Samson, the doctor advised him to work less and rest more, as he was evidently suffering from a nervous complaint. He persevered, and on June 9, 1827, he received the tonsure at the cathedral of Notre Dame.

The Collège Stanislas was an exclusively missionary seminary, a fact of which Francis, who felt no inclination to become a missionary, had been unaware. So, in autumn of the same year, he was transferred to the famous seminary of St. Sulpice, for which the archbishop of Paris granted him a bursary. He was very happy there and spent much time in prayer and study. Towards the end of 1827 he received a fearful shock: a letter arrived from his father, who had heard of his conversion. He pleaded with Francis to return to the Jewish fold; if he failed to do so he would curse him for ever. This letter brought about one of his violent headaches, but he was nevertheless able to receive minor orders before Christmas. Not much later, Lazarus Libermann, brokenhearted at the defection of his favourite son who in his turn loved his father dearly, died without having forgiven him. Francis threw himself into hard work and intensified his prayers, with the result that he frequently suffered from dizziness. After a long rest in the summer he was much better and in Advent 1828 prepared himself to receive the first of the major orders leading to the priesthood, the subdiaconate.

The seminarians of St. Sulpice were at recreation, which

owing to the bad weather took place in a hall. There a letter
was brought to Francis. He recognized the handwriting; it
was from his brother Henoch. Francis went aside to read it.
It contained the most violent reproaches he had ever had: he,
Francis, was responsible for their father's death because of his
unpardonable apostasy from their faith—would he please now
refrain at least from adding to this the most horrible insult of
becoming a Catholic priest. Francis, deadly pale, returned to
join his fellow seminarians. Suddenly he fell to the ground,
his face distorted, foaming at the mouth, his limbs horribly
convulsed. When his violent movements finally stopped his
fellow seminarians carried him to the infirmary. At last his
nervous disease had declared itself: he was an epileptic, and
epilepsy is a canonical obstacle to ordination.

By 1829 all knew that Francis Libermann could not now
become a priest; it seemed to him that the curse of his father
was taking effect. His superiors advised him to embrace another career, but he felt this to be impossible. He was sure
God wanted him to serve Him alone. So it was decided that
he should stay on at the seminary to await developments. But
the seizures continued with varying intensity. Francis, who
had gathered a circle of friends who sought his advice and to
whom he was in the habit of giving spiritual talks, lost nearly
all of them. For during his attacks he looked quite frightening;
his companions were embarrassed to speak to him afterwards,
for epilepsy, like certain other nervous diseases, has a different
effect on others from that of merely physical illnesses. To be
subject to such fearful seizures was intensely humiliating; it
seemed that a man who would suddenly writhe in helpless
convulsions on the floor could not really be the holy, perfectly
disciplined person they had thought him to be. Francis bore
his misfortune with a serenity which surprised his doctor, as
epileptic seizures usually produce severe melancholy. During
the summer of 1830, which he spent partly at the villa
Solitude, the summer house of St. Sulpice, he had only slight
attacks. While there he heard the guns of the July revolution
in Paris, which once more disrupted the life of the nation and

also caused great losses to the Church. When things had quietened down, the seminarians returned to the capital. Francis was dispensed from most of the lectures and instead was asked to give help to the newcomers. In December, when some of his friends were ordained subdeacons, he had yet another major crisis, which greatly perturbed the young seminarians under his care.

His hopes that, despite everything, he might yet be admitted to the priesthood, became increasingly slender. Yet he had evidently a vocation to help in the sanctification of priests, as his superiors realized quite well, since they continued to entrust others to his care. In 1831 he had a vision—a very rare occurrence in his spiritual life—which seemed to express this vocation, though he did not know whether it meant that he himself would never become a priest or the reverse. On July 20, when St. Sulpice celebrated the feast of the priesthood of Christ, Our Lord appeared to him during the High Mass as the eternal Priest and, from his treasure, distributed spiritual graces to the seminarians. Only Francis received nothing. But, when Jesus had finished, He turned to Libermann and entrusted him with the whole treasure. At first Francis took this to mean his permanent exclusion from the priesthood; only later did the real meaning become clear to him.

After long deliberations the archbishop of Paris finally decided to withdraw his bursary. When his superior asked Francis what he was going to do he simply said he was sure God would look after him. His evident holiness had made a deep impression; and so at the end of December 1831, St. Sulpice decided to send him to their house at Issy, to help with the spiritual formation of the students there.

During this time the effects of the disease showed themselves in sudden temptations to suicide, especially when he had to cross a bridge over a river; it cost him all his strength to keep a grip on himself and not to take the quick jump that would set him free from all his misery. Despite these sudden attacks of despair his health improved, as he was given much work out of doors. Besides, his Jewish business

sense proved a godsend to his superiors, who soon entrusted
him with most of the financial affairs of the seminary. But
these rather worldly duties in no way impinged on his
spiritual life and influence. The July revolution had resulted in
a slackening of discipline; therefore he organized "bands of
piety," that is, special groups within the seminary for the most
fervent of the students, as a means of raising the spiritual level
of the whole community. The attacks he suffered at this time
were frequent but very mild; there were no major crises. In
January 1835 he could write to his brother Samson: "My
health is all right, I have not had an accident for a year.
Nevertheless I am not cured, and I do not think God wants
me in the priesthood. If He calls me to it, I am His; He knows
that I am ready to do whatever pleases Him."

In October of the same year two young men entered the
seminary at Issy who were destined to give his life a wholly
new direction. They were Creoles; Frederic Le Vavasseur,
also a convert from Judaism, and Eugene Tisserant from Haiti.
They awakened his interest in the missions and urged him to
form a new missionary society, an idea which attracted him,
though he could not see at that moment how it was going to be
carried out, as there was as yet no hope that he might be
ordained after all.

In May 1837 another of his brothers became a Christian:
Henoch, whose dreadful letter of reproach had once brought
about the first great epileptic seizure. Now Henoch apolo-
gized very contritely for what he had then written. A few
months later the rabbi's sixth son, David, also came into the
Church; and this conversion did much to disperse the melancholy that had seized Francis after another very severe attack
in March. In the summer of the same year he received an offer
that surprised him greatly: the Eudists, a congregation mainly
devoted to education, which had been almost extinguished by
the French revolution of 1789 and had been reconstituted in
1826, were looking for a novice master for their noviciate at
Rennes. His superiors suggested Francis, despite his illness,

despite his still only being in minor orders—surely a most impressive tribute to his spiritual stature.

So, in September 1837, Francis, much to the regret of his two Creole friends, went to Rennes to take up his new duties. Very conscientiously he familiarized himself with the teaching and constitutions of the congregation, which did not differ very much from those of the Sulpicians. Both belonged to the so-called École Française, a school of spirituality which concentrated on the interior states and virtues of Jesus and Mary. At Rennes he was delighted with the fervent atmosphere, while he himself was plunged into intense desolation. As so often happens in the lives of the mystics, exterior and interior trials came together. He found it difficult to get on with the superior, Monsieur Louis, while one of the novices conceived such an extraordinary hatred for him that it could only be called diabolic. However, his greatest affliction was the interior conviction that he was completely useless, that he himself was the cause of all these external difficulties which made his life almost unbearable at that time. "The sufferings which the conduct of this noviciate caused me were so great," he wrote later, "that I should never have thought to be able to bear them. But I can tell you that the greatest of all was to realize that I was quite useless to the Church of God." This situation had at least partly been caused by a major seizure in February 1838. At a conference on one of the feasts of the congregation Francis was asked to say a few words. He had hardly begun when he fell to the ground, and for three quarters of an hour was writhing on the floor, in the sight of the whole seminary, both students and professors, foaming at the mouth, his features distorted and his limbs convulsed. His speech, which had frequently been impeded, now became even worse; sometimes he had to begin a sentence seven or eight times before he could finish it.

In July he was visited by Le Vavasseur, who entreated him not to abandon the plan of the missionary society, for which he had enlisted several new members. Francis hesitated. Many things, above all his continued illness, seemed to militate against undertaking such a difficult enterprise. In the meantime his difficulties at Rennes did not diminish. In the summer of 1839 he went to Issy to discuss the matter still further. There he found a very capable young man, Monsieur de la Brunière, the nephew of a bishop, who had joined the missionary circle. On his return to Rennes he finally received an interior illumination that this was the work God meant him to do. He decided to leave Rennes on December 3, the feast of St. Francis Xavier, patron of the missions.

On November 30th he informed the superior of the Eudist house by letter of his plan, for he felt that he could not trust his nerves sufficiently to explain in person to Monsieur Louis, to whom he had always found it difficult to speak. The superior fumed: it was all due to self-love and pride, Rennes seemed not good enough for Francis, nothing would come of this mad idea of founding a new missionary society. Francis stood firm. Although, from the natural point of view, his contemplative nature dreaded the difficulties and ceaseless activities such a work was bound to entail, yet he was completely sure that it was the will of God for him. He wrote to Samson from Lyons, just a week after leaving Rennes: "I have left Rennes for ever. This is very imprudent —not to say foolish—in the eyes of those who judge matters according to the standards of this world. I had a secure future; I was certain of my livelihood and even of an honourable existence. But woe to me if I seek to be happy on this earth, to be held in honour and esteem. . . . I have left Rennes. I have nobody on earth in whom I could trust. I have nothing, I do not know what will become of me, even how I shall be able to live; I shall lead a life which, in the eyes of the world, is despicable, forgotten, neglected and lost. Many of those who have once loved and esteemed me will disapprove of me; I shall perhaps be treated like a madman, be despised and even persecuted. . . . I cannot tell you at the moment what God demands of me. I will only say that I shall carry on with what He, in his infinite goodness, has inspired me to do."

This letter is evidently written under the violent emotional strain of his departure from Rennes against the will of the superior. He would not tell his brother what he was going to do: in fact he had decided to go to Rome to try to get his plan for a new missionary society approved. He travelled together with Monsieur de la Brunière, who made himself responsible for their expenses. During his journey Francis had many misfortunes. One of the ecclesiastics, whom Monsieur Louis had advised him to consult about his plans, simply laughed out loud; another, whose Mass he wanted to serve, sent him away because his clothes were too shabby. Deeply discouraged he arrived in Rome. But there his old friend Monsieur Drach, who had since been made librarian to the Office of Propaganda, visited him and arranged an audience with Gregory XVI for him and Abbé de la Brunière, which took place on February 17, 1840. The Pope was deeply impressed with Libermann's personality, encouraged him to continue with his missionary plans and placed his hand on his head in blessing. After he and De la Brunière had left, the Pope asked Monsieur Drach who was the man whose head he had touched. Drach gave a brief outline of his history, and Gregory XVI remarked: "*Sara un santo* [This is a saint]."

In March the Secretary of Propaganda gave Francis permission to present a memorandum on his ideas for the new society; but later he was told that before anything could be decided he must be ordained priest. About the same time Monsieur de la Brunière became discouraged; he complained that he was completely isolated and that even "dear Monsieur Libermann" did not understand him; so he decided to go back to France, leaving Francis some money to keep him going. He died a martyr in Manchuria in 1846. Libermann at once moved into much poorer quarters, a miserable attic where he lived in extreme poverty. He spent his days praying and composing a spiritual commentary on the first twelve chapters of St. John's Gospel, where he found the Person of Christ revealed more clearly than in the Synoptics. Moreover, he

drew up a provisional rule for his proposed Society and
carried on his considerable spiritual correspondence; for
though he still was only an acolyte, his spiritual advice was
sought by a growing number of seminarians and also by his
young nephews and nieces, whom he directed with great
patience and understanding.

While he was waiting for developments, the memorandum
he had sent to the Congregation of Propaganda was being
carefully studied, and one day he received a letter with
favourable comments on his plan and expressing the hope that
God would give him sufficient health to become a priest. At
the same time he received news from France that the Irish
Benedictine Bishop Collier, Vicar Apostolic of Mauritius, was
looking for missionaries and was prepared to accept him for
his vicariate.

To obtain a decisive light on his vocation he went on foot
to Loretto, the famous sanctuary of Mary. Again he suffered
many humiliations during this pilgrimage on account of the
poverty of his dress and his humble bearing. He describes
himself once as a "very poor man, both physically and
morally. My external appearance is so wretched that several
times during my journeyings I have been taken for a
criminal and almost was put in prison as such." At Loretto
he prayed almost uninterruptedly for seven days, until he had
the inner certainty that it was God's will that he should
become a priest and found his missionary society, *L'Oeuvre
des Noirs* [The Work of the Blacks]. So, in January 1841,
he went back to France.

He entered the seminary at Strasbourg, where his brother
Samson gave him much valuable assistance, and finally reached
the goal he had desired for so long and was ordained priest on
September 18, 1841, at the age of thirty-nine, not without
some opposition from certain quarters in Paris, where he was
regarded as an adventurer. At his ordination, as at his baptism,
he received mystic graces. Immediately after the ceremony he
writes to Samson: "I was ordained priest this morning. God
knows what I have received on this great day. God alone

knows it, for neither man nor angel can imagine it." And on the same day he tells another correspondent: "Today immense and innumerable graces have descended on me, and I am almost submerged by them: May God grant that I remain as it were drenched in his grace and his divine love."

Purified through much suffering and long years of waiting, Père Libermann was now ready to begin in earnest the immense work which had first been suggested to him by his two Creole students, Frederic Le Vavasseur and Eugene Tisserant. The new Missionary Society began in a small country house at Neuville-les-Amiens, of which Francis took possession on September 27, nine days after his ordination.

He began with two companions, one of them Le Vavasseur (Tisserant was still kept in parish work for some time), whom he trained very carefully, according to the provisional Rule he had drawn up in Rome. The congregation was consecrated to the Holy Heart of Mary: it was to be animated by Mary's own love of Christ and her apostolic zeal, which would overcome all differences of race and class: "We shall do all we can to establish between rich and poor, whites and blacks that Christian charity which brings it about that all men consider themselves brothers in Jesus Christ, so as to extinguish scorn and indifference on the one hand, jealousy and hatred on the other. But this needs great prudence, so as not to lose all."

Father Libermann knew the Christian principles by which his missionaries must be guided—he knew also the difficulties they would have to encounter, both among the pagans and among those who called themselves Christians but whose way of life was sadly at variance with the teachings of their Master. And the missionaries themselves often showed all too human tendencies. Le Vavasseur, though very devoted to his superior, caused trouble because in his view the Rule was not strict enough; he easily flew into tempers, and Father Libermann often found it difficult to calm him. He left for his native Bourbon in the summer of 1842, while the noviciate at Neuville was attracting an ever growing number of aspirants. Father Libermann not only instructed them in the Rule, but even taught them cooking and housekeeping, accomplishments which they would badly need out in the missions, with no one to look after them.

In autumn 1842 Eugène Tisserant was finally allowed to join him; after a short training period he left for Tahiti. So both Father Libermann's earliest companions had gone away, but others came to take their place, among them Ignatius Schwindenhammer, a solid Alsatian who entered in September 1843 and became a great help to Libermann, who said of him that he was "an excellent subject, of outstanding piety, very capable, a good counsellor and well versed in business." He needed a trusted helper, for soon the missionaries out in the West Indies ran into difficulties. There were grave political disturbances which made their work almost impossible. But immediately another sphere open to him: he met Bishop Barron, an Irish-American who had been appointed vicar apostolic for the two Guineas and who was looking for missionaries.

So Father Libermann sent his disciples out to Africa. But the venture met with one catastrophe after another. The climate was murderous; many of the young missionaries—and just the best—succumbed to pernicious cerebral fevers and typhoid. But the founder did not lose courage, though he called his new mission field "our beloved and crucifying Guinea," which "must be saved whatever the cost." For he regarded·the Negroes of Africa as the most abandoned of men, enslaved and exploited; therefore they must be brought the light and love of Christ even in the face of all but insurmountable difficulties. By 1844 it had become clear to him that the greatest need was for a native clergy—a revolutionary idea at that time. In July he writes to Mère Javouhey, herself an experienced missionary and foundress of the Sisters of St. Joseph of Cluny that ". . . a native clergy . . . is the most useful and the most important matter, to which we must devote ourselves with all our strength." In November of the same year he returns to the subject in a letter to Le

Vavasseur: "Without a native clergy it is absolutely impossible to bring salvation to these lands." In contrast to many of his contemporaries he considered the Negroes perfectly capable of becoming priests. Though he himself never left Europe, he studied carefully all the reports and came to the conclusion that "the black men are no less intelligent than the other races," that all they were lacking was the centuries of culture and education the whites had behind them: "The black men are by nature gentle and docile." If they are immoral, it is due to the bad influence of the Europeans who have taught them to drink alcohol and to indulge in other vices. "Their race," he writes, "has suffered so much from us haughty Europeans that it would be an immense happiness for me to do all I can to make amends for the wrong the White men have done."

But his charity was not confined only to the Negroes; it extended to all who, today, are called "the underprivileged." Though the son of Rabbi Lazarus had become a most devoted son of the Church, he nevertheless could not agree with all ecclesiastical regulations. His strongly developed social sense revolted, for example, against the exclusion from the religious life of illegitimate children. He failed to understand the severity of the Church's rules on this point. In fact, these children being far more exposed to temptation than those who grow up in a well-ordered family, he felt that they needed all the more the security the religious life would give them: "I find here a veritable non-sense, a thought that contradicts the spirit of the Gospel. . . . The spirit of the world has been mixed up with the spirit of Our Lord. . . . The world remains always the world; and if it is religious, it mingles the worldly with the religious spirit. The founders of Orders were obliged to give way to the prejudices of the world in order to succeed in their plans; the Church itself had to conform to this in the choice of her priests for fear of being despised. But today this danger no longer exists."[1]

[1] Illegitimacy is still a canonical obstacle to the priesthood and the religious life, but can be dispensed if circumstances warrant it.

In the midst of his many activities and despite his illness Father Libermann never neglected his spiritual life, though he did not like to speak about it. Nevertheless, his spiritual writings and letters allow us glimpses into his soul, for much of what he describes is obviously his own experience. Writing about the Blessed Sacrament, he says, for example: "A powerful force emanates from the tabernacle which exercises such a vehement attraction that one fears to be dragged out of one's place. It seems, in fact, that if this attraction increased one would have to yield to it and would be veritably removed and pressed against the tabernacle. . . . Tears flow in torrents and the delights are immense. This attraction may last fairly long, about half an hour, sometimes more, at other times less." A little further on he writes that "a soul in this state of prayer will have ardent colloquies with the Blessed Virgin. Sometimes it will be reduced to a state of extreme weakness, being scarcely able to breathe on account of its fervent desires and sentiments. It would like to speak most tenderly with its divine Mother all day long."

Libermann knew, however, that these transports of love are not essential to the mystical life; that periods of dryness are not only bound to come but that they can be most fruitful for a man's spiritual development. In line with the great mystics like St. Teresa of Avila and St. John of the Cross, he holds that the phenomenon of "ecstasy is actually a weakness, which is due to the frailty of our organs; but that which causes the ecstasy (that is to say the divine action) is a great favour of God, an eminent grace of divine love which normally produces great effects in the soul. . . . It is rare, however, that this lasts for a long time. It may last for two or three years, but even this seems rare to me. . . . When these graces diminish and gradually disappear, they are sometimes replaced by interior pains (cf. the dark night of St. John of the Cross); at other times by graces of the same kind, but more interior ones and of a higher order. Or, again, these souls leave this state altogether and enter by degrees a more solid, elevated and stabler state; and this seems to me the most desirable, if, indeed, we be permitted to desire anything at all."

It seems from these and many other passages that Father Libermann himself had traversed the mystical way that begins with deeply felt religious experience leading to ecstasy and ends with a permanent, stable union with God that is almost wholly free from the emotions and vicissitudes that agitate the mystical life in its earlier periods.

During the following years, he worked out the constitutions of his congregation and spared no effort to improve the lot of his beloved black men. In May 1845 Eugene Tisserant and his group came back from Tahiti, exhausted and discouraged. But under their superior's invigorating influence they soon recovered, and in November of the same year Tisserant was sent to Senegal as prefect apostolic. But the series of disasters that had accompanied the African missions from the beginning was not yet at an end: the ship in which the missionaries travelled was wrecked and Tisserant was drowned. Besides, there were those human jealousies which occur even among otherwise very devoted Christians: the Holy Ghost missionaries, a congregation at that time almost moribund, regarded the new congregation of the Holy Heart of Mary as a rival, and their superior did all he could to hinder its work. When he died, in January 1845, Father Libermann said Mass for his soul "fearing he might have offended God" in taking this attitude. Under his successor, negotiations began for the amalgamation of the two societies, which took up much of Father Libermann's time and energy during the next three years. But despite all his other preoccupations he never ceased to penetrate ever more deeply into the problems of the African continent so that, in 1847, he could give to the community at Dakar advice that sounds as if it belonged to the twentieth rather than to the first half of the nineteenth century: "Strip yourselves of Europe, of its habits and its spirit. Become negroes with the negroes to fashion them as they must be fashioned, not in the manner of Europe, but leaving them their own character. Behave to them like servants who adapt themselves to the ways and habits of their masters, so that you may perfect and sanctify them." His missionaries must, above all, avoid giving any cause for being identified with the French government, for this would lose them the confidence of the natives; on the other hand they must be sufficiently diplomatic not to offend the powers that be, for this would harm their freedom of action. The missionaries did not always find it easy to follow these instructions which combined intuitive spiritual insight with a wisdom that might be called worldly if it were not so palpably applied only to supernatural ends. In the same spirit, though urging his missionaries to give themselves to their task with the utmost generosity, Father Libermann nevertheless asked them not to expose themselves to unnecessary dangers nor to damage their health by external mortifications. The life of a missionary was sufficiently hard without them; besides, they owed it to the men they hoped to convert to husband their strength; for, "The life of the missionary is a life of love of God and his neighbour, not a life of penance."

In the spring of 1848 France was once more in the throes of a revolution. Far from regretting, like so many of his confreres, that the times were changing so rapidly, Father Libermann wrote on March 20: "We are now no longer in the order of the past. . . . Let us therefore freely and simply embrace the new order. . . ." He himself was the first to act on this principle.

In September of the same year, after lengthy negotiations, his own Missionary Society of the Holy Heart of Mary was amalgamated with the decaying Congregation of the Holy Ghost, and Father Libermann was elected the first superior of the new Society of the Holy Ghost and of the Immaculate Heart of Mary. As such he had to reside in Paris, in the house of the old congregation. There, in order to repair the damages of the revolution, he established a confraternity of priests, the Society of St. John the Evangelist, to help them overcome their isolation and strengthen their apostolic spirit. At one of the conferences he gave to the confraternity he spoke to them about the role of the priest in the new social order that was just making its appearance. "There is one general phenomenon in our age," he said, "that requires a special disposition from the priest: I mean the levelling of the social classes. Hence a new feeling is abroad among the people, which inclines them to esteem and better themselves. It would be dangerous to offend this feeling. From this derives the strict obligation for the priest to avoid all sentiment and all appearance of superiority in his relations with the poor and the workers. He must become small and simple; if he acts thus in the spirit of faith and with a certain tact . . . he will gain the esteem and win the hearts of those with whom his devotion brings him into contact." In reading these almost prophetic words one cannot help feeling that, if this advice had been widely heeded, the position of the Church in France would have been far different at the beginning of the twentieth century from what it actually was.

In fact, Father Libermann organized practically single-handed an apostolate among the workers. In February 1849 he opened the chapel in the house of his congregation to the unemployed, to whom his religious gave spiritual instructions as well as food and clothing: "No finer work could be done both for the society and for our religion," he writes in an appeal to a devout lady to send him funds. In the same year he was attacked by a severe fever, similar to those tropical diseases of which his missionaires were suffering in Africa. He wrote to them joyfully that he was glad to share with them their illnesses, as he could not share the actual work they were doing. He went to Samson at Strasbourg to recuperate, for despite the immense load of administrative work involved in the direction of his Society he kept in close touch with his family. To his great joy one of his nephews wanted to become a priest and three of his nieces nuns.

In the middle of September he returned to Paris, where new troubles awaited him. The new congregation of which he was the head had been placed under the direct authority of Rome, whereas the Holy Ghost Fathers had originally been under the archbishop of Paris. The archbishop, imbued with the spirit of Gallicanism which desired the greatest possible independence from Rome, objected to the new arrangement, under which he had no jurisdiction over the Society, and the greater part of 1850 was filled with intricate negotiations. Father Libermann held firm, but showed such calm, charity, and humility in dealing with this delicate situation that the archbishop's own vicar general finally testified to the "excellent spirit" of the new superior.

The relation between the clergy and the working class was becoming an increasingly burning problem, though it was scarcely realized by the majority of priests and bishops at the time. It was, however, constantly in Father Libermann's mind. In November 1850 he wrote a letter of practical instructions on the attitude of the clergy to rich and poor respectively: "Visit the poor more than the rich, though do not neglect the latter either, as they, too, must be saved; but avoid attentions and flatteries. With the rich be polite and benevolent, with the poor kind, affectionate and charitable, indeed of an effective charity. Avoid dining with the rich, not only so as not to lose the priestly spirit but also because the poor cannot give you dinners. All must be equally dear to your priestly heart. Be, however, more charitable and more persevering with the poor."

He knew that the French working class could be saved only by a convincing display of the authentic spirit of Christ; for he, too, had received an anonymous letter sent out to many of his fellow priests in which they were called reactionaries, assassins, hypocrites, and scoundrels and which finished with the threat: "Crowd of rascals, soon your heads will roll, and with the fat of these swine we shall make lovely torches." Anti-clericalism was rife in France—only burning charity could conquer it.

During the first years of his life as a Christian Francis Libermann had almost been crushed under the weight of his illness and the apparent frustration of his burning desire for the priesthood. Now, in his last years, his heart was torn by the evils of the time, and also by the inadequacy of his own associates. In his correspondence with his missionaries of the year 1851, the last of his life, he emphasizes again and again the need for regularity. His young disciples, only very rapidly trained, were sometimes tempted to strike out a line of their own and so to endanger the community spirit on which their efficacy depended in the long run. So, in addition to all his other preoccupations, he now had to spend his remaining strength on the consolidation of his lifework.

Under this load of correspondence, engagements and frequent travels his always uncertain health began to fail rapidly. In January 1852 he took to his bed, from which he was not to rise again. At the end of the month his two most trusted helpers, Le Vavasseur and Schwindenhammer, were with him, and he appointed the latter as his successor to carry on his difficult and exacting work: "I believe it is you who must sacrifice himself."

Francis Libermann died on February 2, 1852—on the feast of the presentation of Jesus at the Temple, the meeting of the representatives of the Old Law with the Bringer of the New Dispensation—a fitting end to the life of the rabbi's son who had become one of the great Christians of his century.

CHAPTER TWO

Hermann Cohen—Father Augustine Mary of the Blessed Sacrament

(1820–1870)

Paris. Winter 1834. George Sand, the famous novelist, in whose "salon" the cream of the French intelligentsia used to meet, was sitting at her writing desk. A boy of fourteen, dressed like a page, with long dark curls and large, melancholy eyes, was busy rolling cigarettes for her. Young Hermann Cohen's intimacy with the celebrated, and in some ways notorious, lady was a subject of incessant gossip in the literary circles of the French capital. Indeed, he, too, was well on the way to becoming a celebrity in his own right, for besides being a remarkably handsome boy, he was a musical prodigy and pupil of Franz Liszt. Whenever Liszt was invited to play at a *soirée* given by one of the great Paris hostesses Hermann was by his side, and soon the disciple was asked to go to the piano almost as often as his master. It seemed a wonderful career—he was spoilt, admired, fêted—enough to turn the head of any impressionable youth.

Life had not been quite like that in Hermann's home in

Hamburg. His father was a wealthy Jewish businessman, and in his first years at school the small boy had to endure much teasing and sometimes even worse from his fellows, as anti-Semitism was rife in Germany even in those days. He had fought against it by straining every effort to show them that he, a Jew, was really superior to them; and soon he was top of his class. His musical talent was even more remarkable than his intellectual gifts. At first his father objected to an artistic career for his younger son; but his mother supported it very strongly, and when the political unrest of the year 1830 had seriously affected the family's financial position, Herr Cohen, too, gave in to a project which promised early independence for the boy. Hermann began to give concerts in his native city and later, accompanied by his devoted mother, at the courts of several German grand dukes. But his dream was to go to Paris, where Chopin and Liszt were the great attractions for a budding pianist. The grand dukes, charmed with the precocious young artist, gave him letters of introduction to their ambassadors in the French capital. Armed with these precious documents Hermann accompanied by his mother, his sister and his elder brother, set out for Paris. The travellers called at the court of Hanover, at Frankfurt, and at Cassel; everywhere Hermann was overwhelmed with praise and compliments, so it was not surprising that he soon turned into a little tyrant lording it over his family, who became completely subservient to his every whim.

In Paris, under the shadow of the great Liszt, Hermann developed both his musical gifts and the less desirable qualities of a spoilt child prodigy suddenly plunged into the social whirlpool of the gayest city in Europe. Under his nickname, "Puzzi" the fourteen year-old became its darling and met many celebrities, including the brilliant Abbé Lamennais, who presented him with a copy of his *Paroles d'un Croyant*. The book was condemned by Gregory XVI immediately after its appearance (1834) on account of its rationalistic tendencies, but it and its author made a deep impression on "Puzzi." It was his first contact with Christian, even though not quite orthodox, ideas. George Sand, to whose circle Abbé Lammennais and Hermann both belonged, wrote about the young pianist in her articles for the *Revue des Deux Mondes*, and this distinguished testimony became the passport that opened all the drawing rooms of Europe to him.

In the spring of 1835 Liszt accepted a call to Geneva. Hermann was heartbroken, for he was genuinely devoted to his master, and decided to follow him. Liszt's influence was powerful enough to obtain for him a professorship at the *conservatoire* in that city despite his youth—he was only fifteen. Apart from his teaching he gave many concerts and earned a great deal of money, which he spent almost as quickly as he earned it. For in addition to his other rather expensive tastes he now developed a very dangerous passion indeed: he began to gamble. He himself described the beginnings of it. After a concert a wealthy prince gave a dinner for the artists, and afterwards some of the guests began to gamble; "I think," Hermann wrote later, "it was the first time that I saw this kind of thing. I eagerly watched the game, in which large sums of gold and silver changed hands. Then I asked for permission also to be allowed to risk a few francs. This was the start of a passion that has devoured the best years of my youth in an abyss of tortures and faults, without giving me a moment's rest."

After a stay of fifteen months in Geneva, both Liszt and Hermann with his mother returned to Paris, where the young artist temporarily lost his head completely. He insisted on living alone, neglected even his piano, and spent whole nights gambling. However, both the lack of money and the nausea this totally purposeless life produced in his sensitive nature drove him back to his mother. And now another circle received him with open arms: he was introduced to the Princess Belgiojoso, in whose house the slim, seventeen-year-old young man soon became a constant guest. But the soft life in the drawing rooms of the princess and her aristocratic friends once more went to his head. He neglected his music, was soon deep in debt, and fled to Hamburg—but the attrac-

tions of Paris were too strong for him, and after a few weeks
he was back. The princess once more took him up; he
gave piano lessons, accompanied a famous Italian singer,
Mario, and in the autumn of 1838 went to London, where he
gave a highly successful concert. But an increasing restlessness
did not allow him to stay in any place for very long; in the
following spring he had joined Liszt in Italy, and in the
summer of the same year he was once again in Paris. His
conceit and complete lack of self-discipline, which could be
forgiven in a boy, began to lose the young man one after the
other of his friends. The princess was annoyed with him because he compromised himself with a singer called Candida,
and would not listen to her remonstrances; "Hermann," she
wrote, "needs moral protection. His family, I think, is completely subservient to him. Moreover, his profession brings him
into daily contact with people whose life consists in nothing
but pleasure. It is very sad." Two years later, in the spring
of 1841, even his most devoted friend, Franz Liszt, broke
with him. Hermann was genuinely distressed, but soon con-
soled himself with the pleasures of constant travel, musical
successes, and gambling. In this way he spent the next seven
years of his life: "I did not think myself any worse than
most of my companions. I tolerated everything in others,
therefore I, too, permitted myself all sorts of liberties. Sometimes, when the opportunity offered, I did a good deed, but I
had no conscience about also doing a bad one. . . . I do not
exaggerate if I say that all the young people of my acquaintance were living in this way. . . . They were content with
the sorrows and pleasures of this earth and had just sufficient
morality to comply with the requirements of good manners
and not to get into trouble with the secular authorities."

He continued to be obsessed by his passion for gambling
and lost considerable sums of money. Soon he was deep in
debt. So he gambled with borrowed money, ever hoping to
make good his losses. But his losses were always greater than
his gains. He seemed to be caught in a vicious circle from
which there was no escape.

Then, one Friday in May 1847, he was asked to conduct the choir in the small church of St. Valérie in Paris during an evening service. Towards the end of it, the priest took a golden vessel in the centre of which was a small white circle raising it above the heads of the congregation in a cruciform movement. At this moment, Hermann writes, "I felt a strange emotion, as if I had no share in this blessing, which did not seem to be given for me." Nevertheless, he was deeply moved and felt "an unknown relief."

When he left the church he could not understand what had happened to him. For the moment he seemed unable to carry on with his accustomed dissipations. A week later he returned to the church—the same experience. He felt drawn as if by a magnet, and finally decided that he must speak to a priest. The Abbé Legrand, to whom he had an introduction, counselled calm and constancy. A few days after the interview Hermann departed for Germany, where he had to give a concert in the famous spa of Ems. There, on Sunday, August 8, he went to Mass. "At the moment of the consecration," he writes, "I suddenly broke into a flood of tears. Divine grace had seized me with great violence. . . . When I was quite bathed in tears I immediately felt a vehement contrition for my past life. And at once, as if divinely inspired, I offered to God an interior confession of all the faults of my whole life. I saw them all before me, ugly and horrible, inciting the divine wrath. . . . And yet I also felt an unknown peace descending on my soul, consoling me, because the merciful God would forgive me everything and have pity with my sincere repentance. Yes, I felt God had forgiven me and, for my penance, had accepted my firm resolve to love Him above all things and to be converted. When I left the church of Ems, I was a Christian, as far as one can be such before being baptized."

As soon as he was back in Paris he went to Abbé Legrand and asked for baptism. The ceremony was to take place on August 28, the feast of St. Augustine, the greatest convert and doctor of the Latin Church. Hermann prepared for it by a novena spent in silence and prayer, and, like St. Augustine

himself, was attacked by fierce temptations on the eve of
the feast. At the baptism itself he had a mystical experience.
In his description of it the ancient mystical imagery of light is
strikingly combined with a discovery of nineteenth-century
science; he writes: "I felt a movement so vehement and
powerful that I can only liken it to the shock of an electrical
engine. My bodily eyes closed, but at the same moment the
eyes of my soul opened to a supernatural, divine light. I was
immersed as if in an ecstasy of love; my heart, like that of my
patron saint (i.e., St. Augustine) seemed to taste the joys of
paradise and drink from the stream of delight which the
Lord gives to His chosen ones in the land of the living."

At the dawn of the machine age the mystical experience
could be described in a new language: it was still light, as it
had been for the Greek Fathers, for St. Augustine and many
mystics after them; but it was also like something else: it was
like the electrical power which had for so long been hidden
from men.

And this power he felt especially in the Eucharist. For, as
in the case of many modern contemplatives, his mystical life
was centred in the Sacrament of the Altar, which had been
revealed to him already in his first religious experience in the
church of St. Valérie. Following the custom of the time,
he did not receive Holy Communion immediately after his
baptism but had to wait another fortnight. But according to
the notes in his diary he received a eucharistic grace even
before he was allowed to receive the Host. He writes under
the date of September 3: "Mass in the chapel of Our Lady of
Sion: marvel of the power of the Holy Eucharist, even before
my first holy communion." And a few lines later: "Repetition
of the marvel of the communion."

The first eucharistic grace had come to him during an
evening service in May, the month dedicated to Mary. So
Mary remained throughout intimately united with his spiritual
life; indeed, he called her the "Mother of the Eucharist." In
one of his sermons he describes an experience at the time of
his conversion; but from his language it is not altogether clear

whether it was an actual vision or an interior illumination which he clothed in visionary language. Whatever its form, it was a profound inner event that communicated its meaning to his whole future life. Describing it to his audience in the third person he told them how "before his eyes there appeared a light which descended towards him and, while it came nearer, took the form of a living human being—of a woman. . . . Indeed, something divine was reflected in her features: they bore the imprint of a more than angelic goodness, tenderness and gentleness. . . . Who are you? he exclaimed. Are you perhaps that enchanting Rachel who captivated the heart of my ancestor Jacob? Or perhaps Judith, whose conquering beauty brought about the ruin of Holofernes? Are you that Esther, who saved her people by her charm and her love? I am all this, she said to me. And even more than that. I am of thy nation, a daughter of Abraham, Isaac and Jacob, a daughter of the tribe of Levi, of the priestly race. But what is this? she continued. I am the daughter of Jahveh, the Mother of the Messiah, the Spouse of that Spirit who brooded over the waters on the day of creation. . . . I am the Wisdom of which Solomon speaks. The Lord possessed me from the beginning and preserved me from the wounds of the serpent."

Thus he sees Mary as the link connecting his ancient race with his new religion; she, like himself (the name Cohen means priest) from the priestly tribe of Levi, foreshadowed by the great women of Israel, yet greater than them all, brings him Christ, and Christ in the Eucharist. In a letter written much later he explains: "It was the month of Mary (i.e., when he was converted) . . . Mary, the Mother of Jesus, revealed to me the Eucharist . . . Mary led me to Jesus, Mary gave me Jesus! She gave me the Eucharist, and the Eucharist has delighted my heart."

He would have liked best to become a religious straightaway and to spend his days and nights at the foot of the altar. But his old life was still with him—not, indeed, interiorly, for there he had changed completely, but externally: he had no less than thirty thousand francs gambling debts, which he had to pay before he could think of entering the priesthood. So Hermann continued to teach the piano and give concerts. But his nights were no longer spent in the drawing rooms of his rich friends. Indeed, these, especially the ladies, were disappointed with him and regretted that his piety had lost him to the world. Instead he used to pray for many hours before the tabernacle. One evening he went into a Carmelite chapel. He had quite forgotten the time when a sister made a sign to him to leave, as she wanted to lock up. He was indignant, since some women, members of a confraternity, were allowed to stay on, and he told his confessor. "Well then," said the *abbé*, "why don't you look for men to join you, and then we will allow you to imitate these devout women whom you envy so much."

In a short time Hermann found a number of like-minded friends, and on November 22, 1848, in the year when all Europe was in the turmoil of revolution and even Pope Pius IX had been forced to flee from Rome, the small society was officially founded and began their work of nocturnal adoration a fortnight later in the famous Paris Church of Our Lady of Victories. Hermann himself moved with two other young men into the house of the Marist Fathers, where he lived a life of constant work, prayer, and the utmost austerity. Gradually the load of debt began to get lighter, and early in 1849 he prepared to give a last concert which, he hoped, would free him altogether from this burden. To fit himself for this ultimate effort he kept practising scales from morning to night, for scales, he maintained, were the best piano master, and besides, they did not prevent him from reading at the same time—and so his fingers raced up and down the keys while his mind was occupied with the treatise on *Christian Perfection* by Alphonsus Rodrigues, which lay in front of him instead of the music score.

The concert was a tremendous success, for Hermann had put his whole soul into this swansong. When one of the Marist Fathers congratulated him afterwards, he said to him: "Indeed, you may congratulate me—because I have at long last escaped from the world. Now I have finished with it once and for all. With what blissful relief did I say goodbye to it after I had played the last note." He was determined to become a priest, but he had not yet made up his mind whether he would also enter an order. During a retreat his vocation became clear to him: ever since his conversion he had read the works of St. Teresa of Avila and St. John of the Cross; he would become a Carmelite. In a letter to his relatives of August 16, 1849 he wrote about his decision: "You have probably expected that I was going to leave the world and the dangerous profession I practised. But you do not yet know what kind of clerical life I am going to lead. Your worst fears will not be realized; you will not see me walking about Paris in a soutane. . . . I have chosen something else: solitude, silence, retirement, a hidden life of self-denial is to be my lot. I have entered the novitiate of the Order of Mount Carmel, famous for its spirit of penance and love of God." And he continues: "This life is what I have chosen. And when, as I greatly hope, you will one day visit me, you will find a gay and happy countenance and a heart that loves you and will always love you. . . . If one of you should have the misfortune to displease or offend the Lord, I would implore Him to let me do penance for him so that he would not have to suffer for it eternally and we would one day be united to each other in Abraham's bosom."

Baptism had not diminished Hermann's strong Jewish family feeling, and he quite naturally spoke their language when writing to them—for was not Abraham's bosom only another name for heaven?

Hermann had hoped to bury himself in the hidden life of a contemplative order. He was radiantly happy in the seclusion of the noviciate, and even the temporary prohibition to concern himself with anything musical did not damp his spirit. At his clothing on October 6, 1849 he received the name Augustine Mary of the Blessed Sacrament. When he was studying for the priesthood, one of his friends asked him whether the adoration of the Blessed Sacrament, to which he was so attached was not curtailed by his timetable. But he assured his correspondent that nothing was lost: "For who prevents me from offering my studies to Jesus in the sacrament of his love? Can I not learn for love, read for love, argue and philosophize for love? The true adoration, the adoration *par excellence* consists in fulfilling the divine will. Now, as I know that Jesus demands that I should devote all my spare time to study, I must offer Him this kind of adoration. And he is surely better pleased with this than if I revelled day and night in ecstatic feelings against the will of my superiors." This is the authentic attitude of the true mystic: to prefer the will of God even to the most satisfying spiritual experiences.

Eighteen months after his clothing Hermann was ordained priest, on Holy Saturday 1851. He writes that on the eve of his ordination he had only the one idea that the next day he would, as it were, give a new existence to Christ, whom he had killed so often by his sins. As he had been converted by the Eucharist, so his first sermon was devoted to the Blessed Sacrament, which now, through his priesthood, became even more intensely the centre of his spiritual life.

But if Hermann had hoped to bury himself in the solitude of Mount Carmel and give himself up completely to the mystical dialogue with Christ in His sacrament he was mistaken. Indeed, the second half of his life almost seems like a spiritual replica of the first. Then he had travelled all over Europe, delighting enthusiastic audiences with his music; now, far from remaining in his cell, he again was almost constantly on the road, but holding his audiences no longer by his play, but by his word. His superiors soon realized that, precisely through having been very much a "man of the world," well acquainted with the hold vices can gain over one, he was particularly well equipped to stir up the consciences of his hearers. Everyone knew that he spoke from his own experience when he told them that a life completely given over to pleasure was barren and bound to end in bitter disappointment, whereas the intimate relationship with Christ would give them peace and perfect fulfilment. He was not afraid of speaking of himself, of confessing both his unworthiness and the overpowering graces he had received. In 1854 he preached for the first time in Paris, the city where he had had his greatest successes, where people still knew him as the brilliant pianist and reckless gambler. So the large church of St. Sulpice was filled to overflowing when Père Augustin, once best known as "Puzzi," mounted its pulpit. And the first thing he told them was that he must ask their pardon for the scandal he had once given in their city. " 'What right, you may well ask, have you to preach to us, to exhort us to virtue and piety? For we have seen you among public sinners, tossed about by the winds of all sorts of false teaching. You have offended us by your disgraceful behaviour.' Indeed, brethren, I confess that I have sinned before heaven and before you. I know well that I deserve being blamed by you. And I am quite ready to do public penance. I have come clothed in a penitential habit, for I belong to an austere Order, my head is shaved and my feet are bare. Once, in the month of May I entered a certain church, I was still a Jew. The congregation was singing hymns. Mary, the Mother of Jesus, revealed to me the mystery of the holy Eucharist. I began to know It, I knew Jesus, I knew my God, and soon I was a Christian. The holy water touched my forehead, and at that moment all my sins—my terrible sins—were wiped out. God had forgiven me; my soul was all at once pure and innocent. God, my brethren, has forgiven me. Mary has forgiven me. Will you not forgive me?"

The congregation were deeply moved. And then Father Hermann described how he had travelled far and wide looking for happiness. "I searched for it in the poetic nights of a glorious climate, in the clear waters of the Swiss lakes, in the most magnificent scenery. I have also sought it in fashionable drawing rooms, in splendid dinners, balls, and festivities. I have been looking for it in riches, in the excitement of gambling, in romance, in an adventurous life and in the satisfaction of an unmeasured ambition. I have sought happiness in artistic fame and in all the pleasures of the senses and the mind. Indeed, where, O my God, did I not seek it, this happiness, the dream of all human hearts?"

His whole youth had been a never-ending search for happiness. And at last he had found it—where he had never looked for it. "What is this happiness? God alone can satisfy the longing of the human heart. And God has descended into the world in the Person of his Son Jesus Christ; He has become the companion of our pilgrimage, the Bread of our souls. But, someone may say, I do not believe in Jesus Christ. I can only answer: nor did I. And for this reason I was unhappy." There followed a detailed description of his conversion, ending with the words: "Let us love Jesus. There is only one happiness, to love Jesus and to be loved by him."

This personal confession of faith, the complete conviction that radiated not only from Father Hermann's words but from his whole life and being, won him a large number of converts. The most beloved of them came from his own family. His sister, who had once accompanied her young brother on his first journey to Paris, was married to a Jew, Monsieur Raunheim, and had one small boy, George. Hermann loved them both dearly, and Madame Raunheim was very near to the faith. But she dared not accept it because she knew that if she were baptized her husband would take George from her. Two years before he preached the famous sermon in St. Sulpice, in June 1852, he had a very serious talk with his sister at the end of which she agreed to be baptized if she could keep it secret. On June 19, the feast of the Sacred Heart, "on the fifth night after this conversation," as Hermann himself reports, "I poured the holy water over her forehead and gave her the Bread of Life." Four years later George, too, was baptized, in rather romantic circumstances. He had already been attracted to Christ on a visit to his uncle when he was seven, and at his insistence had been allowed to don the dress of a choirboy and cast flowers before the Corpus Christi procession. Naïvely he told his father: "Do you know, daddy, that I have been strewing flowers

before the Lord God?" M. Raunheim was aghast, and fearing that his only son would be induced to become a Christian,
he watched over him most carefully, while his wife, unknown
to any of her family, went to Mass almost every morning.
Only George, small as he was, suspected something and was
heartbroken that he was not allowed to become a Christian
and receive Holy Communion. For many years his great
desire could not be fulfilled. Then, one day he happened to
watch the First Communion of the children of his parish. He
was extremely upset and threatened to cast himself at the feet
of the first priest, tell him his story, and ask for baptism.
Madame Raunheim wrote to Hermann, and in view of the
extraordinary fervor of his nephew he decided to come to
Paris and baptize him secretly. So on the 14th of October 1856
George received his first Holy Communion with the utmost
devotion. For Hermann it was one of the great consolations
of his life. A year later, on the anniversary, he wrote to his
nephew: "Does not the 14th of October tell you all I have to
say to you? When I celebrated Mass this morning, I remembered when I read the holy Gospel that I had read the
same words a year ago, at the solemn moment when you
became a child of Jesus Christ. . . . I am happy at the
sentiments you express in your letter and I share your gratitude with all my heart. I, too, admire the tenderness and
mercy of Jesus and Mary for your soul, and the 14th of
October 1856 will always remain in my heart as one of the
greatest, the most beautiful days of my life."

In the same year Hermann helped to build a new house of
his Order at Bagnères and wrote gaily: "Here I am completely given over to putty, plaster and cement." While he
was hard at work he had the great joy of seeing his Confraternity of the Blessed Sacrament officially confirmed by
the Archbishop of Paris. And in the spring of the following
year he went to Hamburg, where he baptized yet another
member of his family, his brother Albert. In 1859 he restored
the Carmelite monastery at Lyons with the preparation for
which he had been kept busy for the last two years, preach-

ing and organizing subscriptions. In 1860 he was appointed
its first prior. The work had been encouraged by St. John
Vianney, the holy curé of Ars, who, according to Hermann's
own words, had predicted the foundation and sent him
several of his penitents.

At Lyons he devoted himself unsparingly to the apostolate
and made many converts among men and women in all walks
of life. Being himself intimately united to God he exercised a
tremendous influence on others, even on those who had not
set foot in a church for many years. When in June 1862 his
term of office was ended he went to Rome to attend a
canonization. There he met Franz Liszt again, and the two
were completely reconciled. One remark of Liszt, who reported this event to his mother, is very revealing. He writes:
"In the last three weeks I have seen a good deal of him (Father
Hermann) and I like his pleasant, spirited conversation, which
does not prejudice his higher aspirations." In another letter,
to his daughter, dated July 8, 1862, Liszt is even more explicit:
"His joining the Order has improved not only his mind but
also his heart and his manners. . . . He preached here once,
in Saint Louis. His sermon made a great impression. He
touches and wins over all who are not held back by inordinate
pride. The Holy Father has received him with great benevo-
lence. And Cardinal Wiseman has invited him to England to
found a Carmelite monastery. For this Order has wonderful
antecedents in that country through the thirteenth-century
saint, Simon Stock, to whom the blessed Virgin gave the
scapular. Hermann, who has already been Prior in Lyons, will
now probably hold the same office in London, unless he is
appointed the English Provincial."

And so, in his last audience with Pius IX, the Pope gave
Father Augustine his blessing and sent him, "as in the sixth
century one of my predecessors in the chair of St. Peter sent
the monk Augustine, the first apostle of this country."

Hermann admitted that to leave France and his fruitful
apostolate there was a deeply felt sacrifice. He once more
went to Paris, where his friends were horrified to see him

almost destitute and made a collection for him which produced one hundred and sixty francs. With this sum he landed
in England to make his foundation.

England in 1862 had just emerged from the long centuries
of persecution into the "second spring" of Catholic Emancipa-
tion, the Oxford Movement and the restoration of the hierarchy. But still prejudice against the "Roman" Church was
overwhelmingly strong, and the refounding of the old Orders
in the country of Queen Victoria was no easy task. The new
Augustine arrived in England on August 6, the feast of the
Transfiguration of Christ. No doubt he remembered his first
arrival in London, a quarter of a century ago, when, accompanied by the singer Mario, he had won the hearts of the
music lovers of the city by his brilliant playing. His spectacular conversion had not passed unnoticed by the English Catholics, and soon he could resume his apostolic work, even
though in different circumstances, in the capital of the
British Empire.

The nuns of the Assumption in Kensington gave him a
roof, and after two months they allowed him the use of a
small house that belonged to them, where Cardinal Wiseman
presided over the first solemn Mass that was celebrated on
October 15, the feast of St. Teresa of Avila. Hermann had
been accompanied by a few French friars; but he was the
only one to speak English, and so he had to do everything,
even the daily shopping. One of his first objectives was to
introduce the nightly adoration in the city. He found this,
however, more difficult than in Paris, and for two reasons,
which he points out himself. The one was the English love
of comfort; London Catholics were apparently fonder of their
good night's rest than the French. The other he gave as the
greater class consciousness of Victorian Britain, where workmen or small shopkeepers and members of the gentry or the
aristocracy found it equally embarrassing to spend a night
together on a hard mattress to be ready when their turn
came for an hour's adoration. However, gradually all obstacles
were overcome, and on the first anniversary of his arrival in

London the association was established and the first night of-
adoration held in the Carmelite chapel, where many recent
converts prayed before the Blessed Sacrament for the conversion of their friends and relatives.

As the work of the Carmelites was spreading rapidly, more
friars had to be brought over from France, and soon the
house of the Assumption nuns became too small for them.
Hermann had his eyes on a large house and garden in the
neighbourhood, which belonged to a Mr. Bird, an eighty-
year-old staunch Protestant. It seemed very unlikely, indeed,
that the old gentleman would consent to lease his property
to a Roman order; but Hermann followed the example of his
foundress, St. Teresa, prayed ardently to St. Joseph, and
then went to tackle the redoubtable octogenarian in person.
Mr. Bird was greatly surprised to find so much charm and
good manners in a Catholic religious and finally agreed to
lease his house to him. He was, however, not prepared to
sell; and so the Carmelite Fathers installed themselves in their
new home, happy, indeed, but feeling not yet altogether
safe in their new monastery.

Then, oddly enough, *The Times* came to their rescue. In
1864 Hermann attended a Conference at Malines where he
gave an account of the work of his order in England. A
reporter got hold of it and *The Times* published a violent
article in which diatribes against Catholicism in general were
mixed with personal attacks on the Carmelite prior in particular. Mr. Bird read it and was seized with a powerful emotion,
known as the English love of the underdog. Acting on it at
once, he summoned Father Hermann, and then and there
offered to sell his house to him, a proposal that was accepted
with alacrity.

In February of the same year Hermann had one of the
most moving experiences of his English apostolate. Six
Catholic seamen from the Philippines were condemned to
death by hanging at the Old Bailey. On the morning before
the execution Hermann was allowed to bring them Holy
Communion, after they had been reconciled by a Spanish-

speaking confrere. "When they received the Holy Viaticum," he writes, "the terrors of death and the anguish of the ignominious punishment that awaited them within a few minutes disappeared completely before the splendour of the divine life which Jesus came to give them. I have now been a priest for thirteen years, but I have never had such an overwhelming experience of the power of the Eucharist and of the priesthood."

Father Hermann's term of office ended in 1865 and was followed by two years of almost incessant travels, given over to preaching in England, Ireland, Belgium, France, and Germany. Yet in his heart he desired but one thing: to retire into the "desert," that is to say to one of the Carmelite houses where the friars can live a completely contemplative life without any outside obligations. On April 21, 1868, he writes to his dearly loved nephew George from Cologne: "Today I am writing to take leave of you, because our Lord calls me to solitude. . . . I look upon my stay there [the "desert" of Tarasteix near Tarbes] as if it were the forecourt of heaven, I have an inexpressible thirst for it." And six months later he tells him that this sojourn in the "desert" corresponds perfectly to the longings of his soul. But, he continues, his eyes have begun to trouble him; he will have to see a doctor, and, if a complicated treatment should be necessary, he would have to leave his beloved solitude. His fears were realized; the doctor diagnosed glaucoma; he had to wear coloured spectacles, exchange his Carmelite sandals for warm shoes, and cover his tonsure with a warm head-dress; both lamp and daylight gave him intense pain, and he could no longer read even his breviary. The only—very un-certain—hope was a highly dangerous operation by a famous Berlin surgeon Dr. Graefe. Then someone suggested a novena to Our Lady of Lourdes, who had appeared to St. Bernadette just ten years before. He himself has left us a description of his cure: "The Novena began on October 24, the feast of the Archangel Raphael, who had cured Tobias of his blindness. Each day I bathed my eyes in the healing water drawn from the miraculous grotto. . . . On the sixth day of the novena I went on foot from our monastery at Bagnères to Lourdes, as I wanted to make the pilgrimage in conditions offering the greatest chance of success. Already at Bagnères I had experienced a daily improvement of the ophthalmia, and that at the very moment when the water from the grotto had touched my eyes. . . . Finally, on the last day, the feast of All Saints, when I was in the grotto itself and near the fountain, I no longer felt any symptoms of the disease. Since then I have been writing and reading as much as I wished, without glasses, without precautions, without effort or fatigue. . . . I have put on my sandals again and had my tonsure cut; I have obtained what I desired above all, that is to say I can continue my hermit's life in our beloved desert; in a word, I am completely cured and, it is my intimate conviction that this cure is a miracle due to the intercession of the Blessed Virgin."

So Father Hermann could return to his desert, of which he writes in a letter of November 18, 1869: "I taste a profound happiness, a delightful peace in solitude. . . . I have been overwhelmed, inundated during my sojourn in solitude. Nowhere else did I find God so easily; nowhere else did I feel Him so near, never have I tasted the delights of the religious life to such a degree. And frequently I feel as it were touched by the breath of Divinity, inviting me, calling me, urging me to surrender myself to the sacred influence of grace." In this very discreet description Father Hermann gives us a glimpse of his mystical prayer, in which he felt the divine touches of which St. Teresa speaks. Two months later, on January 13, 1870, he is more explicit, for he writes to a sister of Charity, Hermanne de Jésus, who had similar experiences: "These 'assaults' usually come upon me when I am not even thinking of God and am busy reading, writing, or working in the sacristy. Then, whether I want to or not, I must stop whatever I am doing, else the onslaught becomes even more vehement (when I am reading my eyes close spontaneously) until I am before the Blessed Sacrament or gone down on my knees somewhere else, and then I simply have to give in, for it is impossible to resist. I am inundated with torrents of delight, or else a gentle flame penetrates my inmost heart. Sometimes I remain thus immersed for hours in a sea of heavenly delights, and these hours pass like minutes."

Here, in the hermitage of Tarasteix, Hermann was overwhelmed with the graces of the mystical union, the intense joys of the soul totally given to God. But this does not mean that he remained unaware of the needs and problems of the world outside. His interest in his family, especially in his sister, Madame Raunheim, and her son George, remained as keen as ever. Indeed, he found time to draw up for them detailed instructions for their spiritual life, and, when necessary, did not mince his words. "You tell me," he writes to his sister, who had become a Carmelite tertiary, "that you enjoy a good table and eat without depriving yourself of anything. Why do you not rather give your soul a substantial meal by nourishing it daily with solid reading? Perhaps, having first eaten from this spiritual table, you might later be more inclined to mortify yourself at the other."

He was also, of course, profoundly interested in the preparations for the Vatican Council and in a letter of 14th October, 1869 he asks his nephew for clippings from the *Univers*, a Catholic paper, of items concerning his order and the Council, for, "It is important that I should keep informed on these matters." But perhaps George had sent him too many papers, for in a later letter he asks him to send him every three weeks only résumés of everything "concerning our Order, the Church and the Council" rather than newspapers and periodicals, "because I should not like to introduce something not in keeping with the customs of the eremitical life. . . . In this way I shall know all a priest has to know, and you will give me great pleasure in rendering me this service."

The Vatican Council opened on December 8, 1869. Hermann followed it with keen interest. On January 6, 1870, he again writes to George: "I must have the list of the commission of bishops elected for the section of the Council dealing with the Religious Orders. If this is not contained in the numbers you have already sent off, please send it without delay. We must continue to pray fervently for the Council. The Holy Spirit has, indeed, promised his assistance, but through prayer we can obtain even more abundant outpourings of the truth for some particular Council, and we must desire that in this one the veil over several controversial questions may be torn asunder, so that men of little faith may know what a Catholic is bound to believe, and that the sum of the revealed truths may not be diminished. The Gallicans strike a poor figure at the moment, and our Holy Father preaches on humility at every opportunity."

It is clear from this letter that he ardently wished for a definition of Papal Infallibility, which the so-called Gallicans opposed. He left his beloved hermitage in the spring to give a course of Lenten sermons at Poitiers, which he had to cut short, however, on account of ill-health. But in May he was well enough to give Maria, the eldest daughter of his brother Albert, her first Holy Communion. In the same month he was elected to a high office, that of first definitor of his Order as well as that of novice master at Broussey (Gironde). His brief hermit's life was at an end and after preaching two retreats he arrived at Broussey on June 1. The hoped-for definition of the Infallibility of the Pope was promulgated on July 18, 1870—and on the following day war broke out between France and Prussia, an event which completely changed Father Hermann's life. The populace were in great excitement and his German origin would be a danger not only to himself but to his community. So he decided to make one last retreat in the "desert" of Tarasteix, where, as he writes to his sister on August 13, he would offer himself to God "in order that we might be spared so many misfortunes. Nevertheless, I bless His loving Hand for whatever happens, for He is as lovable when He chastizes as when He caresses." In October, after some unpleasant adventures, for at Grenoble he was taken for a Prussian spy, he arrived at Montreux, where a number of refugees were in need of a priest. But his apostolate in Switzerland was short-lived, for at the end of November he was asked to go to Spandau, near Berlin, to minister to 5300 French prisoners of war. It was exhausting work. He describes his day in a letter to his sister of December 6, 1870: "Each morning a company of about four hundred soldiers is conducted in military fashion to my Mass, where I preach them a sermon. In this way they all have attended once in twelve days. Then I go to the hospital to visit the sick, and in the afternoon I go to the barracks to see those who are well." Among the sick many had typhoid, dysentery, and even smallpox. Father Hermann, weakened by penance and intense activity had little physical resistence left. He caught smallpox and soon was lying in bed with high fever, his mind wandering, his face pale and sunken. The night before his death he made his last confession and received once more the Eucharist, which had been the centre of his life ever since his conversion, more than thirty years before. He died at Spandau on the morning of January 20, 1871.

CHAPTER THREE

Isaac Thomas Hecker

(1819–1888)

In 1897 a book appeared in France that sparked off a violent controversy. It was the none-too-faithful French translation of Walter Elliott's *Life of Father Hecker*, to which the very progressive Abbé Felix Klein had added a long and highly laudatory preface. The *abbé* was one of a small group of priests who fought against what seemed to them the "reactionary" forces in the Church, and he thought to have discovered in Father Hecker a most valuable ally. His alleged teachings were grouped together under the heading "Americanism" and were reproved by Leo XIII in his letter *Testem Benevolentiae* (1899). For a long time Father Hecker's name remained under a cloud: only in very recent times has he emerged from it, for today the Church herself approves the "progressive" ideas that sustained his tremendous apostolate.

Isaac Hecker was a native of New York of German parentage, the youngest of three brothers. The family had originally been Lutheran, but Mrs. Hecker had felt an early attraction to Methodism, of which she became a devout adherent. Isaac was sent to elementary school when he was

seven but his education was cut short when, in 1831, the
family was in financial difficulties. He was first apprenticed
to a publishing house, but soon joined his two brothers, John
and George, who had established a bakery. His work opened
his eyes to the social question and for a time he became
interested in the Equal Rights party, an offshoot of the Democratic party which tried to improve the lot of the workers
but failed, owing to the selfishness of its representatives.
Deeply disappointed, and without any religious faith, Isaac
was left with the vague feeling that he was called to something, but without knowing what this "something" might be.
His work in the now flourishing bakery could not really
satisfy him, and his education had remained extremely sketchy.
The family spoke only German, and his English was bad.

At this juncture he met a man whose influence was going
to give his life a new direction. In March 1841 Orestes Brownson, a thinker and lecturer then at the height of his fame,
spoke in New York on "The Democracy of Christ" and
the "Reform Spirit of Our Age." Hecker himself gave as the
gist of the lectures that "Christ was the big Democrat and the
Gospel was the true Democratic platform." Isaac and his
brothers were profoundly impressed with the man from
Boston and arranged another lecture for him on Independence
Day, and after that a course of lectures the next year. Under
Brownson's influence, Isaac now began to study the German
philosophers. Early in 1842 Brownson spoke on "Civilization
and Human Progress," stating that unaided human reason
was unable to ensure progress unless it was helped by the
reason of God, "speaking not only to the heart, but through
revelation and the traditions of the race." At this time
Brownson stayed with the Heckers and had many conversations with Isaac, who was sixteen years his junior. There was
one question especially that worried the younger man and
which he formulated thus: "How can I be certain of the
objective reality of the operations of my soul?" To find the
answer he dipped more deeply into Kant, Fichte, and

Hegel, but these difficult thinkers could give him no help and rather confirmed him in his subjectivism.

Then, in the early summer of 1842, something extraordinary happened. Isaac began to lose all interest not only in his philosophical books but also in his work. The bakery, the family concerns, even social reforms, suddenly lost all their meaning, all their importance. There was only one reality that mattered, and that reality was God. He developed an insatiable desire for prayer, for contemplation and, to his own dismay, found himself neglecting his work in order to commune with this new-found Reality. Very soon he began to have some strange experiences, one of which he described in detail in his diary several months after it had occurred: "I saw (I cannot say I dreamt, for it was quite different from dreaming as I thought, since I was seated on the side of my bed), a beautiful, angelic, pure being and myself standing along-side of her, feeling a most heavenly pure joy. And it was as if . . . our bodies were luminous and they gave forth a moonlike light which I felt sprung from the joy that we experienced. We were unclothed, pure, and unconscious of everything but pure love and joy, and I felt as if we had always lived together and that our motions, actions, feelings and thoughts came from one centre. And when I looked towards her I saw no bold outline of form but an angelic something which I cannot describe, but in angelic shape and image. It was this picture which has left such an indelible impression upon my mind, and for some time afterwards I continued to feel the same influence, and do now so that the actual around me has lost its hold on me . . . I am charmed by its influence, and I am conscious that if I should accept anything else, I should lose the life which would be the only existence wherein I could say I live."

Similar remarkable experiences came to him several times. Their reality is proved by their result: they changed his life completely and finally led him into the Church. More, there is very little imaginative embroidery in this vision; its main effect is one of light and joy, which the mystics have always held to be one of the criteria of divinely caused experiences.

The consequence of this new interior life was that he felt with growing conviction that work in the bakery could no longer satisfy him. He must follow this strange call, even though he had as yet no idea where it would lead him. But he was terrified of having to tell his family—for how could they understand what he could not explain even to himself? However, they realized that something had happened to him that caused him anxiety, and as they were a closely knit, devoted family, both his mother and his brothers treated him with great kindness and fully supported his decision to go to Boston to discuss his difficulties with Brownson. In his conversations with his older friend it became increasingly clear to him that a life in business was not his vocation, that to continue in it would mean to turn his back on what had become the most precious thing in his existence.

Isaac was not the only American at this time who desired a life away from the concerns of money-making and ceaseless external activity. In various places groups had formed who were trying to live a more natural life on the land, divided between farming and intellectual pursuits. Many of them were Transcendentalists and followers of Emerson, whose basic religious belief may be defined as the conviction that "the highest revelation is that God is in every man." One of these groups was the community of Brook Farm, founded by George Ripley about a year before on co-operative lines. Brownson, realizing that for the time being, at any rate, Isaac found it impossible to return to his family, suggested he should go there to see whether this kind of life would suit him. In January 1843 the troubled young man set out for the new venture.

At the farm he divided his time between contemplation and study, for a while he also made the bread for the community. But the thought of his family was troubling him. He feared that they might think he despised them among the highly intellectual members of Brook Farm. In March, therefore, he returned to New York to discuss matters with them, and with their approval next month he temporarily joined the community, but giving up baking for them in order to devote himself solely to spiritual and intellectual pursuits. He began to study French and Latin, attended lectures on Kant, and read Hume and Goethe.

Among the many interesting men and women at the Farm was Almira Barlow, a very beautiful and intelligent woman, twelve years older than himself and the mother of three sons. She had separated from her husband and soon fell deeply in love with Isaac. He himself admitted in his diary that Almira had come nearer to his heart than any other human being. Nevertheless, he could not return her passion. Ever since his vision of the angelic being he had felt that he could never marry, that his life must be given to a greater love than any woman could kindle. Moreover, he was now beginning to be interested in the Church. He read the famous *Symbolik* of the German theologian J. A. Möhler, a "presentation of the doctrinal differences of Catholics and Protestants according to their public confessional writings." The publications of the Oxford Movement, of Newman and Pusey, also played a part in this new interest, which was fanned by Brownson. Together the two men would often discuss these writings as well as the Christian doctrines of Original Sin and man's need of redemption. Within a few months Isaac had travelled far away from the Transcendentalists' tenet of human self-sufficiency. But the Catholic Church still seemed strange to him. He wrote in his diary after attending a service that he felt it could not give him what he wanted, though, a few days later, he thought it would fulfil all his needs. Nevertheless, he did not feel the desire to join it.

His difficulties increased. Owing to the comparatively high costs of life at Brook Farm he could not stay there indefinitely. So in July 1843 he went to a recently established similar community called Fruitlands, near Harvard, which was very austere and less expensive. But this, too, could not satisfy his aspirations. In August he went home. His brothers agreed that he should work at the bakery only in the mornings, so that the rest of the day would be left free for prayer and study. His mode of life was extremely strict: his food consisted of apples, potatoes, nuts, and unleavened bread; he drank only water and even that in very limited quantities. He also tried to introduce social reforms in the family business and established a reading room for their workmen. But he soon realized that he could not achieve any appreciable results by his individual efforts and his thoughts turned to the Church—though he was not sure which he would join, the Episcopalian or the Catholic Church. In March 1844 he called on influential members of both, but without coming to a decision. The manner of Bishop John Hughes of New York, who presented the Church exclusively under its authoritarian and disciplinarian aspects repelled him, and he wrote in his diary: "The R. C. Church is not national with us, hence it does not meet our wants, nor does it fully understand and sympathize with the experiences and disposition of our people. It is principally made up of adopted and foreign individuals." This description, though quite untrue of the Church as such, was nevertheless not without foundation as far as some of its representatives were concerned; many of his later difficulties were caused precisely by such narrow interpretation of the essence of Catholicism.

Next month Isaac went to Boston to discuss his problems with Brownson, then himself considering whether he should join the Catholic Church. From there he went to Concord to study Greek and Latin under the guidance of a competent graduate of Harvard, George Bradford. But very soon he found that his prayer life was becoming so intense that it encroached on his studies. He went through a period of ardent devotion overflowing into his whole being, so that he wrote in his diary that he "would die and be with God which is only desiring to live in a diviner life which I feel within." It became increasingly impossible for him to study, for as

soon as he forced himself to do so his mind went blank and
his memory was gone.

In June matters had come to such a pass that he decided
to write to Brownson for advice. His friend answered by
return of post. He told him that, though there was much that
was good in his state, nevertheless it was fraught with danger:
"The power to control your thoughts and feelings, and to
fix them on what object you choose is of the last necessity,
as it is the highest aim of spiritual culture. Be careful that
you do not mistake a mental habit into which you have fallen
for the guidance of the All-Wise. . . . You have not won
the victory till you have become as able to drudge at Latin
or Greek as to give up worldly wealth . . . You cannot
gain this victory alone, nor by mere private meditation and
prayer. You can obtain it only through the grace of God,
and the grace of God only through its appointed channels.
. . . Do you really believe the Holy Catholic Church? If
so you must put yourself under the direction of the Church."
Then he tells him that he himself has begun to take instructions with a view to becoming a Catholic. And he ends
his long letter: "There is no use in resisting, you cannot be
an Anglican, you must be a Catholic or a Mystic." A Catholic
or a mystic. Brownson at that time knew nothing about
Catholic mysticism; he himself had come to the Church by
way of philosophical reflection and argument—Isaac's strange
experiences seemed to him nothing but daydreaming and
dubious feelings. For a moment Isaac was terrified that in
joining the Church he might have to give up his interior
life. Nevertheless, Brownson had pointed out to him that
he was in conscience bound to do so if he thought the
Catholic Church to be the true one. He went to Boston for
a consultation with the Bishop, who sent him to his coad-
jutor, Bishop Fitzpatrick. He took a line very different from
that of Brownson: Isaac's experiences had not been illusions;
he had been guided by the Spirit of God who had brought
him to the threshold of the Church. And the bishop gave

him an introduction to Monsignor McCloskey, the coad-
jutor of New York.

Once Isaac had made his decision to become a Catholic,
he was inundated with deep peace. He returned to New
York and resumed his old life, baking in the morning and
praying and reading in the afternoon and evening. On August 2, 1844 he was received into the Church. The bishop
discreetly questioned him about a possible vocation to the
priesthood, but for several months he could not make up
his mind, though he left the firm of his brothers and began
to study seriously, this time with greater success than before. After many hesitations, due to his feeling of unworthiness, he finally decided to become a priest. But he still did not
know whether he should become a secular or a religious, and
if the latter, which order he was to enter. In May 1845 he became acquainted with the Redemptorists, who at that time
catered almost exclusively to the German immigrants. But
recently two young Americans, Clarence Walworth and
James McMaster had applied for admission to the congregation. Suddenly Isaac's mind was made up. When he heard
that these two were due to leave for the noviciate in Europe
the following afternoon, he told his brother George, who
had followed him into the Church to pack his suitcase, while
he travelled overnight to Baltimore to obtain the permission
of the Provincial, Father de Held, to join his compatriots.
After hearing Mass next morning he was given the permission
and rushed back to New York where he arrived just in
time for the boat to Europe. And so, on August 27, 1845,
the three young Americans arrived at Portsmouth and from
there went to St. Trond in Belgium to begin their noviciate,
since at that time the American Redemptorist houses were
attached to the Belgian province of the congregation.

Isaac's year in the noviciate was happy, though at first
the novice master treated him rather harshly. As the novices
had to tell him all about their spiritual life, Isaac had to
reveal his extraordinary experiences, and the master, in
accordance with the usual practice of the Church, put their

supernatural origin to the test by making sure of their recipient's virtue. And so, when the other novices were allowed to go for a walk, Isaac would often have to stay in the monastery to clean the stairs. After nine months the novice master had convinced himself of the reality of his spiritual life and even granted him the, in those days, very rare privilege of daily Communion. Towards the end of his noviciate Isaac began to read for the first time the works of the Catholic mystics such as St. John of the Cross, St. Catherine of Genoa, and St. Teresa of Avila, and at last began to understand what had happened to himself, and that his hitherto incomprehensible experiences had not been daydreams or illusions, as his friend Brownson had thought, but were part and parcel of the mystical life.

After his profession Isaac was sent to the house of studies in the southern part of Holland, where much less time was given to prayer and more to learning. This he found difficult, for he had never had a regular education, and the fact that the lessons were given in Latin did not help. Nevertheless, all went well at first, and though the results of his efforts were not brilliant, they sufficed. But in the second year there happened again the same thing as before: he was so strongly drawn to prayer that he found it impossible to follow the regular schedule. But how could he expect to become a priest if he could not acquire the necessary knowledge? Isaac himself wrote an account of what he thought was God's will for him. He was convinced that God was calling him "to America to convert a certain class of persons amongst whom I found myself before my own conversion; I believe that I shall be the vile instrument which He will make use of for the conversion of a multitude of those unhappy souls who aspire after truth without having the means to arrive at and possess it." But "to convince me that this work will not be mine and that I shall only be the mean instrument for the accomplishment of His design He wills me to be deprived of all human means, so that I shall not attribute His glory to myself." For this reason Isaac thought that if he were allowed to acquire what was absolutely necessary for the priesthood in his own way, without regular lessons, "God would abundantly supply all else of which I have need." His superiors decided to dispense him from the usual courses, and the outcome justified this move: though working quite on his own he obtained good marks in the various examinations and even did better than his two fellow Americans. In 1848 he was sent to England, to complete his studies at the Redemptorist house at Clapham, near London. A year after, on October 23, 1849, he was ordained priest by Bishop, later Cardinal, Wiseman. Eighteen months later he returned to America.

The Dutch Father Bernard Hafkenscheid, then the American Provincial, had asked for him and his companion, Father Walworth, to begin extensive mission work in their homeland, and himself trained them and two other English-speaking Redemptorists for their work. Immediately the missions became a tremendous success, and under Father Bernard's guidance Father Hecker developed into a very good speaker. The small band of American priests were asked to give missions throughout America, and the Redemptorists were no longer regarded merely as an order catering to German immigrants.

Then, just when Father Hecker and his friends were looking forward to a period of ever-growing expansion of the American missions, Father Bernard's term of office came to an end and he was not reappointed. He was followed, early in 1854, by Father George Ruland, a Bavarian of quite different temperament. Being a German himself he was far more concerned with preserving the original character of the Redemptorist houses in America than his predecessor; though a devoted religious, he was not open to new ideas and his main concern was to uphold strict religious discipline, regardless of the needs of the apostolate in a new country, so different from his native Bavaria. A clash between him and the go-ahead, mission-minded Father Hecker was almost inevitable.

However, at first all seemed to go well. In the summer of 1854 Father Hecker began to extend his apostolate: he had started to write a book destined to make converts, which he entitled *Questions of the Soul*. In it he retraced in part his own way into the Church, the problems of -human destiny, the insufficiency of purely humanitarian ventures such as he had encountered at Brook Farm and Fruitlands, the disappointment with the Protestant version of Christianity, finally leading to the fulfilment of all man's aspirations in the Catholic Church. The work was positive, scarcely controversial, and inaugurated a new approach to the apostolate. It was immediately welcomed not only by Catholic journals but also by part of the secular press, though violently attacked in Protestant publications. Encouraged by the success, Father Hecker soon planned another book, called *Aspirations of Nature*, in which he would set out the relations between reason and faith. In 1856 he had the opportunity to put his ideas into practice. During a mission in Virginia many non-Catholics had attended, and so Father Hecker resolved to try out the experiment of special lectures, designed chiefly for them and proving that the Church was not hostile to reason, but, on the contrary, fulfilled all its needs. These lectures, too, were very successful, and he was gradually led to the conviction that his real vocation was to work among non-Catholics for the conversion of his country.

But he realized that, as things were at the moment, such work was hampered on all sides. The small group of missionaries were distributed among a number of Redemptorist houses, so that it was extremely difficult to co-ordinate their efforts. Besides, the fact that both language and customs in these houses were German prevented more American vocations, which were essential if the mission work envisaged by Hecker and his associates were to succeed. The only solution of these problems would be the foundation of an American house with English as the normal language and missions, not parishes, as the principal work of the religious. This plan had been suggested to Father Ruland in 1855, but he had rejected it as premature. Indeed, he had a very poor opinion both of the United States and its inhabitants. One of his chief complaints was that Americans were not brought up to "blind obedience," as were the children of his own country, and indeed, of almost all Europe at that time, that they had far too much freedom and independence. This also expressed itself in the religious life, and in consequence Father Ruland was inclined to see rebellion and disobedience everywhere. In his view a mainly American house, run by American superiors could only spell disaster to all religious discipline. He unburdened himself of his fears to the General in Rome, Father Mauron, who trusted him completely and hence conceived very unfavourable opinions of the American character in general and the American missionaries of his own congregation in particular.

Meanwhile the latter grew more and more convinced of the necessity of establishing an American house, a plan which was favoured also by several bishops. Father Walworth outlined his ideas to his superior, who immediately wrote to Rome that he was afraid that the American Fathers were "driven more by natural than by supernatural motives and that is why I fear their plans are not free from danger." In July 1857 matters came to a head. The General, alarmed by Father Ruland's fears, wrote from Rome that a purely American house would mean the destruction of the Redemptorist Congregation in that country, though, in his conversations with the missionaries, Father Ruland had showed himself in favour of such a foundation. At the same time the provincial informed them that two new houses were to be opened in the West Indies and in Quebec respectively, for which English-speaking Fathers would be needed. This was "disastrous news" since it would mean the dispersal of the group of missionaries and the final abandonment of any hope for an American house. If this blow were to be averted, action would have to be taken, and taken quickly. The only hope seemed to be for one of the American Fathers to go to

Rome and explain the situation to the General, who appeared to have completely misjudged the situation.

There was, however, one snag in this: though the Redemptorist constitutions allowed for a simple religious to go to Rome to see the general on urgent business, there had quite recently been a case of a Redemptorist from America taking such an action without any real reason, as a consequence of which the general, Father Mauron, had issued a circular stating "that no one is permitted to leave America of his own will under penalty of expulsion from the Congregation automatically incurred." After many discussions Father Hecker came to the conclusion that this prohibition did not apply to him, as it had been issued in consequence of a case entirely different from his own; besides, it had not yet become officially the law of the order. He therefore set out for Rome—his brother defraying the expenses of the journey—armed with a sheaf of letters and recommendations from important ecclesiastics supporting the plan of an American house.

What followed can only be explained by the utter difference between the situation in the United States and that in Europe in 1857. The Communist Manifesto in 1848 had been followed by revolutionary outbreaks in many parts of the old continent, in the course of which Father Mauron himself had to flee for his life. Hence it was not so surprising that, totally ignorant of conditions in the New World as he was, he should have reacted violently against anything that smacked of insubordination. Despite his years in Holland and England, Father Hecker, on his part, was almost equally ignorant of European conditions and even more so of Roman protocol. He had three private conversations with Father Mauron, who simply refused to discuss the advisability or otherwise of an American house and confined the talks to Father Hecker's disobedience in coming to Rome without his general's permission. These discussions were followed by a meeting of the consulta of the congregation, before which Father Hecker expected to be able to explain his case in greater detail. Instead, the general stated the matter as he saw it; Father Hecker was given no chance to defend himself, but at the end of the meeting was handed a document which decreed his expulsion from the congregation, because he had violated his vows of obedience by undertaking this journey as well as his vow of poverty by accepting the money for it from his brother.

Father Hecker was aghast. "You condemn me then without a hearing?" he asked. The assembled Fathers simply nodded in affirmation. Isaac, whose actions had only been prompted by his fervent apostolic desires, saw himself ignominiously expelled from the congregation which he had merely wanted to serve to the best of his ability.

Father Hecker was not going to accept his fate without a fight—not for the sake of his own personal reputation, but because he realized that, as a religious expelled from his congregation the stigma attached to his name would prevent him from carrying out any of the plans he had so much at heart; besides it would harm also his fellow missionaries who had thrown in their lot with him. So the next months were full of activity, while he was trying to interest all possible persons in his reinstatement. Fortunately he found one very influential adviser in Cardinal Alessandro Barnabò, the prefect of the Congregation of Propaganda, a remarkably liberal-minded man who, moreover, as head of the congregation devoted to spreading the faith was particularly interested in Hecker's ideas. His reception in Rome had shown Father Hecker the lack of understanding for the American mentality, and to counteract these prejudices he wrote two important articles for the Roman periodical *Civiltà Cattolica,* entitled "Present and Future Prospects of the Catholic Faith in the United States of North America." In them he deliberately painted a somewhat rosy picture of these prospects in order to offset the widespread ecclesiastical prejudices against his country. The two articles appeared in November and December 1857. A little before, his

Aspirations of Nature had been published in America and, like its predecessor, was very favourably received.

In the meantime Hecker's efforts to have his name cleared were beginning to bear fruit. In December 1856 he converted an American artist who was known to several influential members of the Roman Curia, and this success made a great impression, as it seemed impressive evidence of the truth of his statements in the *Civiltà Cattolica*. He was gradually acquiring "status" in Rome. In December he submitted a formal defence, drawn up by a canon lawyer, and one week before Christmas he was granted an audience with Pius IX, who gained a very favourable impression of him, though he told him that: "In the United States, there exists a too unrestricted freedom. All the refugees and revolutionaries gather there and are in full liberty." Since then the Church has travelled far, and Pius IX would no doubt have been surprised to hear that only a little over a century later a Catholic would be president of "the refugees and revolutionaries" who, in his view, made up the country.

Father Hecker left the Pope's presence delighted with the warm reception the Pontiff had given him. Meanwhile, many more precious documents were added to his growing dossier which were to help him finally to clear his name. Besides, an Irish-born bishop whose diocese was partly in Canada, partly in the United States, warmly defended him in an audience with the Pope. In the course of the conversation Pius IX suggested that the problem would best be solved if the American missionaries severed their connection with the Redemptorist Congregation and formed an independent missionary community. In January and February 1858 very outspoken letters from the American hierarchy arrived in Rome, with favourable comments on Father Hecker's plans and activities. Nevertheless, his case dragged on. Father Mauron firmly refused to readmit Father Hecker, and the Pope himself was in a difficulty. If he annulled the Decree of Expulsion he would offend the Redemptorists as well as many cardinals and the Germans; if he did not, this would be a blow to the Congregation of Propaganda as well as to the American bishops and the cause of the Church in the United States. The delays were naturally very irksome to the ardent missionary, but, as he himself wrote, they laid in him "the foundations of something much greater than the world imagines: that of becoming a saint. For I am sure my present opportunities on that score are abundant and thank God, His grace is more abundant."

Finally the Pope acted. On March 8 Father Hecker had the satisfaction to read that Pius IX dispensed him and his companions from their vows and ordered them to pursue their missionary work under the direction of the local bishops. The decree contained not a word of criticism, but rather emphasized their zeal "in the prosecution of the holy missions." At last Father Hecker was free to devote himself completely to his one great ideal: the conversion of his country.

After a final audience with Pius IX, in which he thanked the Pope for his kind help, Father Hecker left for America, where he arrived early in May and immediately began to organize his little group—there were four of them besides himself—for the work they felt called to do. What he had in mind was a highly trained community entirely devoted to the apostolate. He felt that what he needed for his purpose was a company of men, distinguished not so much by faithfulness to a set of rules as by initiative and vision. He therefore preferred that his followers should bind themselves not by vow, but by agreement—a precedent having been set by the Congregation of the Oratory, to which, among others, Cardinal Newman and Father Faber belonged, and which is nowadays widely followed by the secular institutes. The first weeks after Father Hecker's return were naturally filled with deliberations about their new mode of life. They finally agreed to work under the authority of the archbishop of New York. Henceforth they were to be known as the Congregation of Missionary Priests of St. Paul the

Apostle, under whose patronage they placed themselves, or, shortly, as Paulists.

As soon as they had worked out the principles by which the community was to live they resumed their mission work, though they had not yet a house of their own, but depended on the hospitality of Father Hecker's relatives and friends. Soon, however, donations poured in, so that they were able to buy a site, and in spring 1859 they rented a small house near to it and began to live in community there until, in Advent of the same year, they could move into their own building and combine their missionary activities with parish work.

Soon the new church of the Paulists attracted a large congregation, for they preached on subjects not usually discussed in other churches in New York or even in the United States. Father Hecker told his audiences that the Catholic Church was universal, that it was as much at home in America as in Europe; that it did not suppress freedom but gave it its proper direction, that reason was a divine gift complemented by, but not opposed to, faith. Besides preaching to adults Father Hecker was particularly concerned with the education of the young, and his Sunday school became a model to many others. Work began to accumulate, and soon more men joined the new community. In 1862 another activity was added to parish work and the giving of missions: Father Hecker began now on a larger scale the lectures to Protestants which he had inaugurated when he was still a Redemptorist. These lectures were entirely positive: he always presupposed the good faith of his hearers, and he would insist that Catholic Christianity took a far more favourable view of human nature than Protestantism did. He corrected mistaken ideas, drew attention to difficulties, and ended up with an exposition of arguments favouring the teaching of the Church. Among the most popular subjects he discussed were: How and Why I Became a Catholic, The Church and the Republic, The Sacraments, as well as controversial themes like Materialism and Spiritualism. While often arousing the antagonism of the Protestant clergy, Father Hecker's lectures were much appreciated not only by his audiences but also by the secular press which gave them good publicity.

Soon, however, Hecker realized that the spoken word alone, whether on the platform or in the pulpit, was not enough. He needed a wider audience, and this could only be reached by the printed word, for, as he once wrote, "evidently the special battlefield of attack and defence of truth for half a century to come is the printing-press." His two books, *Questions of the Soul* and *Aspirations of Nature* had run through several editions and were still selling well; but what he felt was most needed was a magazine which would deal with questions of the moment from the Catholic point of view. And so, in April 1865, the first number of a new magazine made its appearance, *The Catholic World,* a monthly publication catering to a wide range of interests and served by a fine staff of contributors, among whom Hecker's old friend, Orestes Brownson, appeared most frequently. There were articles on social and political questions, on religion and science, often from a controversial angle, as well as short stories and poems. Though the subscription list was comparatively small, Father Hecker soon gave his mind to other literary plans: he founded the Catholic Publication Society which issued books and pamphlets, many of them devoted to combatting the demand that religion should be completely banned from the schools. At the second plenary council of the American episcopate held at Baltimore in October 1866 Archbishop Spalding of Baltimore invited Father Hecker to address the assembled bishops on the subject of Catholic literature as a missionary force, and his speech made a deep impression. The next year he attended the Catholic Congress at Malines, in Belgium, from where he went to England and Ireland to contact publishers to discuss his literary plans with them. For it was Hecker's idea —also advocated and partially realized three quarters of a century later by Maximilian Kolbe—that many Catholic men

and women might find a real vocation as printers, type-
setters, and illustrators, performing this work today in the
same religious spirit as the monks had copied their manu-
scripts in the Middle Ages. He was greatly encouraged in
his work by a letter he received from Pius IX early in 1869,
in which the Pope commended the work he and his community had undertaken, especially the apostolate of the press.

In November of the same year he once more went to
Rome to the Vatican Council—but this time not as a harassed
religious "under a cloud," but as the representative or
"procurator" of the Bishop of Columbus, who was prevented
by illness from attending in person. When it was found that
as such he would nevertheless not be allowed to attend the
Council on account of the large number of prelates, the
Archbishop of Baltimore appointed him his theologian, an
office which permitted him to read all the documents issued
by the Council and so to be completely informed of its
deliberations. Naturally Father Hecker again met many old
friends and made a great number of new ones, he visited many
of the shrines of the Eternal City, especially the Basilica of
St. Paul, where he prayed for the success of his own community and its work. He also preached before large con-
gregations and sent articles to *The Catholic World* to keep its
readers informed of the progress of the Council.

The Council had opened in December 1869; by May 1870
it showed no signs of coming to an end. Father Hecker felt
that his presence was needed at home. So, after brief visits
to Assisi, Venice, and a few other Italian places, he went to
Paris where he embarked for New York. In October he
started a new magazine, *The Young Catholic*, which proved
an immediate success. It contained several series of interest to
growing boys and girls such as "A Boy's Letters from Rome"
and "Catholics Who Have Helped Build America."

Ever since he had returned to America from his first years
with the Redemptorists Father Hecker had led a life of
incessant work and travel; with many troubles and excitements thrown in for good measure. Besides, as he himself

admitted, his youthful dietary experiment with nothing but fruit and potatoes for his food had harmed his constitution at an early age. Now, towards the end of 1871, the constant strain began to tell. The headaches from which he had been suffering for many years grew steadily worse; besides, his doctor diagnosed angina pectoris. There was nothing for it but complete rest, and in the summer of the following year he took an extended holiday in the South. But on his return to New York, early in 1873, his health had not improved, and his brother George urged him to go to Switzerland for a cure. So he once more travelled to Europe, arriving at Ragaz, not far from Liechtenstein, in August.

The Alpine air and the freedom from any worries benefited him, but as soon as letters from home arrived asking about the possibility of his return his headaches and depressions came on again. The only thing to do was to put any such thoughts out of his mind and simply to vegetate. Later in the year, however, he was well enough to go sightseeing to Lucerne, Geneva, and elsewhere. In November he went to Paris, and there some American friends suggested a trip up the Nile. He and his party embarked at Marseilles for Alexandria, and from there went up the river to Cairo. They spent Christmas at Ekmeer and then went further south, returning to Cairo in the early spring of 1874.

Despite the long months of inactivity Father Hecker was not much better and could not think of resuming work, even though the community wrote how much they missed him. Before returning to Europe he made a pilgrimage to the Holy Land, visiting all its most famous shrines and having the joy of saying Mass in the Church of the Holy Sepulchre, in the very place where, according to tradition, the body of Christ had been placed after He had been taken down from the Cross.

On his return to the Continent, he found Germany in the throes of the *Kulturkampf*—a struggle between the Church and Bismarck's new *Reich*, which tried to suppress Catholic education and to curtail the freedom of Catholicism in every possible way. This had been one of the consequences of the destruction of the temporal power of the papacy after the seizure of Rome by Victor Emmanuel (1870). These events had left Catholics in Europe stunned, and the prestige of the Church greatly damaged. Father Hecker, deeply disturbed, could not understand the inactivity of both clergy and laity in the face of these calamities. So, early in 1875, he wrote a paper entitled "An Exposition of the Church in View of Recent Difficulties and Controversies and the Present Needs of the Age." In it he criticized the European Catholics of his time for a surfeit of external devotions while neglecting the spiritual side of the Christian life. The Church, too, had been rather repressive in the past; soon the time would come for her to encourage greater individual activity. He foresaw an increasing influence of the Anglo-Saxon races in the future as against the almost exclusive predominance of the Latin peoples in the past, and this would mean more freedom for the individual, because the Anglo-Saxon countries were accustomed to democratic government as against the feudalism still prevalent on the continent of Europe. Non-Catholics could see only the outer and human side of the Church; "we" he ended, "must by our own Catholic life and actions bring these people back into the Church by an appeal to their intelligence of the inward and divine."

When the paper was finished he took it to Rome, where it was approved by many influential clerics, including Cardinal Manning. Though preparations were being started to have it published there, it was declared "inexpedient," and so it was brought out in London and immediately afterwards translated into French and published also in Paris. Though appreciated by many who saw more deeply, the work roused much criticism and was held in certain quarters to be infested with illuminism and mysticism—the latter having become a term of abuse in the second half of the nineteenth century, when mystical experience was rated low and often confused with illusions. In the spring he returned once more to Radaz. He dreamt of visiting Russia and India, but a letter from New York, showing that his community was in urgent need of guidance from its founder, decided him to return. He landed in New York in October 1875, after an absence of over two years.

He did not, however, resume community life for the time being, since his health could not as yet stand it, but he stayed at the house of his brother George, occupied mostly with writing articles for *The Catholic World* and with giving spiritual direction. Four years later he went back to the house of his Society and took up once more at least part of its government. Now that his activities were so drastically curtailed, he had more time to read, and it is significant that, apart from the Bible, St. Thomas Aquinas and St. John of the Cross were his constant companions. He particularly treasured Père de Caussade's treatise on *Abandonment to Divine Providence* with its teaching on the present moment as the principal means of sanctification. During these last years Father Hecker went through the interior trials which St. John of the Cross calls the "Night of the Spirit." He was terrified of the divine judgment and became increasingly aware of the avenging Majesty of God, who left him to an overpowering feeling of his own human weakness without giving him any support.

In 1887 he published a collection of his articles and essays including his *Exposition,* and in 1888, the year of his death, he published an article in *The Catholic World* called "Things That Make for Unity" which, in the light of recent developments in the Church, seems almost prophetic. In it he wrote that "the tendency of the religious minded is nowadays toward unity as it was to disunion centuries ago." He continued asking if it were not better now to stress points of agreement rather than to emphasize the differences. He answered in the affirmative, but cautioned that it must be done wisely. "Why," he concluded, "should we, under Providence, not start a movement toward unity set in our day, just as in the sixteenth century the perversity of men brought about a disunion of sects?" The last article he wrote, "The Mission of Leo XIII," gave another proof of his correct anticipation of future trends. In it he foresaw not only an increasing separation of Church and State in Europe, but also quite a different composition of the College of Cardinals, until then overwhelmingly Italian. The democratic trends of the time "would result in bringing the Papacy and the Episcopate closer together and both into direct communication with the people. . . . It would result in the College of Cardinals being made a representative body of all mankind—the religious senate of the world."

In the latter part of the year the angina pectoris which had been latent for so long began to take its toll. But, as death drew nearer, the fear of God's wrath and the night of the soul that had affected him disappeared completely. Instead, he was filled with the sense of the presence of the Holy Spirit who had been his guide ever since he had begun to search for the truth and the meaning of his life. Calm and serene, he waited for the end. On December 2, 1888, he breathed his last.

Nine years later the controversy broke out which has been mentioned at the beginning of this chapter. It was the time when Modernism was just making its appearance, when the Church had to fight against rationalistic tendencies in her own ranks. In those days bold new ideas were bound to be suspect, and when, through the translation of Walter Elliott's *Life of Father Hecker* his views and methods became known in France, many clerics saw in them dangerous novelties and, by a one-sided interpretation, found in them a new heresy dubbed "Americanism."

Today this controversy has long been forgotten. Many of Father Hecker's ideas which seemed once so revolutionary have become generally accepted in the Church: the apostolate of the press, the greater participation of the laity in Church affairs, the inclusion of all nations and races in the College of Cardinals—seventy years after his death these are no longer the bold visions of a priest who combined great apostolic activity with an intense mystical life, but a commonplace. And the Church in America, the country he had to defend against so many prejudices, has been gaining in strength ever since, as Isaac Hecker had told incredulous audiences that it would.

CHAPTER FOUR

Contardo Ferrini

(1859–1902)

Towards the end of the nineteenth century the Church in Italy was in a very bad state. In September 1870 Victor Emmanuel had seized Rome and Pope Pius IX lost the last vestiges of the temporal power the Church had enjoyed in the Middle Ages. He became the "Prisoner of the Vatican," and Italy was given over to not only anti-clerical but even atheist politicians. Matters were not improved by the Papal decree "Non Expedit" (1868), by which Catholics were forbidden to take part in any civil elections. This meant that the government of the country was completely left in anti-Catholic hands, and, naturally, that education at all levels was taken out of the hands of the Church and made the concern of secular authorities. A young Catholic intellectual growing up in such an atmosphere would have to face very grave problems.

This was precisely the situation into which Contardo Ferrini was born. Both his parents were devout Christians. His father was a professor at a technical college who wrote learned treatises on electricity, heat, and other scientific subjects. His mother, a very forceful woman, had no understanding of intellectual work and thought nothing of interrupting her husband, and later also her eldest son, to make them run errands for her. In 1861 his father bought a villa at Suna, on the Lago Maggiore, where his family would go for their holidays and which became the centre where, in later years, parents and children would reunite. Contardo was a happy and lively little boy who loved to play at soldiers, but he was abnormally sensitive. Once, as he was singing, an uncle told him that his voice was not very pleasant, a remark he took so much to heart that he never sang again. When he was six years old he was sent to school at the Institute Boselli, where he made excellent progress in languages but very much less in arithmetic, which he disliked.

It seems that the only time Contardo fell in love was at the tender age of eleven with an English girl ten years his senior who was staying at his home and who subsequently became a nun. But a year later occurred an event that turned his thoughts in quite a different direction. In April 1871 he made his First Communion, having prepared for it by a fortnight's retreat under the direction of the Ursuline nuns of San Carlo. This first Holy Communion worked a decisive transformation in him. The high-spirited boy became very quiet and studious and showed an intense devotion to the Blessed Sacrament and to prayer. Nine years later he wrote a letter to his younger sister when she made her First Communion, which evidently reflects his own experience. He tells her that: "It is the day of high resolves which should last throughout our life . . . the offering of our poor heart to its Creator, a promise of love, an answer to the tenderness of the God who made us, the sweet converse between child and father, the fulness of worship. All coldness will melt, peace and joy will come, self will be annihilated, and we shall have the fulness of love which should yet be prudently hidden from others. Never again shall we be moved by passion, nor by the doubts and torments that trouble worldly people.

You will pass through the world without understanding how evil can attract mankind."

It seems from this letter that Contardo thought such an intense experience quite normal; it did not occur to him that it was a special, we may well call it a mystical, grace that made him realize so clearly the intimate union between Christ and His creature which happens in eucharistic communion and that produced such lasting effects. But just this realization, joined as it was to his extraordinarily sensitive temperament, was to cause him great sufferings during the following years of puberty and adolescence. In the secular school he attended neither piety nor purity were greatly esteemed, and once his fellows had discovered that he would blush at the slightest coarse remark they took cruel advantage of this easy way of amusing themselves. This made Contardo very unhappy. Even during vacation in the country he could not always escape from being teased on this account, and he was soon nicknamed St. Aloysius, after the young Jesuit who had been famous for his outstanding purity.

These difficulties, however, did not prevent him from giving his mind to his studies. He was particularly interested in languages, and in addition to the Latin and Greek he learned at school, he studied Hebrew and Syriac under the guidance of the prefect of the famous Ambrosian library in Milan. This choice of languages was stimulated by his profound interest in the Bible, which he wanted to read in the original. His love of the Scriptures was allied to a great inclination for legal questions, a combination which is not as strange as it might appear at first sight, seeing that a large section of the Bible itself deals with laws, and that all priests have to possess a certain knowledge of canon law for the exercise of their ministry. So the very first treatise Contardo wrote, when he had just gone to the University of Pavia at the age of seventeen, had for its subject the juridical capacity as evidenced by the Hebrews. This early work was published only after his death; it showed already the brilliance of the young scholar's mind, for no less a personage than the Great

Rabbi of Milan said of it that it merited serious consideration, "especially on account of the subtle studies on which it is based and for the learned deductions which the author draws in masterly fashion from the Mosaic Laws by quoting in support of his thesis the opinions and observations of the best commentators of the sacred text. We admire especially how he has succeeded in condensing in a short study such a wealth of citations, references and passages and compared them with each other; here we have evidently a profound critical study of the Biblical text." This is, indeed, no mean praise from an expert on the Old Testament for the work of a boy of seventeen. It also shows his ability to combine the deep spiritual understanding with which he approached the Word of God in prayer with an objective, purely scholarly exposition of it which is very rare.

Though Contardo's intellectual powers were recognized by everyone, professors and fellow students alike, he was a butt of frequently very crude jokes on account of his retiring ways and his piety. In the winter this was particularly unpleasant, for there was only one heated room in the students' house, so the only way of escaping from the teasing of the others was by going to his own icy study. One day, as Contardo came into the lounge with a bucket and a shovel to take some of the burning coals to his room to warm himself, one of the students upset them all over the floor, so that he had great difficulty putting them back into his bucket without causing damage. On another occasion, when he was dean of students and as such was responsible for silence being kept in the room of studies, they continually disobeyed his orders and finally kicked up such a row that he saw no other way than to gather up his books and retire to his room.

Naturally such behaviour wounded the sensitive young man very deeply. The more so, as it seemed to show him that he was quite without any influence on his fellowmen, whom he would so willingly have led to Christ. All the apostolic desires so natural to a Christian of his devotion and intelligence seemed doomed to frustration, as his personality only appeared to arouse derision. At that time he wrote: "To despise the world is natural for the Christian soul which sees things as they really are; but disdain for those who are in the world would be very wrong, for they are our brothers." As he realized that he would not be able to spread the Kingdom of God by direct apostolic activity and that even the good example he tried to set seemed only to arouse scorn and dislike, he felt good for nothing and came to see only gradually that prayer and suffering can also be the most effective means of the apostolate. These years at Pavia were thus a time of intense purification—not through mysterious supernatural interventions, but through the very natural reactions of the sensitive, retiring character of a true Christian scholar to his insensitive and at times brutal, unbelieving environment.

This, however, does not mean that Contardo was quite without friends. On the contrary, when he had found a like-minded young man his attachment went deep, and he shared with him all his intimate life. He would introduce his friends to the writings of Newman, whom he greatly admired; he would pray with them and write long letters to them especially to Vittorio and Paolo Mapelli. Many of these letters were almost small religious essays expressing his beliefs and aspirations. His own spiritual life was intense. He went to Mass almost every day and to Holy Communion much more frequently than was usual at that time. His devotion centred in the Eucharist and was very liturgical; he followed the Mass in his missal—also very rare for a layman in those days.

Contardo's piety was allied to a very strong sense of the beauties of nature. He loved the mountains and was an excellent climber; his father had introduced him to this sport when he was a small boy, and at the age of seventeen he made his first attempt to reach the summit of the Monte Rosa, though he was not successful at that time. Later he became an expert and climbing was his favourite relaxation throughout his life. He needed such an outlet for his physical energy, since his work kept him at his desk almost all day long. At

Pavia he also developed a taste for Greek civilization and became the favourite pupil of the professor of Greek language and history. So at the end of his academic training, he chose for his thesis a subject which combined this new interest with his old one in legal matters and wrote on the profit a student of law may draw from the poems of Homer and Hesiod. Again he stresses also the religious aspects of the law. For he demonstrates in this work that the Greek law knows divine sanctions. Its underlying concept is that the punishment of all crime, whether public or private, is reserved to Jupiter and that the earthly punishment is regarded as executed in the name and in the place of the Deity. The judges act not in their own name, but as representatives of the Godhead—a view which, though present in ancient and medieval jurisprudence was no longer accepted in the Italy of the late nineteenth century. The lucidly reasoned and extremely well-documented exposition earned Contardo the highest praise from his examiners; indeed, his thesis was considered so brilliant that the faculty ordered its publication, a very unusual honour. He now had to decide on a profession; he chose the law, with the view to a university career.

He also wrote his first religious book on a *Way of Life for a Young Student*, in the form of letters to the Mapelli brothers. In it he combats especially freemasonry, then of great influence in Italy and violently anti-Christian, to whose hatred of the Church he opposed Christ's way of love. He advises his readers to practise purity, his own favourite virtue, and humility, and to see Christ in their neighbour, whom they were to help both spiritually and materially.

Contardo's brilliant examination had won him a scholarship for the study of Roman law in Berlin, where there were such famous scholars as Mommsen, Pernice, and Zacharia von Lingenthal. So in December 1880 he left his native city for the capital of Bismarck's Reich. His father had had some misgivings: would Contardo be able to keep his faith intact in this citadel of Protestantism? He need not have worried. Not only was Contardo's faith far too deep-rooted to be shaken, but his experiences in Berlin, as later those of Jerome Jaegen, actually strengthened it. For the German Catholics were just then emerging from the *Kulturkampf*, the struggle between Bismarck's government and the Church already referred to in the chapter on Isaac Hecker. This attack on the freedom of the Church and her members had considerably strengthened the faith and devotion of German Catholics, so that Contardo found in the Catholic circles of Berlin an atmosphere of fervour quite different from the indifference or even hostility of Italian students. The Catholic students of Berlin were well organized, went to Mass and the Sacraments with exemplary regularity, and belonged to such charitable institutions as the St. Vincent de Paul Society. Contardo was greatly edified by all he saw, as well as by the clergy which he found by and large much better educated than their Italian confreres.

Thus the two years he spent in Berlin were far happier than his student life at Pavia. His habits were very austere; he stayed at a hostel run by Ursuline nuns and divided his days among work, prayer, and contacts with congenial fellow students and professors. The latter were greatly impressed by his ability; no less a personage than Theodor Mommsen considered him the most gifted student of ancient Roman law, in which he had specialized. Contardo took his work very seriously. In the summer of 1881 his family wanted him to return to Suna for the vacation; but though he would have preferred it, he felt it his duty to go to Copenhagen instead in order to examine a manuscript that was essential to his studies. As he himself expressed it: "I have two important duties: to prepare myself as well as possible for the career God has destined for me, and to correspond to the best of my ability to the intentions of the Italian government who have facilitated my stay here. Thus I can be at peace, knowing that I am fulfilling these duties honourably." In the autumn of the same year, after consultation with his confessor, he made a vow of perpetual chastity.

Many of those who knew him best were surprised that he

did not choose to become a priest, that he did not decide to enter an order such as the Jesuits or the Benedictines, where he could have combined a life of prayer with scholarly work. When someone broached this subject he would say that he was not worthy. Perhaps, after the unhappy experiences at Pavia, he may have felt he had not sufficient gifts for making contact with and influencing his fellow men, that he was not enough of a leader to be able to cope with the problems confronting the Italian clergy at that time. His vocation, as he saw it, was neither the pulpit nor the confessional, but the professorial chair. But in his case this vocation had to be lived as a strict discipline, unrelieved by the joys and relaxations of either family or intensive social life. It was his way of offering himself to God: a scholar and celibate in the world.

In 1882 he returned to Italy, sure of his calling, and far happier than after his harrying student years in Pavia. He continued his research in Milan and Rome, and in the summer went to Suna for a climbing holiday. At that time ancient Roman and Byzantine law had its finest representatives in Germany, and the Italian government welcomed it that now one of their countrymen of outstanding ability was taking up these studies which had recently been neglected in the very land where Roman law had originated. So late in 1883 a new chair was created for him at Pavia for research into the sources of Roman law, and he delivered his inaugural address in June of the next year.

It was only to be expected that the brilliant young professor, tall, handsome, and a fine sportsman, should have been considered a very eligible son-in-law by mothers with marriageable daughters. Contardo's own mother, too, was anxious to find him a wife. His replies to the various proposals made to him show a lighthearted sense of humour, not without a touch of sarcasm. Once his mother extolled the wonderful dowry one young lady would bring him, whereupon he asked drily: "Would it not be possible to marry only the dowry?" On another occasion she explained to him how much a girl would inherit on the death of her father, fol-

lowed by more on the death of her mother, and by another
lot on the death of her uncle . . . when Contardo interrupted
the flow of explanations with the words: "Yes—but so many
corpses!" Once a prospective mother-in-law herself took him
in hand and insisted that he should go for a walk with her
and her two daughters. Afterwards she asked hopefully
which of her two girls he liked best. "The third, Madam," he
replied without hesitation.

Ferrini's university duties left him only comparatively
little time for prayer. For him his work was in itself a
service of God, for it was the duty He had laid on him and
he took it as much as a divine vocation as if he had become
a priest. Nevertheless, besides going almost daily to Mass and
Holy Communion, he gave at least a quarter of an hour to
mental prayer and hardly ever missed a visit to the church in
the afternoon. If his prayer time was short, his colloquy with
God was all the more intense. Those who saw him, lost in
God before the altar after he had received Holy Communion,
realized that his interior life had reached mystical heights.
"Only our feet should touch the earth," he once wrote, "our
soul should be absorbed in God. That calm and uninterrupted
absorption ought to be an image of the Sabbath of the
Trinity."

Nourished by prayer, his scholarly output was tremendous.
During his four years at Pavia, from 1883 to 1887, he
published two major works on the Roman law and prepared
a third. In them he threw out a multitude of brilliant ideas
which were to inspire later research. The only criticism
made by his colleagues was that his references were frequently
wrong. This was due to the speed with which he worked so
that he was not always careful to verify his quotations, a
fault often to be found in original thinkers. He himself was
the first to admit his mistakes when they were pointed out to
him and good-naturedly submitted to the teasing of his friends
when they had found yet another reference that was not
quite correct.

In 1887 Contardo was appointed to the University at

Messina as professor of Roman law: for it was the policy of the Italian government to move their teachers and officials freely about the country so as to counteract local patriotism and unify the land. Ferrini was not happy about this move. Not only was he separated from his family by the whole length of Italy, but the natives of Sicily were very different from those of Northern Italy. Ferrini, himself a hard worker and outstanding scholar, demanded serious application from his students; but this was impossible to obtain in Sicily, where everyone seemed devoted only to the principle of *dolce far niente*, sweet laziness. He felt that he could make no headway with the students of Messina, and so, when in 1889 the chair of Roman law in the famous university of Bologna fell vacant he applied for it.

Everyone agreed that Ferrini was the best qualified of the candidates competing for it, nevertheless he was unsuccessful. The chair was given to Giuseppe Brini, whose supporters spread the rumour that Contardo did not really want to go to Bologna, that he meant to go to Pavia; besides, Brini had written a book on *Marriage and Divorce in Roman Law,* in the preface to which he had said that it was meant to prepare the way for legislation for divorce in Italy, which seems to have been one of the reasons why the government preferred him to Ferrini. The latter knew very well that, on merely scholarly merits, the chair ought to have gone to him; for humility is allied to truth, and it is no virtue for a man to pretend that he does not have the qualities which he knows he possesses. But, having pointed out why he should be given the professorship at Bologna, he never had a word of blame for those who had prevented his success and accepted that of his rival without any adverse comment.

In the meantime three other universities asked for Ferrini: both Parma and Modena wanted him, while Messina hoped to retain him. The minister offered him the choice, and Contardo opted for Modena. He left Messina in August 1890 and after spending another holiday in his beloved mountains, took up his new post in the autumn of the same year. At

Modena his students fully appreciated their famous teacher.
He had by now perfected his method. His chief concern was
to present his subject in the simplest and clearest possible
way, leaving aside inessential detail that would only confuse
his hearers. Hence his lectures were crowded and his pupils
were devoted to him. For he not only taught them, in the
vacation he would also sometimes take parties of them to the
mountains, frequently acting himself as guide. In addition to
being a great lover of the mountains, the silence and majesty
of which he found brought him nearer to God, he also was
very knowledgeable about geology and botany and full of
interesting information which he would vary with quotations
from both classical and modern poets.

Apart from these holidays the young professor continued
his austere life, which aroused the admiration of his Jesuit
confessor who wrote of him: "To see a man in the flower of
his youth, a university professor of profound learning lead
the life of a perfect religious, the life of a saint, this is truly
a spectacle worthy of the angels. How impressed we were
seeing him go to Holy Communion, which he received nearly
every day, returning from the altar with folded hands and
lowered eyes, and all this so simply and naturally that one
easily realized that he saw Jesus in the divine Sacrament and
felt Him present in his heart." In 1886 he had become a
Franciscan tertiary, following the recommendation of Leo
XIII who, four years before, had urged Christian men and
women to join the Third Order of St. Francis to combat the
evils of the time. Contardo took his membership very seriously
and quietly practised such inconspicuous austerities as taking
no sugar in his coffee or refusing second helpings in addition
to the asceticism his devotion to learning demanded from
him.

In 1894 his former German teacher Zacharia von Lingenthal died; and he left his pupil all his unpublished works and
notes to edit, a mark of confidence and respect that touched
Ferrini very deeply. In the same year he had the happiness
of returning to his own university of Pavia, and in 1895 he

was finally transferred to Milan, the home of his family. Here at Milan more responsibilities were added to his already overcrowded life. So far he had abstained from taking part in any elections or other political activities in obedience to the Papal decree, "Non Expedit," though many good Catholics refused to do so. If asked for his reasons he explained that, even speaking from a merely human point of view, the Pope had more opportunities for forming his opinions than the ordinary faithful; besides, he would receive supernatural lights when taking his decisions. Nevertheless, early in 1895 a situation arose when he felt that he could not in conscience refuse to concern himself with the political future of his native city. The municipal elections were hotly contested, and Ferrini was asked to stand as a Catholic candidate in order to bring his outstanding legal knowledge to the struggle against anti-Christian socialism which was threatening the Church. At that moment relations between the papacy and the Italian government had temporarily improved, and so Ferrini consented to stand, though with a heavy heart, since his peaceful, contemplative temperament was ill-suited to the struggles of the political arena. In the February elections the radical socialists were defeated and an anti-socialist coalition came into power. Ferrini spoke but rarely at the meetings of the assembly, though he attended them regularly. But his character as well as his legal knowledge assured him a silent influence on his fellow-citizens, who were well aware of his high principles and, indeed, his holiness. In fact, in the caricatures of the time he was almost invariably represented with a halo.

Contardo was deeply concerned with the social problems of his time. In 1891 Leo XIII had published his great encyclical *Rerum Novarum* on this burning question. Soon after becoming a City Councillor Ferrini outlined his own ideas on the subject. He was convinced that "words of hate serve only to disturb hearts and to create mischievous dissension." In his view, "Moral remedies alone can meet the case; but to ensure their acceptance an educational campaign will be needed to destroy the deceptive arguments and paradoxes of the socialists and remove the false illusions they create." Men should "work together to gain their freedom by courage, then they will find life worth living. Enlightened kindness and consistent action will prepare the way for the increasing betterment of the lot of the disinherited."

The combination of sustained research and political activity tired him out. In a letter to a friend he described his over-crowded days: "I have no time to rest or take recreation. I cannot relax. It takes a great deal out of me to give two courses of lectures; then, this year, I have as well to edit a Greek manuscript which takes up a good deal of my time. Besides, there is my work on the council as well as my private affairs. . . . For, after all, I have obligations to my family and my friends, for I am partly a lawyer and partly a professor not only for outsiders but also for my own." For he never refused to help those who came to him for advice and was often involved in difficult cases. For example, should a totally depraved mother be deprived of the custody of her son? Ferrini favoured such a course which, however, aroused a certain amount of opposition among those who maintained that a child had to remain with his mother in all circumstances. Nor was it always easy to maintain the balance between his duties as a councillor and the at that time often very narrow views of the Roman clergy, who were in deadly opposition to all that concerned the new secular Italian state.

The unveiling of a statue of King Victor Emmanuel, in September 1896 provoked a bitter discussion. The King had become for many a symbol of the modern secular state, opposed to the power of the Church. On the other hand, if the Catholic councillors were to absent themselves from the ceremony this would only provoke the anti-clerical government even more. So the councillors, guided by Ferrini, decided to be present at the unveiling. When this act came to the knowledge of the *Osservatore Romano*, the official organ of the Vatican attacked him and his colleagues vio-lently, though they had made it clear that they did not mean their presence to condone the anti-clerical tendencies of the government but regarded the statue as a tribute to the liberation of Italy from foreign (Austrian and French) oppression. The controversy caused much sorrow to Contardo, who wrote to his friend Paolo Mapelli: "Have you seen the *Osservatore* recently and what he has said against us? May God preserve us from all the evils which a misguided zeal can cause us." How right was his conciliatory attitude appeared clearly when, as an answer to the attack, the non-Catholic councillors threatened to deprive the clergy of their right to teach religion in the schools.

Ferrini saw only too clearly the perils into which the apathy of the Italian bourgeoisie, impervious to the danger signals, would lead his country. In February 1898 he wrote to a friend: "Only too often do those who govern us fail to do anything that could influence the masses. Here in Milan the socialists make constant and remarkable progress, the good middle classes notice nothing, but as soon as they will realize what is going on they will be horrified. The only people who oppose the forces of socialism as best they can are the priests, who organize conferences, relief, cooperatives, rural funds to prevent the masses from letting themselves be duped by the vain mirage of social transformation. During the present carnival they organized no fewer than thirty amateur theatres to keep the workers away from the public houses, which are real hotbeds of socialist infection. But our good citizens notice nothing—let us hope they will not have to pay for it too much."

He saw with surprising clarity what was coming; for he added: "I do not think it possible that socialism will succeed in establishing itself; the masses which belong to the party are not very clear about what they want to do and have no programme. But that class hatred will lead to an explosion, a revolution, a catastrophe, that is only too probable and perhaps too near." Events proved Ferrini right. In April street fighting broke out in Milan as well as in many other Italian cities; the rebels were shot at by the police, and the

Catholics were no longer allowed the freedom of association because they had taken up a sympathetic attitude towards the workers. At the next election they were ousted from the government, and thus Ferrini's short political career came to an end.

The last years of his life he spent entirely in the service of scholarship and education. He was of the opinion that academic education and our civilization as a whole suffered from a lack of appreciation of the world that God had made. "We ought," he wrote, "to make a large place in our education for cultivating the sense of the beauties of nature, a precious quality reserved for privileged souls. Poor youth! They grow up shrivelled, miserable in body and soul, without ideas, without courage, knowing no other landscape than the boulevard, no other horizons than those they discover from a balcony, no other spectacles of nature than those they read about in books." We must remember that these words were written at the end of the last century, when youth movements and scouting had not yet been thought of. With the rare insight into the needs of the time which is to be found so often in the mystics, Ferrini anticipated these developments, because he pitied the young men who were growing up in an increasingly specialized society, becoming more and more divorced from their roots in God's creation. "Poor youth," he said again, "without conscience and without dignity, occupied only with fashions, novels, the theatre, and which has never ventured to the edge of a precipice, nor trodden the snow on the summit of a mountain." In his view the decadent European youth of the *fin de siècle* could only very gently be led back to the true vocation of man through contact with the simple things of life, as Contardo himself loved to talk to the peasants he met on his climbing expeditions and to children.

Like most holy people, the learned professor loved children, and they were very fond of him and would obey him more easily than their own parents. Once a small nephew of his was very bad-tempered and would only stamp his foot and say, "No, no, no," to whatever his mother asked him to do. Contardo watched the scene for a few minutes, then he took the boy by the hand and went into the garden with him. "Now then," he said, "I think we had better bury Mr. No. Here is a good place for it—take your trowel and make a nice grave for him, and then we'll see that he will never come out again." The boy understood, and though "Mr. No" did at times still come out of his grave, he did so much more rarely and went back to it more quickly than before.

Ferrini treated his students, too, with the same psychological understanding and tact. Dressed in black, he would begin his lectures in a low voice, so as to concentrate their attention entirely on his words; then gradually he would raise his voice until his audience was completely captivated and followed every word of his lucid expositions of even the most difficult and complicated subjects. Through the kindness he combined with his outstanding scholarship he exercised a quiet apostolate among his students, though he never referred directly to the faith. To do this would, indeed, have been very imprudent. As the professor of a state university Contardo was obliged to give his time to instructing his hearers in the subject he was commissioned to teach; to have used his position for purposes of the apostolate would have been a breach of trust. His vocation was to the indirect apostolate, to bearing silent witness to the Christian truth in a world that was hostile to it. The very fact that a first-class scholar should also be a devout Christian made a deep impression on his colleagues and students. Rationalists as most of them were, they tended to think that religion was only for the simple-minded, in accordance with the saying of the German poet Goethe: "He who has art and scholarship also has religion; he who has neither of these, ought to have religion." They all knew that Ferrini went to Mass almost every morning; they would see him walking in the Corpus Christi procession, usually carrying the canopy over the Blessed Sacrament, or kneeling down when he met a priest carrying It.

How did he combine his exacting scholarly work with an intense life of prayer? He himself answers this question: "Even in the daily occupations there must be what I call the intimate communications between God and His creature. . . . This will mean remembering the holy thoughts of the morning Mass, a remembrance that comes to us, consoling us, in the course of our daily work. This will be a glance towards our Father in the midst of our daily cares, an act of love springing almost unconsciously from our lips, but recorded by the angels and lifting our heart up to God." Thus the intimate union with God he had experienced during the Mass accompanied him throughout his day, giving all his work a supernatural value and significance. And of this work itself he could say, in his preface to a learned treatise on legacies and trusts: "I am happy to be able to say of myself that I have always sought the truth and never what is fanciful, uncertain or merely sparkling."

His scholarly mind and his feeling for what is essential expressed itself also in his attitude to his religion. He scarcely concerned himself with secondary devotions but went straight to the heart of the faith, to the Trinity, the Incarnation, the Eucharist. For "the end of Christian prayer," he wrote, "is our transformation into Jesus Christ. . . . This calm, tranquil absorption must reflect the union within the supreme Trinity as the Saviour has said in His last discourse."

Even before Ferrini embarked on his short political career his health had been indifferent. From 1892 onwards he had suffered each year from attacks of influenza. Nevertheless, he never took much notice of his health. His work absorbed him so much that he could not tear himself away from it; his holidays, too, were very strenuous, as he spent them always climbing, and though he would return from them tanned and full of vitality, his doctors feared for his heart. But he had no forebodings of an early death. At Easter 1901 he planned to go to Palestine with a friend, to see the Holy Places. But then the pressure of work was so hard that he could not make time for it. For, among other things, he was involved in the controversy following the intention of the government to introduce divorce legislation and wrote a long preface to a work by another legal expert, opposing it. He deferred the Palestine project till later in the year, but again had to put off the voyage, because his heart condition would not allow it. In January 1902 he had touches of rheumatic fever. Nevertheless he continued to work very hard. The examinations were the worst part of his professorial duties; they tired him out completely. In August 1902 he wrote: "I have been harried by the examinations and the prize lists and have emerged from them, on July 10, more dead than alive, through fatigue and the heart."

After the university term was over he went to Suna to recover. There he went to Mass early every morning, then studied, bathed, and spoke to the peasants, many of whom would come to him for advice. In September he had to attend a conference in Rome, from which he returned even more tired than he had been at the beginning of the vacation. Once, as he went for a walk, he drank water from a stream. The doctors thought that this was responsible for the typhoid which he developed within a fortnight. At first he disregarded his illness; he even still went climbing. On October 4, a Saturday, he felt shivery; nevertheless he insisted on going to Mass next day. On his return home he fainted, and soon he was in a delirium. Characteristically, in his lucid moments, knowing that he was going to die, he repeatedly asked: "Have I done my duty?"

Contardo Ferrini died on October 17, 1902. He was beatified in 1947.

CHAPTER FIVE

Elisabeth Leseur

(1866–1914)

Is it possible to combine marriage with mysticism? Do not the cares as well as the joys of married life preclude that intense union with God which is the essence of the mystical experience? But, we may ask, countering these questions, would God, who is good and who desires to be most intimately united to his reasonable creatures, deprive a man or woman of the possibility of this union merely because he or she is living in a state which has itself the rank of a sacrament? True, mystics are rare, because the mystical union presupposes much self-denial and the practice of all the Christian virtues to a high degree; and even if these conditions are fulfilled God will not always give it. Nevertheless, even though the celibate state ranks in itself higher than marriage, the married life offers its full quota of opportunities for self-sacrifice and the practice of Christian charity, and the marriage vows are as secure a foundation for developing the Christian life as are the vows of religion. Perhaps there are many more married mystics than we know, because they are more hidden: their daily work often prevents them from writing down their experiences, and their families have no opportunity for making them known. It may well be questioned whether a woman like Elisabeth Leseur would have become known at all, had not her husband become a Dominican after her death and published all those letters, journals, and meditations of hers which she had written without any idea of their ever seeing the light of print. But from time to time divine Providence reveals one of these hidden mystics, whose outward life does not seem to differ at all from that of other "ordinary" Christians; and then we realize by how many various ways God leads men and women to Himself, to union with Him even in surroundings that would seem to preclude any really intense Christian life.

Elisabeth Leseur, née Arrighi, was a true "Parisienne": slim, dark, attractive, gay, and very elegant. She came from a highly cultivated milieu, belonging to the best French bourgeoisie. Her parents were conscientious, practising Catholics: Elisabeth was intensely devoted to both of them. She was the eldest of five children, four sisters and one brother; Juliette, six years her junior, was her special favourite with whom she shared all her experiences. Elisabeth was given the best education then available for a French girl: she was sent to a day school run by two maiden ladies, where she was instructed in such subjects as music, modern languages, and arts and met other girls belonging to the same social class as herself. Her main interest, however, was her catechism lessons in preparation for her First Holy Communion, which she began eighteen months before that event, in the autumn of 1877. Throughout this period she kept a kind of spiritual diary, astonishingly mature for a girl of eleven, though we have to take into account that French girls of that period were brought up very differently from present-day American or English children. The First Holy Communion especially, received at a much later age than nowadays, was an event that required long, careful preparation and dominated the entire outlook and upbringing of a young girl of good Catholic family: often the mother herself would accompany her daughter to the classes and supervise the essays she was required to write, the girl would be encouraged to have a "rule of life," to fight against her faults, and to count her "acts of virtue" as was St. Thérèse of Lisieux, though she belonged to a lower stratum of French society than Elisabeth.

Like the Carmelite saint, Elisabeth, too, was full of resolutions which she tried to keep as faithfully as she could: at Christmas 1877, when she was just eleven years old, she writes naïvely: "I have prayed much and made lots of resolutions . . . which I hope to keep. . . . I have made a rule of life, as mademoiselle has advised me to, and I will now describe it in my diary: First I must get up at half past seven, I have half an hour to dress, say my prayers and eat my breakfast, and at eight o'clock I must start work till ten o'clock, when I write my diary, and at half past ten I must practise the piano. Lunch is at eleven, and from noon to four o'clock I go out or play. At four I do my account of the catechism lessons till half past five; then I do my homework until dinner, which is at half past six; then I play, read or do needlework, and at nine I go to bed."

A few weeks later Elisabeth had her first meeting with death, at the funeral of the father of her teachers. She notes down her thoughts on this occasion, which were obviously inspired by her catechism lessons, but show how deep an impression these religious instructions had made on her: "Yes, death is a terrible thing, a cruel separation from those one loves; but after that, what will not be the joy of those who are going to find again the loved ones they had lost! One must prepare well for death; one ought always to seek to embellish and adorn one's soul and not one's body, for the soul will appear before God, and what will not be the shame of the wicked to see that they have profited so little from the graces that God has given them!"

Elisabeth made very serious efforts to "adorn" her soul. One short entry in her diary, among many others, shows clearly how earnestly she struggled against her faults: "My day was good," she writes. "There was a moment when I was going to be impatient with my little sister Marie. Fortunately

I stopped short, having remembered all my good resolutions in the morning." For, with the help of a book, she made a short meditation every morning. This was at times accompanied by very strong religious emotions, for once as she was meditating on heaven, she was so carried away that she cried out, "My God! Heaven!" to the great surprise of her nannie who entered just at that moment and thought she was play-acting. Despite all her efforts there was, however, one fault which at that time she found impossible to overcome: she was very headstrong and could not bring herself to admit that she was in the wrong. Besides, she was much given to teasing, which was not always appreciated by her family and friends.

Elisabeth was very disappointed that it was so difficult to get rid of her faults. In March 1879, when she was twelve and a half, she wrote sadly: "To think that in a month and a half I shall make my First Communion, and I have not yet done anything!" In May, just before making her retreat in preparation for the great event, she wrote: "I am disconsolate; I have lost the two years God has given me to prepare myself . . . Shall I be worthy of the good God descending into my heart? No. This frightens me." Fortunately Elisabeth was a very level-headed girl, or the intensity of this long preparation at such an impressionable age might have seriously disturbed her emotional life. Jansenism was still strong among the French Catholics of the time; small children were impressed with the anger of God, who would be offended by their slightest fault; perhaps it is not surprising that so many lost their faith as soon as they grew out of these artificially nursed fears.

During the retreat Elisabeth regained her peace of mind, and her First Communion was pure bliss. "O, how can I express the happiness I tasted at this moment! I possessed Our Lord; He belonged to me; I was no longer alone. . . . I listened to the good God who spoke to my soul, who said to me all the time: I belong to you; you possess me. And I said to Him: Thank you, my God, for I am very happy." The absence of all embroidery, the sheer simplicity of this dialogue between Christ and the young girl is astonishing and points to a very deep spiritual experience that might almost be called mystical.

But this does not mean that Elisabeth became at once a model of all virtues. Her obstinacy remained, and her mother had to reprimand her repeatedly not only for failing to admit her faults but also for laziness: subjects she disliked, such as mathematics or botany, she would neglect, while she enjoyed music and literature. She continued her education until the age of nineteen, then she lived the life of a well-to-do French girl waiting to get married. Theatre and opera, balls as well as holidays by the sea or in the Swiss mountains filled her life, though all these amusements never made her neglect her religious duties.

Elisabeth first met her future husband, Felix Leseur, when she was twenty-one. Her elegance, beauty, and gaiety as well as her culture and her intelligence attracted him at once. He had studied medicine but had then entered on a career of political journalism. Both were of the same social standing, their families were delighted. Felix and Elisabeth danced together and talked together, until in May 1889, his parents asked her parents through mutual friends, for the hand of their daughter in the formal manner customary in nineteenth-century France. They were married in July of the same year. Both were radiantly happy, and Elisabeth wrote to her parents that she had found in her husband all she desired, that she had the fullest confidence in their future.

There was only one fundamental question on which they differed: during his medical studies Felix had lost his faith completely, the fashionable atheist French literature contributing its share. His library contained almost exclusively anti-religious authors such as Voltaire, Strauss, Renan, Loisy, and others. Before his marriage Felix had promised to let Elisabeth practise her religion without any interference; at first he had done this and even sometimes accompanied her to Mass. But the circles in which he moved belonged to the anti-clerical French professional classes, he himself was a confirmed atheist, and precisely because he loved his wife very deeply he would have liked her to share his convictions.

As we have seen, Elisabeth had been an exceptionally devout young girl, and she remained a good, practising Catholic also during her engagement and in the first years of her marriage, which, however, were spoiled by ill-health. Almost immediately after her radiantly happy honeymoon she developed an abdominal abscess, which had opened into the intestines. She was critically ill for some time. She recovered, but the fistula did not close, and though this did not make Elisabeth an invalid, it nevertheless imparied her health and made her much more susceptible to fatigue as well as to other illnesses.

After being bedridden for many months Elisabeth could at last take up her domestic duties. Her husband's position and inclinations involved a great deal of entertaining; he liked a good table and an elegant home, and Elisabeth adapted herself quickly to her new life, which made the recollection to which she had been accustomed increasingly difficult. Felix had to go back to the office of his paper about midnight and hardly ever went to bed before two or three o'clock in the morning. Their evenings were very rarely spent at home: there were theatres, music halls, dinners, and parties practically every night. The young couple moved in an animated circle of politicians, writers, musicians, and artists, completely out of touch with and mostly actively opposed to Christianity. Gradually Elisabeth's faith showed signs of weakening. Though she had much time to herself during the day, she gave up prayer and instead developed her intellectual life. She took lessons in Latin and, being an excellent linguist, she was soon able to read Virgil and Ovid in their own tongue. Later she added Italian and Russian to her accomplishments. In the summer there would be exciting vacations, sometimes with other members of their families, or else trips to other European countries. In short, she led the existence of a leisured, well-to-do woman of the end of the last century, which seemed very unlikely indeed ever to produce a sustained mystical life. Of course, there were sufferings, the quite-sudden death of her father and that of her young sister, but her happy marriage helped to allay these bereavements.

Her many worldly distractions and the sustained efforts of her husband combined to estrange her from the Church. Felix put her through a veritable course of anti-Catholic reading; about 1896 she began to have serious doubts and soon she ceased to practise her religion. In the spring of the same year they made a trip to North Africa. Her letters from there contain interesting descriptions of scenery and people, she also mentions a visit to the cathedral of Carthage and to the White Fathers, but in a completely detached way, without any religious feeling—St. Augustine, St. Cyprian, the African Fathers who, a few years later, were to play an important part in her life, are not so much as mentioned. She sums up her impressions in her diary: "Our journey has come to an end, and I have the most exquisite and unforgettable memory of it. This good life together, so free from the stifling conventions of the great city and from social prejudice, this constant companionship with unspoilt nature, this contact with a new art form and a civilization so different from our own, all this makes travelling an excellent thing, wholesome for the body which it develops and invigorates as well as for the spirit which it renews, enlightens and transforms."

Next year Elisabeth and her husband went to Bayreuth, because they were both ardent devotees of Wagner. There they heard *Parsifal* no less than three times, and Elisabeth wrote that "in this admirable work the religious sentiment is expressed in a way such as I have never seen it expressed in any other work, however great; here one experiences the divine fragrance of pardon, love and purity which is both pacifying and moving." That the romantic religiosity of Wagner (incidentally the favourite composer of Hitler) could affect her so deeply proves that she had travelled far from the faith of her girlhood; and her family were grieved to realize that she no longer went to Mass at all.

Such was her state of mind for about two years when, in the summer of 1898, she one day asked her husband for a book, because she had run out of reading matter. Felix thought that he might deal the death blow to her faith if he gave her the notorious *Life of Jesus* by the French atheist Ernest Renan. This writer saw in Jesus nothing more than a very impressive Jewish rabbi who later lost his Jewish faith, was under the illusion of being the Messias, and preached a religious revolution. While professing to admire his religious genius, Renan reduced Christ to a mere man, denying all his miracles and, of course, his resurrection.

Elisabeth read this book, which had destroyed the faith of a great number of Christians, and, strangely enough, it produced on her the exactly opposite effect. Having perused it she said to herself that this most certainly could not be the truth about Jesus. The strange edifice of historical facts and personal hypotheses which Renan had erected, combined with the somewhat hypocritically sounding professions of admiration for the founder of Christianity, left her with the profound conviction that, whatever the truth about Christ, it was certainly not such as Renan presented it.

Paradoxically enough the brilliant fireworks of Renan's imagination stirred Elisabeth's interest in her religion and she resolved to make a proper study of it. First of all she turned to the Gospel accounts themselves, which Renan had manipulated out of all recognition. This renewed contact with the Person whose life they describe revived the fervour of her early years. Her husband was furious when he realized that the book he had recommended to his wife had the exactly opposite effect on her from what he had expected. He redoubled his attacks and his mockery, but these confirmed her all the more in her return to the practice of Christianity. By the end of 1898 she was once more firmly established in the Catholic faith and determined to deepen it day by day through prayer and reading.

In the summer of 1899 Elisabeth and Felix travelled to Russia, and her impressions of that country, eighteen years before the October revolution, are very interesting, indeed. As she knew the language, her observations are particularly relevant. She wrote in a letter to her mother immediately after they had left for Turkey: "In Russia I could only write to you a few quick words, for our time was taken up. Besides, what can one tell in a country where everyone is watched and spied upon! We have left Russia without regret. We began to feel suffocated; heavens, how good it is to belong to a free people! One cannot imagine what it is like for a great nation to be without a press, without freedom, without intellectual life. This becomes quite odious after a time. . . . This unfortunate people, kept stupid by alcohol and religion [she is, of course, referring to the state-sponsored, rather superstitious Russian orthodoxy encouraged and directed by the Tsarist government] really arouses one's pity. Only—what will be the awakening? And to think that, through the vagaries of politics, we have become the allies of these people!"

What will be the awakening? Elisabeth, with her natural intelligence sharpened by the spiritual insight her inner life gave her, saw beyond the outward manifestations of religion; the dreadful reaction, which came only after her death, would not have surprised her. Her stay in Turkey came as a great relief after Russia, especially as Turkey had been very open to French influences ever since Aimée Dubucq de Rivery, a cousin of Napoleon's wife Josephine, had been captured by corsairs and become the favourite of the Sultan Abd ul Hamid I and the mother of his son, Sultan Mahmoud. For Elisabeth had her full quota of French devotion to *"la patrie,"* and when, one night in Smyrna, she saw an approaching cruiser flying the tricolor, she dissolved into tears, for "here a particle of the fatherland was passing before our eyes, or, rather, all the fatherland, personified in this vessel and this piece of material, luminous like our genius."

After her return to Paris she began a spiritual diary which

was published after her death, and which reflects the ascent
of this French society woman to God.

The very first entry, under the date of September 11, 1899,
presents the programme of her new life: "For a year I have
been thinking a great deal and praying very much. I have
constantly tried to enlighten myself, and through this perpetual exercise my mind has matured, my convictions have
been deepened and my love of souls has grown. What is
there greater than the human soul, or finer than conviction?
We must create in ourselves a 'new spirit,' the spirit of understanding and fortitude. We must renew ourselves and live
our interior life intensely. We must pray and act. Every day
of our life must carry us closer to the supreme Good and
Intelligence, that is, nearer to God."

So Elisabeth's spiritual life was to be based on strenuous
intellectual effort. Once her faith, however fervent, had
been unquestioning acceptance; hence it could fairly easily be
shaken. Now, through her struggle with unbelief, it became
enlightened and firm. She realized with perfect clarity that
she could not hold her own in a highly intellectual, anti-
Christian society unless she really studied Christianity and its
doctrines, unless she was acquainted with historical evidence
and philosophical reasoning. For almost as soon as she had
recovered her own faith she felt drawn also to the apostolate; not, indeed, to outward activity but to the silent,
intellectual, and spiritual influence on her surroundings. "I
want to love," so she writes a week after that first entry,
"with a special love those whose birth or religion or ideas
separate them from me; I want to understand them, for they
need to be given a little of what God has given me." She
realized that in order to give them such understanding, she
would have to submit herself to a strict intellectual discipline,
that she would need to study philosophy, because "it throws
light on many things and produces order in the mind." She
cannot understand why philosophy "is not made the crown of
feminine education. What a woman so often lacks is true
judgment, the habit of reasoning, the steady, individual work-

ing of the mind. Philosophy could give her all that, and free her from so many prejudices and narrow views which she transmits assiduously to her sons, to the great harm of our country."

For Elisabeth religion was not only emotional activity as for so many pious women; on the contrary, it was above all a highly intellectual pursuit, satisfying the mind and integrated into the whole human life. As we have noticed before, when the mystical life begins to develop, intellectual penetration increases; Elisabeth, too, is in advance of her time—and not only in her views on the education of women, which are all the more remarkable as she was a society lady, not, like Edith Stein, for example, a university lecturer. Her own experience had shown her that, in our time, it is not enough to practise one's religion from habit, that its deeper understanding can safely be left to the clergy who have studied it. She was one of the first lay women to realize not only the importance of the lay apostolate but also its indispensable foundation: a thorough knowledge of the essential doctrines of Catholicism.

In the building up of this solid basis she had almost no outside help; on the contrary, her husband and his friends looked on her inner development with distaste and did everything in their power to arrest it, while she had not yet found a priest to guide her beyond the normal spiritual direction given in the confessional. So she had to rely largely on reading; and, to counteract her husband's exclusively anti-Christian collection of literature she began to assemble a library of her own which contained only solid Catholic reading. When he went through her books after her death, Felix Leseur was astonished to find among many others, Biblical commentaries, works by St. Jerome, St. Augustine, and St. Thomas Aquinas, as well as mystics like St. Teresa and St. Francis de Sales. Equipped with such theological armour and assisted by daily mental prayer Elisabeth soon became more than a match for her unbelieving surroundings.

Nevertheless, her married and social life did not suffer from these spiritual pursuits, rather the contrary. She continued to take an active part in all her husband's travels and amusements. Apart from being much occupied with the World Exhibition in Paris in 1900, the Leseurs visited Spain and North Africa in the spring and the Rhineland in the summer of the same year, travelling from place to place: Burgos, Madrid, Seville, Cadiz and Tangier, Gibraltar, Granada, Toledo, Barcelona; Mainz and Luxembourg, Cologne and Coblence, Treves and Metz. Would not Elisabeth's prayer life be affected by these constant changes which her husband enjoyed more than she herself? But she had an extraordinary capacity, so frequent in the mystics, of finding spiritual food everywhere. So she could write on May 29, 1900, just after her return from Spain: "After five weeks of travel I resume my ordinary life, but I take it up, I think, in rather different conditions. During this journey I have reflected and prayed a good deal and I have looked clearly into myself and my life." She continues that she has definitely given herself to God and that, in her prayer during this journey, she has realized quite clearly what God wants of her. She must bring those dear to her, especially her husband, "whom I love more than all," to God, but "not by controversy and discussion can I show them what God means to a soul. Only through struggling against myself, through becoming, with his help, more Christian and more valiant, shall I bear witness to Him whose humble disciple I am. By the serenity and strength I mean to acquire I shall prove that the Christian life is great and beautiful and full of joy." This she proposes to do by cultivating her mind in order to make others know that God is the highest Intelligence.

Her social life brought her into contact with the most burning problems of the day; the social question loomed large on her horizon. But she knew that it could be solved only on a Christian basis, more, that it was too large to be settled once and for all: "This question," she writes, "which will last as long as the world, can advance only through Christianity; that is my firm conviction. . . . Every Christian ought to interest himself in the crisis through which the people are passing. . . . New apostles ought to arise for new needs; those workers, peasants and labourers of any kind who constitute the majority of the people must be shown the true Source of all freedom, justice and change. If we do not make God known to them we shall have failed in our most important and pressing duty."

She tried to practise what she preached as far as her circumstances would allow her. Early in 1903 she founded a boarding house for working girls, where they would find a family atmosphere and religious encouragement. But her lack of experience proved fatal to such an undertaking and it had to be liquidated two years later. She also collaborated in the *Union familiale*, an organisation devoted to the education of the children of workers, where she taught the catechism. Moreover, she restrained her husband from spending too much on luxuries. She had plenty of beautiful jewelry, but for him she could never have enough. So one day, when he proposed to give her yet more rings, designed by the best Paris artists, she pulled him up short. Having assured him that this offer did not please her at all, she told him that she had quite sufficient adornments for her social status: "I do not consider that I have the right to devote to selfish vanities large sums that could be used far better for helping so many unfortunate people. If you really want to give me pleasure, give me the money you have set aside for these costly superfluities and allow me to use it for charities."

In April of the same year, 1903, the Leseurs once more travelled to Rome. There Elisabeth had an audience with Leo XIII, then quite near his death, who impressed her deeply. A few days later she had a mystical experience after confession and communion in St. Peter's: "I felt in myself the living presence of the blessed Christ, of God Himself, bringing me ineffable love. His matchless Spirit spoke to mine, and for a moment all the infinite tenderness of the Saviour entered into me. Never will this divine trace be destroyed. In that unforgettable minute the triumphant Christ, the eternal Word, He who has suffered and loved as a man, the one living God, took possession of my soul for all eternity. I felt myself renewed by Him to my very depths; I was ready for a new life, for the duty and the work His Providence intended for me, and I gave myself and my future to Him without reserve. . . . On my return I found myself once more in an atmosphere of sarcasm, criticism and indifference. But nothing mattered; the flame of Christ was still burning within me."

This profound experience, described still so vividly three months later, after her return to Paris, gave a new vigour to her spiritual life which was still further deepened by the fact that she had just found a spiritual director in the French Dominican, Père Hébert. Her most intense suffering was caused by the complete lack of understanding of her tenderly loved husband, "the great spiritual separation between myself and Felix," a subject to which she returns again and again in her diary. Besides, the constant distractions provided by her social life began to weigh more and more heavily on her. The best times for her were the summers. In 1902 they had built themselves a house at Jougne, in the French Jura. There they would spend the vacation with Elisabeth's family; for, having no children of her own, she was devoted to her nephews and nieces, and took an active part in their upbringing, especially in their religious formation. Anti-clericalism and socialism had not yet penetrated into that hidden corner of France, and Elisabeth enjoyed the peaceful, patriarchal atmosphere, though she asked herself anxiously how long this blissful state could continue: "The so-called advanced party will destroy all this—but will the people be happier? . . . Will the hatred that is being sown be able to replace what one wants so inconsiderately to destroy?"

The first rumblings of the revolutions the twentieth century was to bring could already be heard, and not only in the political sphere. So far the stability of family life had seemed indestructible: now she met for the first time the breaking up of a marriage in her own circle. A Jewish couple with whom the Leseurs had been very friendly were seeking a divorce.

Elisabeth was profoundly shaken. When the wife, who had fallen in love with another man, affirmed her right to happiness, Elisabeth called it: "Her right to the unhappiness of others." Several years later she absolutely refused to entertain in her home an intimate friend of herself and her husband who had married a divorced woman. It was the only time when Elisabeth and Felix had a veritable scene. He raged and stormed at her intolerance; she firmly told him that the Church forbade divorce with good reason; it was a real scourge bound to destroy society; if she opened her house to divorcés she would not only act against her conscience but give scandal to others. Felix gave in: he realized that for all her intense charity and understanding, Elisabeth would never compromise on a question of the Church's law.

At the end of 1903 a dark shadow fell over Elisabeth's life: her most loved sister Juliette was suffering from pulmonary tuberculosis and her life was in constant danger. She and Juliette had a great deal in common, and Elisabeth loved her not only as a sister, but almost as a daughter. The entries in her Journal at this time are full of Juliette: "Great suffering, on Juliette's account," "The cruel distressing trial of Juliette's illness and the fear of the future, the knowledge of our poor mother's grief, my usual afflictions, a bad state of health and a painful oppression of mind and body—all these now make my life a sacrifice which I offer to God for Juliette." The time spent with Juliette was most precious to her, "she moves and edifies me more than I can say. I love her soul, and I think she understands mine." She knew that, except for a miracle, Juliette would not live. She summed up her feelings in the words: "I suffer, I adore, and I pray."

After a year of anxiety, alternating with occasional rays of hope, Juliette died. The entry in Elisabeth's diary on that day consists of one brief line:

April 13th   †   1905.

Six weeks later her niece Marie made her First Communion. Despite her grief Elisabeth wrote for her a small treatise, "The Christian Woman," in which she described the ideal which she herself was so anxious to realize. "To your husband," she wrote, "you will be a friend and companion, and to your children a guide and the embodiment of moral fortitude. . . . You will meet many human beings on your way, but go by preference to the weakest, most embittered and most abandoned, and whatever may be your own trials and sorrows, know how to rejoice with those who rejoice and to share in the happiness of others." Her social preoccupations, too, are reflected in her counsels: she tells her niece that she ought to make every effort to improve the material and moral condition of others, particularly of the masses. The religion she teaches is virile and thoughtful, apt to sustain a young girl throughout the vicissitudes of her life.

Elisabeth resumed her diary almost three months after Juliette's death, freely expressing her grief; indeed, the loss of this sister left a wound in her heart which never quite healed. Though he did not understand her religion, her husband's love was her greatest consolation, and she prayed with even greater insistence for his conversion. Nevertheless, her loss combined with her own very indifferent health caused her frequent depressions, and she would accuse herself in her diary of not being sufficiently even-tempered and of talking too much about herself and her troubles. "I have spoken even too much of You, my God, for in this world that does not know You we should be very careful about what we say of You. . . . I believe it is my duty in awaiting the divine hour to preach Jesus Christ only through my prayers, my sufferings and my example . . . every part of me must speak of Him without mentioning His name; I must be an influence, not a profession of faith." With this aim in view Elisabeth also resolved to watch over her dress, "to make myself attractive for God's sake," as St. Francis de Sales had already counselled his "devout woman."

But to combine her social duties with an interior life that was growing ever more intense and reached the mystical sphere was not easy. Elisabeth felt that she could only achieve this if she established a very strict and well-thought-out

timetable. So in October–November 1906 she drew up a
Rule of Life full of sanctified common sense, which allowed
her to develop her mystical life in her own worldly sphere,
without neglecting her duties as a wife and hostess. Apart
from morning and evening prayer she would make a daily
meditation, for "meditation is necessary for my soul, it is a
daily nourishment without which my spiritual life would
wither." It was especially necessary to her because she could
not attend daily Mass, and at that time went to Holy Communion normally only once a fortnight, though more often
if it could be done without causing trouble. Communion was,
indeed, her greatest joy, after which she often experienced
mystical union with Christ, who communicated to her a new
life that "can neither be described nor explained." Yet she
deprived herself of it because she felt it her duty to give her
husband no cause for complaint; in fact, she resolved to be
even more reticent with him on religious matters than before.
He should come to know her faith by its fruits—only thus
would he, too, one day be converted. For Elisabeth was firmly
convinced that Felix would eventually become a Christian;
she repeatedly mentions his future conversion in her diary; in
her Spiritual Testament, dated October 15, 1905 and addressed to him she writes explicitly: "When you also shall
have become His (the Father's) child, the disciple of Jesus
Christ and a living member of His Church, consecrate your
existence, transformed by grace, to prayer and self-giving in
charity." Shortly before her death she even predicted that
he would become a religious.

Her Rule of Life also contained provision for regular
periods of more intense spiritual activity: one day each month
was to be devoted to what she calls "a little spiritual retreat,"
when she would go to Mass and Holy Communion, be as far
as possible without any worldly contacts, give more time to
meditation, examine her conscience and her life, and prepare
herself for death. Besides, there would be an annual retreat of
several days. Elisabeth did not practise any extraordinary
austerities; her health was too bad, in any case, and she felt

that her main duty both in the interests of her husband and of her apostolate was to watch and improve rather than strain it. She accepted whatever sufferings came her way, and besides used the small ascetical practices open to anyone in the matter of food and drink and foregoing small comforts and luxuries.

During the following years her health deteriorated considerably. An old liver trouble became more pronounced, and from the end of 1907 she was condemned to an almost entirely sedentary life, though she still accompanied her husband on his travels. As this new mode of existence gave her more time and peace for prayer, her mystical life developed rapidly, as well as her apostolate among her friends, who came in increasing numbers to ask advice and guidance. This growing influence was due in large measure to the graciousness with which she surrounded her spirituality; like her contemporary Teresa of Lisieux she believed in the efficacy of the smile: "To cover my sacrifices and voluntary mortifications with a veil of smiles and gaiety which will keep them unknown. To show only grace and sweetness in my home, my dress, my manners and my welcome." In her Lenten resolutions, too, this emphasis on smiles and cheerfulness is very noticeable. If, in earlier ages, the mystics sometimes appeared as grim ascetics who thought laughter incompatible with true spirituality, modern saints—we need only think of a Teresa of Avila or a Francis of Sales—have increasingly insisted on the joy of the Christian existence and the apostolic value of the smile. For Elisabeth Leseur this outward expression of the happiness union with God brings to the mystic became more and more important, as well as an ever deepening understanding of others, however far removed in their convictions from her own luminous faith. In one of her periodical resolutions, dating from October 1910, she stresses the need for showing sympathy and indulgence to others, while deprecating controversy. Anticipating our contemporary emphasis on mutual understanding in the place of bitter dispute she resolves "to avoid all religious discussion."

For she is convinced that "the struggle between intellects will never open a way to God, but a ray of charity will sometimes throw light on the path of some poor distressed heart and lead it to the goal."

Elisabeth was also extraordinarily modern in her attitude to the liturgy. While most women of her time were still content to say the rosary during Mass and took hardly any notice of the great seasons of the Church she wrote in her diary: "The Catholic liturgy has a great charm for me; I love to live, during the course of the year, the great common life of the Church, uniting myself to its joys and sorrows . . . re-living our Saviour's life, His incarnation and death and ascension; to tell Him my faith and love through the mouths of the prophets and fathers and saints of the ages."

During her last years Elisabeth's illnesses multiplied. In 1911 she had to be operated on for a tumour; immediately afterwards she wrote a very tender letter to her husband, full of love and gratitude for all he had done for her—for divine love often intensifies human love, and for Elisabeth Leseur love for God and love for her husband nourished each other. So she could write that one could be very detached from human concerns and live a deeply spiritual life and yet appreciate the interests and beauties of the world and enjoy love, nature, and art even more profoundly than unbelievers. Felix, in his turn, was deeply impressed by the patience with which Elisabeth endured her constant illnesses. Though not yet any nearer to Christianity, he realized that her joyful acceptance sprang from her religious faith, and he ceased to attack and ridicule it. In the next year, 1912, both went to Lourdes. Felix had been there thirty years before and been disgusted with the commercialized atmosphere, so he was very much prejudiced. But, under his wife's influence, he now began to see the other, the religious side of the famous place of pilgrimage, and he found himself not wholly out of sympathy with the manifestations of devotion he witnessed. But his deepest religious impression came from Elisabeth herself. She had gone to pray at the grotto and Felix had followed her. When he saw her kneeling, completely absorbed in contemplation, he hid himself to watch without disturbing her. He had before his eyes, as he wrote later, a spectacle that reminded him of what he had heard about the saints. She was quite motionless, and there was a radiance about her which he could only describe as supernatural. He was deeply troubled, and though he soon forgot the experience in the rush of his life in Paris, a seed had been sown in his soul which was to bear fruit in years to come.

In the spring of 1913 Elisabeth's health deteriorated; she suffered from violent headaches and sickness; after a temporary improvement during which her husband thought her cured, the disease returned: he realized only gradually that she was suffering from an incurable cancer. For six months painful crises were followed by brief improvements, intense suffering alternated with periods of hope, during which she resumed her life of prayer and her reading. But the disease progressed inexorably. A few days before her death, in April 1914, she awoke from a short sleep with an expression of intense anxiety and told her sister that they must pray a great deal. She replied that they were, indeed, praying much for her. But Elisabeth did not mean that: "No—but we must pray for all those wounded, for all those poor wounded." The sister could not imagine what she meant, but Elisabeth insisted on the need to pray for the wounded. A few months later the sense of her words had become clear.

Elisabeth Leseur died on May 3, 1914. Her husband was reconciled to the Church three years later and subsequently became a Dominican priest. His wife's prayers and sacrifices had not been in vain.

CHAPTER SIX

Charles de Foucauld

(1858–1916)

Charles de Foucauld, French officer, explorer and contemplative, combined to an astonishing degree an almost prophetic awareness of modern trends and problems with the incredible austerity of a Desert Father. His life was as extraordinary as his personality, broken in the natural, unified in the supernatural sphere.

Charles became an orphan at the age of six: his father had to leave his young family when his doctor discovered that he was suffering from tuberculosis. The mother died of a miscarriage brought about by the shock of the separation; the father a few months later. The boy and his younger sister were brought up by their maternal grandfather, a retired colonel of seventy whose home was at Strasbourg, the capital of Alsace. Charles had been profoundly attached to his mother, a sincere Christian whose dying words were: "My God, not my will but Thine be done." Her death robbed him of the feeling of security and continuity so indispensable to a child of his age; he retired into himself, became abnormally sensitive and at the same time aggressive, hating the noise and teasing that went on at his school. His happiest time was the holidays, which he spent in the home

of his mother's sister, where he attached himself particularly
to his cousin Marie. Eight years his senior and deeply religious, though not in the least narrow, she soon gained a
profound influence on her young cousin, which lasted
throughout his life. During the Franco-Prussian War in
1870–71 his uncle took his family to Switzerland; the occupation of France by the Prussian army and the annexation
of Alsace by Bismarck greatly affected the sensitive boy,
who thus lost his childhood home a second time and went
with his grandfather to Nancy. There, in April 1872, he
made his First Communion; his cousin Marie had come from
Paris for the occasion and gave him *Elevations on the Mysteries*, a treatise by the famous seventeenth-century theologian Bossuet. It was the first Christian book he read—and
the last for many years to come.

For by the end of the year Charles was invaded by doubts
and began to lose his faith. He was growing up in an age of
scepticism. During the lifetime and especially after the
death of Auguste Comte (1798–1857), the ideas of the
founder of French Positivism had penetrated deeply into the
intellectual life of the country: there was no absolute truth,
everything was relative. Charles' teachers subscribed to the
same philosophy; they allowed their pupils to read widely
without giving them either intellectual or moral guidance.
At the age of fifteen, just about a year after his First Communion, Charles had ceased to be a Christian; he delighted
in Voltaire and Montaigne: "Nothing," he wrote later,
"seemed sufficiently proved to me; the very fact that such
different religions were believed with equal faith seemed to
me to condemn them all." A year later his doubts and restlessness were aggravated by an event that unsettled him still
further. His cousin Marie married and became Vicomtesse
de Bondy. No doubt his attachment to her went much deeper
than is usual between cousins; if any one could still make
Christian values attractive to him it was she—now she, too,
had left him alone. Without faith, without any deep human

affection, Charles became listless: nothing seemed worth the effort.

In August 1874 he passed his so-called "first baccalaureate" and decided to enter the military academy of Saint-Cyr, as he had always wanted to become a soldier. Before being admitted he had to study for two years at another institute, where the discipline was extremely strict: the boys had to rise at 4:40 A.M., were allowed hardly any time off, and had to work almost incessantly. By the second year Charles was in full revolt: he did scarcely any work, had violent outbursts of fury, broke all the rules—in fact, he had become what is today called an "angry young man" or a "beatnik." But in those days "angry young men" were not fêted, they were disciplined; and so, in March 1876, Charles was sent back from school. This punishment which endangered his whole career, shocked him into making a tremendous effort; for the next three months he worked at home under a private tutor and, in June, passed the entrance examination for Saint-Cyr, where he was admitted in October.

But the energy he had displayed in the spring was short-lived; immediately after his examination he had fallen back into a state of indolence, indeed, he had become so fat that, when he entered Saint-Cyr, he could not find a uniform large enough to fit him and had to have one specially made for him. He hated physical exercises, had consistently bad notes in "deportment," tried to be alone as much as possible, and occupied himself with reading the Greek and Latin classical authors; in fact, his mode of life might have suited a scholar, but not a professional soldier.

In February 1878 his grandfather died. The love for the old colonel who had brought him up had prevented Charles from indulging in the worst excesses; now this brake too had been removed. Seven months later he came of age and gained possession of his considerable inheritance. He suddenly lost his listlessness and wanted to "live." Having been made sub-lieutenant, he entered the cavalry school of Saumur (on the Loire) in November; there he gave full rein to his new

desire for a life of unrestrained pleasure. He shared rooms
with a young nobleman, and soon their quarters became famous for the elaborate dinners given there. He absented himself from his duties without permission, spent vast sums of
money, organized one party after another. His friends admired his tact as well as his keen intelligence and fine memory,
but his superiors criticized his insufficient sense of duty and
his lack of seriousness. Towards the end of 1880 his regiment
was transferred to Algeria. Charles took with him one of his
mistresses, and after a few months of riotous living was sus-
pended from the army for "indiscipline and notorious mis-
conduct." He went to Evian, on the Lake of Geneva, with
his mistress, deaf to the remonstrances of his family and
friends.

But such a purposeless life could not satisfy his restless
spirit for long. When, a few weeks after his arrival in
Evian, an insurrection broke out in Algeria and his own
regiment went into action, Charles left his mistress, rushed
to Paris and offered himself again for the army. He was
reinstated and, in June, returned to Africa. There a new side
of his character appeared; the indolent young *bon viveur*
was suddenly transformed into a brilliant, resourceful leader
whose men were devoted to him. For eight months he
fought against the insurgents; then he was sent to the garri-
son of Mascara. There he began to study Arabic; for he had
fallen in love with Africa. The Mohammedans made a deep
impression on him, he wanted to study them: besides, the
military life of the last months had stirred his spirit of adventure, and the African desert had fanned in him a taste for
limitless horizons.

Early in 1882, therefore, he resigned from the army in
order to become an explorer. His family were infuriated at
what they took to be just another of his irresponsible whims;
besides, he had spent no less than 110,000 gold francs of his
inheritance within less than four years. In June 1882 they
struck a counter-blow: he was placed under a legal trustee,
who summoned him to Nancy for a discussion. Charles in-

sisted on his expedition, and to the great surprise of every-
body accepted the condition of preparing himself for it by
first leading the life of a poor scholar with a monthly allow-
ance of 350 francs instead of the 4000 he had hitherto been
used to spending. A year later, in June 1883, he undertook
his exploration of Morocco, being the first European to
penetrate into the interior. For eleven months he traveled
through desert and hostile country, suffering great hardships,
braving many dangers, and indefatigably taking notes, an
achievement which won him the gold medal of the French
Geographical Society in 1885.

On his return, however, in May 1884, he was again seized
by his old restlessness and went back to the life of dissipation
he had led before the African campaign. But about the same
time he met once more his cousin, Madame de Bondy. Her
mature Christian personality, the silent love and understanding she showed him, made a deep impression on him. He
broke with his current mistress, then thought of marrying a
girl unacceptable to his family, and in the autumn of 1885
went back to North Africa to collect supplementary material for the book on his explorations in Morocco which
he was preparing. Next spring he was back in Paris, where
he installed himself in an apartment near his cousin, near
also to the church of St. Augustine, where the famous Abbé
Huvelin, director of such eminent men as Baron von Hügel,
Pasteur, and Gounod was parish priest. The life of his cousin,
who attended Mass every morning and seemed to radiate
sheer goodness, filled him with increasing admiration. At
the same time, strange to say, he was also greatly impressed
by the religion of Mohammed with its emphasis on the majesty of God, which he had come to know well during his
travels in Africa. Yet he felt even at that time that Islam
did not draw the logical consequences of its belief: the utter
transcendence and holiness of God required a more profound
self-giving, expressing itself in a life of chastity and sacrifice,
a life he found realized in the house of his relations and
which began to appear increasingly beautiful to him. Marie

de Bondy, however, watched in silence the gradual transformation of her once so gay and reckless cousin, following
the advice of Abbé Huvelin that the best means of convert-
ing a person is to show him that one loves him.

Charles began to go to church, praying desperately: "My
God, if You exist, make Yourself known to me." Then he
thought that it would be a good idea to discuss the doctrines
of the church with an intelligent priest. His cousin recommended Abbé Huvelin, and so one morning towards the end
of October 1886, Charles entered his confessional, explaining
that he had not come to make his confession but required
some information about the Catholic faith. The *abbé*, not
usually given to dramatic gestures, told him to kneel down,
make his confession, and go to Holy Communion straightaway. "At once," De Foucauld writes in a letter to a
friend, "I believed that there was a God, I also understood
that I could not do otherwise than to live for Him: my
religious vocation dates from the same hour as my faith."

Grace, as the Schoolmen tell us, builds on nature. Charles
de Foucauld's was a restless temperament, due no doubt at
least partly to the shocks of his childhood and adolescence,
the death of his parents, and the marriage of his beloved
cousin. He had an adventurous spirit that could never stay in
the same place for long; besides, he was capable of tremendous sacrifices and feats of endurance, as his exploration of
Morocco had shown. All these qualities remained with him
after his conversion, in his ceaseless quest for the work that
God meant him to do. Therefore he needed more than many
others a firm guide to steady him, and the wise direction of
Abbé Huvelin was to provide just this for the next twenty-
four years, until Huvelin's death.

The *abbé* implanted in him a great love for the Eucharist
and, in an age when Holy Communion was still a rare event
in the lives of most Catholics, allowed him frequent reception of the Sacrament. At the same time he calmed his impetuous desire for entering an Order and told him to wait.
Charles obediently continued his normal life and prepared

his fundamental work, *Reconnaissance au Maroc,* for print, which was published in February 1888. Nevertheless, his one preoccupation was to find out where God wanted him. One sentence in a sermon by Abbé Huvelin had made an indelible impression on him: "Our Lord has taken the last place in such a way that no one can take it from Him." If Christ had done this, then, De Foucauld concluded, the only way to imitate Him is also to "take the last place" as thoroughly as is at all possible. How could he realize this ideal most perfectly?

He read the Gospels and the Lives of the Fathers of the Desert. In August 1888 he visited a Trappist monastery, where he saw a lay brother in such a dirty and patched-up habit that he was profoundly impressed with the monks' spirit of poverty. In November of the same year, at the suggestion of Abbé Huvelin, he set out on a pilgrimage to the Holy Land. We do not know the reason for this advice; perhaps the *abbé* hoped that such a journey to the places where Christ Himself had lived would serve to clear and pacify the mind of his restless penitent. In fact, this pilgrimage gave the life of De Foucauld a new direction. At the midnight Mass in the grotto of Bethlehem he prayed with an intensity of devotion unknown before. But soon something else stirred his imagination: the humdrum, utterly simple daily life of the Holy Family at Nazareth, which appeared to him—though not in accordance with historical truth—as one of complete abjection. Jesus was for him the despised manual worker; the French nineteenth-century aristocrat was unaware of the fact that manual work was held in high honor in Israel. He had found his religious ideal which he wanted to imitate as closely as possible: the spirit of Nazareth as he conceived it, a spirit of abasement, of utter poverty, of total sacrifice.

This experience of Nazareth was very much in line with, and probably also largely influenced by, what is called the French School of Spirituality, the chief representative of which was Bérulle. This school stressed particularly the humiliated states of Jesus in his incarnate as well as in his eucharistic life in the sacrament of the altar. No doubt Abbé Huvelin who followed the École Française, had already turned De Foucauld's thoughts in this direction; but the actual experience of the surroundings in which Jesus Himself had lived gave to the idea a new freshness and a directness that demanded immediate action. It also harmonized with a devotion he had recently learned from his cousin Marie: the devotion to the Sacred Heart, which was at that time very much the fashion in France.

When, in February 1889, Charles returned to France his confessor no longer made him wait but told him to look for a suitable order. After making a retreat at the famous Benedictine abbey of Solesmes and after many deliberations, he decided to enter a Trappist monastery. As Charles so ardently desired to follow Christ in complete poverty Abbé Huvelin suggested a very small and poor abbey, Notre Dame des Neiges, which had the added advantage that it had an even poorer daughter foundation at Cheikhlé, near Akbès, in Syria, quite near the Holy Land, where Charles could go if he wanted to live in still greater austerity and nearer to Nazareth.

And so, on January 15, 1890, he took leave of his family, especially of his beloved cousin Marie. He was in tears when he said good-bye to her, and the very next day he wrote her a heart-rending letter: "My eyes shall never again see yours." He asked how he could possibly live without her for the rest of his life, as in the past years he had so rarely been separated from her. It was the letter of a man who loved deeply, passionately even, but who offered this love to God. Throughout his life he continued to write to Marie de Bondy; there was no experience he did not share with her, and his last letter, written on the very day of his death, twenty-six years later, was addressed to her.

The enclosed existence at La Trappe, subject to many rules and regulations, was not easy for the vigorous young man of thirty-two, used to a life of travel and adventure.

He asked a friend to rejoice with him in "this new existence, wholly made up of sacrifices, to keep Him company whose life on earth has been nothing but sacrifice." Sacrifice is the supreme proof of love—this is the reason why he had entered the monastery, to prove his love for Christ. In this sacrifice of love he found peace, as he emphasized again and again in his letters, a peace that was the effect of an ever closer union with Jesus, the centre of his existence. Used as he was to physical hardships, the penitential side of life at La Trappe, the cold and the fasts, were not at all difficult for him. His days passed in prayer, spiritual reading, and manual work, "in imitation of Him and in union with Him"; but he continued to feel the separation from his loved ones very deeply and even more keenly when, in June of the same year, 1890, he was transferred to the Trappist priory at Akbès, so that he wrote to his cousin on the eve of his departure: "It seems that I shall feel all the waves which, one after the other, will increase the distance between us; it seems to me that my only consolation is the thought that each one is another step towards the end of my life."

There was another almost unbearable sacrifice: he could not even write to those he loved in private: he was a religious, his superiors had the right to read his letters. The demands of monastic obedience lay heavily on the modern officer and explorer, used to organizing his private life according to his own ideas. Nevertheless, he persevered. At Akbès he continued his noviciate under the guidance of a deeply spiritual and understanding Trappist, Dom Polycarpe, and a Carmelite saint: Teresa of Avila, whose works he had already begun to read before becoming a monk. Her intense love for Christ and her apostolic spirit struck a responsive chord in his own heart, and her books remained his favourite spiritual reading throughout his life, taking second place only to the Gospels.

But despite the excellent direction of Dom Polycarpe and the profound peace he has experienced ever since becoming a Trappist, Brother Marie-Albéric, as he was now called, was not satisfied. The poverty of his monastery was severe by most standards, but not by his. He complained that the monks were not living in the poverty he ascribed to the life of Jesus at Nazareth, not even in that he himself had known during his sojourn in Morocco. Nevertheless, he looked forward to his profession, which would bind him even more completely to Christ, and which would take place on January 2, 1892. A few weeks later his superiors decided that he was to begin his studies for the priesthood. Brother Albéric was greatly upset. Being a priest did not at all fit in with his ideas about taking the last place and being absolutely poor. But after some delays due to circumstances, he began his studies in spring 1893. He admitted that they interested him, but, as he wrote to Marie de Bondy, "they are not as good as the practice of poverty, of abjection, of mortification, short, of the imitation of Our Lord, which manual work provides." He could not give up his own interpretation of the imitation of Christ; and soon the discrepancy between this and the will of his superiors began to prey on his mind. There seemed only one way of living to the full this life of total abjection and poverty of which he dreamed: to found his own Order.

He knew what he wanted: a monastery entirely without income—no doubt inspired by the foundations of St. Teresa —where the monks lived from day to day by the work of their hands, reserving nothing to themselves but giving to the poor all that was not wanted for their immediate needs. More, there were no longer to be choir monks and lay brothers; all would have to work with their hands. All the old distinctions were to be swept away, and with them the elaborate monastic liturgy: the prayer that Charles de Foucauld envisaged was open to all and needed no training: assistance at Mass, recitation of the rosary, and mental prayer. A revolutionary programme, indeed, for the end of the nineteenth century—and for a young religious of three years' standing.

Brother Albéric communicated his ideas to Abbé Huvelin

in September 1893. The *abbé* did not reply until the following January. Then he told him, not surprisingly, to continue his studies at least until he had been made a deacon and practise the virtues, especially obedience to his Rule and his superiors. As to wanting to found an Order of his own, he told him unmercifully that he was not at all fit to guide others. Charles bowed to the judgment of his director, but it cost him a good deal. The following years were one continual trial, for he was constantly torn between his overwhelming desire to follow Christ in the most abject poverty and contempt, and his obligation to obey his superiors and continue his theological studies. To be sure, they were interesting: "But did St. Joseph know all that much?" he asked in yet another letter to his cousin. Marie de Bondy sent him a holy picture with a quotation from St. Bernard (the founder of the Cistercians, the religious family to which the Trappists belong) on obedience; Charles replied that he could not place obedience to men above obedience to God. Nevertheless, he would do what Abbé Huvelin told him.

During a retreat in 1895 his last doubts were removed. He was sure that his vocation was to what he called "the life of Nazareth." He would leave La Trappe as soon as his director considered that the moment had come; and Abbé Huvelin himself, who had tried so hard to hold de Foucauld's restless spirit to his vocation, realized that this had become impossible. In June 1896 he gave him the formal permission to leave.

But the *abbé* could not make the final decision: that rested with Foucauld's monastic superiors, to whom he had made his vows. And they ordered him to go to Rome for two years to complete his theological studies. Charles was dumbfounded—but he obeyed; he was convinced that the will of God was manifested to him in this further delay of his plans by those who had authority over him. And so, at thirty-eight years of age, he joined the young students at the Roman College: "old, ignorant, unaccustomed to Latin, I find it very difficult to follow the courses. . . . I shall be an ass in theol-

ogy as in everything else," he complained to Marie de Bondy.
Any time his studies left him he spent in adoration of the
Blessed Sacrament, which had become as dear to him as to
Father Hermann Cohen. He slept very little, and in church
he remained motionless for hours, gazing at the tabernacle.

In December 1896 there was a further shock: he was told
that he was to study three years instead of two. And in
less than two months, on February 2, 1897, he had to make
his solemn vows, which would bind him to the Order for
life, unless he obtained a dispensation from the Holy See,
which was very unlikely. He was torn between his desire to
do whatever his superiors told him and to follow what he
was convinced was God's will for him. Then, at the end of
January, his agonizing problem was solved by the Trappist
General himself who told him to leave the Order so as to
follow Christ in abjection and poverty as he desired. Charles
was overjoyed. In February 1897 he left the Trappist house
in Rome and embarked at once for Palestine in order to become a servant in a religious house, to be approved by
Abbé Huvelin, under whose obedience he once more placed
himself. Besides, he made a vow of chastity and one of "perpetual poverty, by which I undertake never to have more,
whether as property or for my use, than a poor workman."
And so he set out for an unknown destination in Palestine,
arriving at Jaffa on February 24.

He traveled on foot to Jerusalem, and from there to Nazareth, where he found work as a servant of the Poor Clares.
Dressed in a blue workman's blouse, he installed himself in
a small shed belonging to the convent: he served Mass, ran
errands for the nuns, swept and cleaned the chapel and
drew holy pictures, especially of the Holy Family and of
St. Francis, which the sisters distributed. Above all: he
prayed. His timetable was frightening. He rose at two or
three o'clock in the morning, said his office and then wrote
meditations on the Gospel and the Psalms until the ringing
of the Angelus, when he went to the Franciscan church.
There he heard Mass, received Holy Communion and said

the rosary. At six o'clock he returned to the Poor Clares, where he prepared the altar and prayed till Mass began at seven. After serving it he made his thanksgiving; then he worked. From ten o'clock to twelve he prayed again and read a spiritual book. After allowing a quarter of an hour for his midday meal he continued work till five o'clock, interrupted only by Vespers. After Benediction he remained in prayer, interrupted only by a light meal and some sleep, until the next morning. His prayer was very simple: he contemplated the Host, that was enough for him; for he was wholly united to Christ. His meditations were made almost exclusively on the Bible and the Scripture commentaries of St. John Chrysostom: a return to the sources of Christianity very unusual at the end of the nineteenth century. But Abbé Huvelin insisted that he also read dogmatic theology, and though this had not at first been part of his spiritual programme, he soon came to recognize the importance of a solid doctrinal foundation and could write to his director that it did him a great deal of good and was transforming his interior life. Again at the *abbé's* suggestion he began to read St. John of the Cross, as well as Père de Caussade's Abandonment to Divine Providence, and, of course, his beloved Teresa of Avila.

Those first months at Nazareth were extremely happy: he could live to the full the life of which he had been dreaming for years, in the very place where the Holy Family had been living almost two thousand years ago, in poverty and constant prayer.

But was this to be all? Through his meditations on the Gospel Brother Charles, as he was now called, had found out that Christ had not only lived the silent, hidden life of Nazareth. He had also lived the life in the desert, and after those forty days of fasting had entered on his public life, a life of travel and preaching and constant encounter. De Foucauld's innate restlessness and love of adventure now took the form of longing for a more directly apostolic life. He wanted to travel about to collect money for the support of the nuns; but the *abbé* objected. Then, in July of 1898, the abbess of the convent at Nazareth sent him with an urgent letter to Mother Elizabeth of Calvary, the superior of the Poor Clares at Jerusalem. Mother Elizabeth was a forceful woman with three foundations to her credit: she considered Brother Charles wasted in his state at Nazareth and decided that he was to go to Akbès to fetch a young friend of his, Brother Pierre, who had also left the Trappists because he was disappointed with their life. The two, with a few more companions if they could find them, were to live the religious life in the shadow of the Poor Clare convent at Jerusalem.

Brother Charles embraced this plan with alacrity. He set out at once for Akbès; on the way there he composed a Rule of the Hermits of the Sacred Heart which he and his disciple were to follow. But when he arrived, he found that Pierre had no intention to follow him. Very disappointed he returned to Jerusalem; but Mother Elizabeth already had another idea for him: he was to be ordained priest, become chaplain of her convent, and at the same time gather disciples round him and form a community. Brother Charles was enthusiastic. His meditations on the life of Christ had quite removed his earlier prejudices against the priesthood; here seemed the ideal opportunity to realize his plan of a religious foundation according to his own heart, with a minimum of external ceremonies and set prayers and a maximum of austerity, contemplation, and manual work. "I dream," he wrote to Abbé Huvelin, "of something very simple and involving only a small number, resembling the first very simple communities of the early Church." The *abbé* tried to quieten him. He was to remain in solitude; if God really wanted him to make such a foundation He would surely give him a sign. Brother Charles realized himself that the various plans of Mother Elizabeth had upset his life of prayer. Having returned to Nazareth in February 1899 he wrote to the *abbé* that on the one hand his heart wanted to close all the books and remain a servant, spending his life in adoration of the Blessed Sacrament, whereas on the other his head told him that he could do more for God if he became a priest, chaplain to the Poor Clares and founder of a community. The *abbé* once more told him firmly to stay at Nazareth, and Charles himself was relieved to return to his quiet life there after the upsets caused by the energetic Mother Elizabeth. He entered on a long retreat which gave him back his peace of mind. From then on he called himself Brother Charles of Jesus, for during this retreat he had completed his "Rule of the Hermits of the Sacred Heart of Jesus," based on the Rule of St. Augustine, as this was more supple than the Rule of St. Benedict. Its essence is the hermit's intimacy with Christ in the Blessed Sacrament, radiating out into a life of charity, hospitality, and friendship for all men.

Even in Nazareth, however, he was soon full of new plans. In spring 1900 he had the idea of becoming an infirmarian at a home for old people in order to pay for a poor widow who wanted to enter there. But a few days later he wrote to Abbé Huvelin about something quite different. He had heard that the so-called Mount of Beatitudes was for sale at a low price: he wanted his relatives to buy it and build a chapel; then he wanted to become a priest and live there as a "Hermit of the Sacred Heart." He felt that his life at Nazareth was too easy: "The good Sisters make my life so pleasant that I can no longer feel the Cross of Christ," as he wrote to his director at the end of April. He wanted to return to France and be ordained, then go back to Palestine, for, as he said in the same letter: "My place is in a hermitage, in the desert."

Abbé Huvelin was opposed to these constant changes. He sent a cable, followed by a letter, strongly advising him against the plan. But Charles had already made all the preparations for the purchase of the mountain and was determined to carry out his idea: Within a month he wrote no fewer than eight long letters to the *abbé*—he evidently had a bad conscience about acting against the advice of his spiritual guide —in which he explained his plan in great detail and with many repetitions: his undertaking was a eucharistic work, he wanted to gather a religious family round the Blessed Sacrament, Abbé Huvelin was to make all the arrangements for his ordination—he was even to ask the authorities for permission to use a portable altar when travelling, like the missionaries. All this before he was even ordained! Small wonder that the *abbé* was somewhat disconcerted by the impetuous demands of his excited correspondent.

Then, against his director's advice he embarked for Europe apparently to conduct some negotiations for the Poor Clares in Rome he arrived in Paris on August 18, 1900, to the great surprise of the *abbé* who had consistently urged him to stay at Nazareth. However, Abbé Huvelin agreed to his ordination. Thus, after finishing the business of the Poor Clares in Rome, Brother Charles settled down at his old monastery of Notre Dame des Neiges to prepare for the priesthood. There he gradually abandoned the idea of returning to the Holy Land: he wanted to go back to Africa, to settle somewhere in the Sahara, "where I shall be able to remain at the foot of the Blessed Sacrament night and day, in silence and seclusion."

Having been ordained subdeacon in December, early next year (1901) Brother Charles was learning to say Mass. But his instructor had no easy task. As soon as the new subdeacon began to say the prayers at the foot of the altar he became so recollected that he could not continue—he entered into profound contemplation and had the greatest difficulty coming back to the words and gestures required from him. For he had long reached the prayer of mystical union, in which a man becomes unaware of his surroundings and is completely plunged into God.

Brother Charles prepared for his ordination by a month's retreat; the night before he spent in adoration of the Blessed Sacrament. He was ordained on June 9, 1901. At first he had hoped to spend a year at Notre Dame des Neiges to mature in the priesthood and then to leave for Nazareth, an idea thoroughly approved by his director, who was as usual trying to steady his restless penitent. But almost immediately after he had become a priest a year of waiting proved too difficult for Brother Charles, besides, he had by then quite given up his plan to return to Nazareth; instead, Africa, his old love, drew him again most powerfully, especially in view of the many Mohammedans there who knew not Christ. The *abbé* gave his consent, if the ecclesiastical superiors approved; "for," he wrote, "God speaks through their voice, too, which has the greatest authority, and by which the value of those other voices must be judged." No doubt these "other voices" were inspirations that came to Brother Charles in prayer and urged him to go back to Africa, coinciding with his own deepest desire.

On September 9, 1901, he left for Algiers, without having seen his cousin again: "I am greatly moved by the thought of having been so near you, of having not seen you again and of now leaving once more," he wrote to her; perhaps this permanent separation from Madame de Bondy, his deepest human attachment, was the greatest of the many sacrifices of his life. At the end of October he arrived at Beni-Abbes, an oasis on the Northern outskirts of the Sahara, where he intended to exercise a silent apostolate of prayer and charity both among the Muslims and the French soldiers stationed there. In order to win the Arabs to Christ he dressed himself like an Arab, and a very poor one at that: he wore a coarse, long, white robe; his head was covered with a tarboosh from which flowed a folded linen cloth as a protection against the sun; the only distinguishing mark was a red heart made of serge which was fastened to his breast. He lived in a small hermitage and was once more trying to follow a severe timetable: He rose at four, and after saying the Angelus, the *Veni Creator*, and Prime and Terce, celebrated Mass, finishing his thanksgiving about six o'clock. After breakfasting on some dates and figs he made an hour's adoration of the Blessed Sacrament. Until eleven o'clock he wrote letters or did manual work; then he said the other two Little Hours of the Breviary which were followed by an examination of conscience. Dinner was at half past eleven, and until Vespers at five thirty he prayed before the Blessed Sacrament, meditated on the Gospels and read theological books. Supper was at six, followed by an explanation of the Gospel for the soldiers, if there were any, and Benediction. He then said the rosary and Compline and retired at eight, only to rise once more for Matins and Lauds at midnight. He wanted to live the life of a hermit; but, as has happened to so many hermits from the time of the Desert Fathers onwards, his life of union with God soon attracted a surprising number of people who passed through the oasis or were living there. The soldiers proved far more pious than he had expected; many came every evening for an explanation of a Gospel text followed by Benediction of the Blessed Sacrament. Then there were the travellers whom he received, the natives to whom he distributed medicines, guests for whom he had to find lodgings; in fact, within three months of his arrival at Beni-Abbes he had sixty to a hundred callers a day. No wonder that his whole timetable with its hours of contemplation and eucharistic adoration went to pieces, so that he wrote already in February 1902: "I have not a moment for reading and hardly any time for meditation." He had almost literally become "the universal brother" to whom everyone turned for help.

But the work was too much for him alone; he looked again, as he had done already at Nazareth, for companions to assist him. And again, as at Nazareth, they did not come. He attributed this to his own lack of holiness; but he was told by an experienced missionary that his rule was too rigid and his life too austere. Perhaps, too, the time was not yet ripe for the idea of such communities outside the accepted cadres of the religious life. He continued to pray and to help all who came to him. In his conversations with the travellers he heard much about Morocco, the country he had once visited as an explorer, and the complete absence of priests there. Soon he decided to extend his apostolate: he wanted to go to Morocco, with a vanguard of similarly devoted men and women—for now he envisaged also communities of "Little Sisters of the Heart of Jesus" to prepare the ground by prayer, example, and friendship for the active missionary work. For one thing was becoming increasingly clear to him: neither the Mohammedans nor the pagans of Africa were as yet ready to be converted to Christianity. Ignorance and prejudice were far too great for that. What was needed were small centres of authentically Christian life, cells which would diffuse a practical knowledge of the charity of Christ. Thus would be established personal contacts which might, in time—and Brother Charles had realized by now that it might take a very long time indeed—lead to conversions.

A meeting with an old friend of his, Henry Laperrine, now in charge of the oases of the Sahara, brought his plans to maturity: he would go farther south and live among the nomad Tuaregs who appeared to him as the most abandoned people. For them he would say Mass, pray, and adore the Eucharist in a country where active missionary methods were impossible because of severe persecutions; besides, he would study their language, translate the Gospel, and gain their trust and friendship. He had no illusions about the difficulties and dangers of this plan; besides, the nomad habits of the Tuaregs would force him to follow them through the desert; more, it would be very difficult for him to obtain permission to say Mass without a server. It would be a life of utter loneliness, without any human support whatsoever.

Brother Charles had no hesitation. No one was more in need of Christ than the Tuaregs, no one but himself appeared to be able to live as a Christian among them. His ecclesiastical superiors gave the necessary permissions, Abbé Huvelin approved. So, after a number of delays caused by fighting in the neighbourhood of Beni-Abbes, finally he set out for the Hoggar mountains in May 1905. In August he arrived at the oasis of Tamanrasset, where the caravan with which he had travelled left him. There, accompanied by one servant, surrounded only by nomads, he built himself a hut and intended to live once more as a solitary. But just as at

Beni-Abbes, his solitude was soon invaded by natives asking
for needles, medicines, corn, so that his work on a French-
Tuareg dictionary progressed more slowly than he had anticipated. In the following year he returned temporarily to
Beni-Abbes and had the great joy that at last a companion
presented himself ready to share his life. But the young
brother, unused to the extreme austerity of de Foucauld's
regime, broke down and left him three months later on the
way back to Tamanrasset. Brother Charles was in a great
difficulty: he had counted on the young brother to serve his
Mass, and he had no permission to celebrate without a server.
Should he return to Beni-Abbes, or go on to Tamanrasset
and risk being unable to say Mass for months, till the necessary permission arrived? He chose the second course, for, he
wrote in July 1907: "As I am the only priest who can go to
Hoggar, whereas many can celebrate the holy sacrifice, I
believe it is more profitable to go to Hoggar despite everything, and to leave the means of saying Mass to God." This
meant giving up even the greatest joy of his day for the
sake of his silent apostolate; for those who witnessed his
Mass realized that it was the centre of his mystical life; as
one of them wrote: "I have never seen anyone say Mass like
Père de Foucauld. I thought I was in the Thebaid. It was
one of the greatest impressions of my life."

So, in July 1907, he arrived at Tamanrasset quite by himself. For months he was unable to say Mass, because the
permission to say it without a server failed to arrive, and
there were hardly any French travellers who stopped at his
hermitage. Even at Christmas he was entirely alone: "Alas,
no Mass today! . . . Till the last minute I had hoped some-
body might come, but there has been nothing, no Christian
traveller, no soldier, and no permission to celebrate by myself. For more than three months I have had no letters. . . ."
Without a friend, without Mass, without the sacraments,
he was greatly distressed; God seemed far away, but the
Tuaregs needed him, especially at the moment, because
rain had not fallen for two years; there was a famine, and

Brother Charles had a provision of corn, which he distributed to the needy. Once more he dreamed of a new form of religious life, of lay nurses, "in lay clothes, but altogether given to Jesus," of associations of good Christians, who would show the Africans a truly Christian spirit, who would sell them pretty cottons cheaply rather than alcohol, who would exercise an apostolate of authentic Christian charity. He had hard words for the colonizers of Algeria—half a century before the beginning of the present troubles in that country: "In our Algeria, one does, so to speak, nothing for the native population; the civilians seek mostly only to increase the needs of the natives in order to draw the more profit from them, they look exclusively to their own interest," he wrote to Abbé Huvelin in November 1907, and a year later to Madame de Bondy: "I am ashamed for our country and our time to see that so little is done. Not that nothing is done, but that so much less is done than could and should be done."

Brother Charles tried, at least by his own mystical life of sacrifice and adoration, to do all he could for the poor natives who knew not Christ. For his was not the life of an ordinary missionary; there were no striking conversions nor stirring adventures. His apostolate was wholly spiritual, wholly contemplative. It involved a certain amount of travel; but it always ended in the poor little hut of a chapel that held the mainspring of his existence, the Blessed Sacrament. He himself had made a formal promise "to employ all the moments of my life to save the members of Our Lord who are about to be lost: by prayer, penance, example, my own sanctification, goodness, the Holy Sacrifice, the Blessed Sacrament, the foundation of the Little Brothers and the Little Sisters of the Sacred Heart of Jesus, the conversion of Morocco and the other countries which the Sacred Heart will indicate." He was allowed to use all but the last two means; for the religious foundations of which he dreamed were not realized until after his death, and even now the conversion of Morocco is as far away as in his own time.

For the conversion of the Mohammedans, which he so ardently desired, is very much more difficult than the conversion of pagans, since Mohammedanism is a kind of heresy rather than a totally different religion; it is monotheistic like Christianity, includes Christ among its great prophets, but makes far less stringent demands on both the moral life and the understanding, appealing far more to the lower instincts than the exalted doctrine of the Church. Brother Charles realized this only too well, therefore his apostolic method was to break down barriers by constant prayer, a life of suffering and penance, and intense charity to the natives. And his greatest suffering was precisely the total failure to convert anybody.

At the beginning of 1908 he felt this sacrificial part of his vocation with particular intensity. Not only was he deprived of saying Mass, he also could see no results of all the years of labour and striving. "For myself misery and extreme poverty," he wrote to the *abbé*, "for the others not the slightest good. A tree is known by its fruit, that shows what I really am." Exhausted both physically and spiritually he broke down and had to stop all work; despite their own poverty the Tuaregs collected all the goats that were still yielding milk to feed him. He realized more and more that the most efficacious means of the apostolate are, in the long run, those that Christ and the apostles had used: poverty, suffering, persecution—in short the Cross.

In a few weeks, however, he had recovered, and when, at last, the permission arrived to celebrate Mass without a server, he was full of joy. But in his months of deprivation he had realized one thing: that the most important means of the apostolate is not the adoration of the Blessed Sacrament in the monstrance or the tabernacle; it is not even the Mass, at least not the Mass by itself; it is the complete self-giving of a man, his own transformation into Christ. Echoing St. Paul he wrote: "To let the Heart of Jesus live in me, so that it may no longer be I who live, but the Heart of Jesus who lives in me, as He lived at Nazareth."

This transformation into Christ is considered by all the great mystics, above all by St. Teresa of Avila and St. John of the Cross, to be the last stage of the mystical way here on earth that prepares a man for his final union with God in heaven. It is also regarded as the most effective means of the apostolate, because the prayer of the contemplative who is so closely united to God has a tremendous power, even though its effects may not be immediately apparent. Brother Charles' vocation was clearly to this contemplative apostolate even though his ardent nature would have liked to be able to bring about more tangible results; he himself knew this well enough, for he could write: "I see that all that is not the simple adoration of the well-Beloved is so utterly null and void that my hands grow limp as soon as I leave the foot of the Tabernacle."

So his days were spent much more quietly than is usual for a missionary. True, he received many more people in his hermitage than would seem consistent with his love of solitude; but the rest of his time, apart from his constant work on a Tuareg grammar and dictionary, was given over to silent converse with Christ in the Tabernacle or exposed in the monstrance. He hoped all from the Eucharistic Presence in a land where It had till then remained unknown and from the charity he himself tried to radiate. "I try as much as I can," he wrote, "to show, to prove to these poor estranged brethren that our religion is all charity, all brotherliness, and that its emblem is a Heart." This is why he wanted his Little Brothers and Sisters to wear a heart on their habits, the sign of the love of Christ which is so completely opposed to material force and exploitation.

As the years in the desert passed, Brother Charles desired ever more intensely not only to live like and with Jesus, but to save with Him through His sacramental Presence, and, if need be, through giving his own life. He also envisaged centuries before his sacrifices would bear fruit. If only he could find companions to share his sufferings and his hopes. But just these were still denied him.

Despite all his setbacks the desire to make a foundation continued to grow in him. For this purpose he traveled to France early in 1909. He now envisaged a Union of Brothers and Sisters of the Sacred Heart of Jesus, who, like Aquila and Priscilla, the companions of St. Paul (Acts 18:18 and 26: Romans 16:3 and elsewhere) would exercise their silent influence among the natives, who had so far only met Christians with very different ideas.

For it had been his experience that the Mohammedans were incapable of abstract thought and discussion: they could only be converted by example: "When they will see men and women who are more virtuous and wiser than themselves . . . and who are Christians, they will be very near to saying to themselves that these men and women are perhaps not mistaken, and they will ask God to enlighten them." For this reason Charles de Foucauld laid so much stress on the lay apostolate, which was in his time—only half a century ago—so novel a concept that he could write to Abbé Huvelin: "The ecclesiastical and the lay world know so little of each other that the former cannot give to the latter. It is certain that by the side of the priests we need Priscillas and Aquilas, who see what the priest does not see, who penetrate where he cannot penetrate, who go to those who avoid him and evangelize them by their good influence." For the absence of conversions was due to the mediocrity of Christians, their lack of charity and their contentious spirit.

The plan of Brother Charles was approved; but he still found no companions and returned to his solitary life at Tamanrasset in June. In the following year 1910 the death of Abbé Huvelin, his guide for twenty-four years, increased his loneliness. Yet he was not discouraged. In 1911 he returned to France; his plans had been submitted to Rome, but there was no answer. So he continued his desert life as before, developing, with increasing age, like St. John the Apostle the spirit of love, regarding "every human being as a beloved brother," banishing "the military spirit." Similar views were expressed in his book *The Gospel Shown to the Poor*

People of the Sahara, in which he urged the preparation of the active apostolate among them by the practice of charity and prayer. Besides, he was always at work on the Tuareg dictionary. In the spring of 1913 he traveled again to France, this time in the company of a young Tuareg whom he wanted to show how French Christian families live. At last he was beginning to have some success: in 1909 he had received the ecclesiastical approbation for his proposed Association of Brothers and Sisters of the Sacred Heart, that is to say Europeans who bound themselves by special rules to pray for the heathen population of the colonial countries. Now, four years later, this Association had forty-nine members. The advice this "hermit of the Sahara" gave them sounds quite surprisingly up-to-date: "We must extend our relations" he wrote to one of the members, Joseph Hours, "also with the non-practising Christians, trying to have cordial and affectionate relations with them and gaining their esteem and their confidence, and thus to reconcile them to our faith. In France, too, one must be a missionary like in a pagan country, and this work belongs to all of us, Churchmen and laity, men and women." In this work class distinctions must be overcome: "to act, to pray and to suffer— these are our means." In the following years he was fully occupied with organizing his confraternity. He intended to return to France in 1915 to improve its organization, but the first World War put a stop to this plan. In June 1915 he finished his Tuareg dictionary, which he had begun eleven years before, at Tamanrasset. In October 1916 he wrote once more to Joseph Hours, this time about the "mystical priesthood of the faithful soul who offers itself and offers Jesus to all the intentions of the Divine Saviour . . . and who, like Jesus, makes the salvation of men the work of its life."

This had been his own great ambition, but all his wholehearted efforts seemed to have come to very little; as he had sadly written a year before: "Tomorrow it will be ten years that I have said Mass at Tamanrasset, and not a single con-

vert." His life seemed a failure. And now the war had penetrated into Africa. The Senoussi tribe was in full revolt; the
Tuaregs, too, were affected. De Foucauld's hermitage was
fortified; on December 1, 1916, he was there, all alone, when
one of the tribesmen called him out. As soon as he came out
his hands were bound on his back; he was to be a hostage
and guarded by a fifteen-year-old boy with a rifle while
other tribesmen pillaged his hermitage. Suddenly there was a
commotion: two soldiers were in sight. Frightened, the boy
lost all control and fired; Brother Charles was killed on the
spot without even uttering a cry. Three weeks later, the
monstrance with the Host, before which he had been praying, was found in the sand—thrown away by the plunderers
as a worthless object.

But his work that seemed doomed to failure during his life
is bearing fruit after his death. Today the Association Charles
de Foucauld and the Mission de Foucauld continue his apostolate, and the Little Sisters of Jesus, in their blue habits,
are working in Africa as well as elsewhere and have even
reached the television screen.

CHAPTER SEVEN

Hieronymus Jaegen

(1841–1919)

Engineering, banking, politics—there can hardly be any professions less easily compatible with the mystical life than these. At least, so it would seem at first sight. A head for figures and a soul attaining to the mystical union, parliamentary sessions and ecstatic experiences appear to be mutually exclusive. Yet they need not be. The life of Hieronymus Jaegen shows that they can be combined, indeed that business efficiency and a very elevated mystical life can be merged into one harmonious whole.

Hieronymus, or Jerome, to give the easier English form of his name, was born at Treves, the ancient Roman colony, the birthplace of St. Ambrose, where St. Athanasius had spent his exile from his see of Alexandria and Jaegen's patron saint, Jerome, had pursued his studies. Jaegen's parents were simple people; his mother's father was a boatman of the Moselle, his father an elementary school teacher. The family were devout Catholics who did everything to give Jerome a good education. He was a good pupil who after a two years training at a commercial school won a scholarship that enabled him to go to Berlin to complete his studies at the technical college of the Prussian capital.

At that time Berlin was an overwhelmingly Protestant city. Of its half million inhabitants only 25,000 were Catholics, served by eleven priests who administered three parish churches and three convent chapels which were open to the public. Jerome arrived there in the autumn of 1860. The intellectual climate of the capital was still dominated by the pernicious philosophy of Hegel, who had taught at its university from 1818 to 1831. The young student from the provinces was determined to keep his religious faith despite the disintegrating influences of Berlin society. He therefore at once joined the Catholic students' association, the Marian Congregation, the Society of St. Vincent de Paul, and the church choir. Thus the time left free by his studies was well filled with Catholic activities. Besides, he found an excellent confessor in the students' chaplain, Eduard Müller, who devoted his whole life to the formation of the young men entrusted to his care. Jerome wrote of him later: "My energetic confessor soon got rid of my sins and demanded, if at all possible, daily spiritual reading and the systematic practice of the virtues, about which I had to report to him in the confessional. Thus I was soon fully occupied with striving for Christian perfection."

His work for the Society of St. Vincent de Paul had a lasting influence on Jerome's social outlook. There, he wrote, "class consciousness and pride soon disappear. The love of the poor for Christ's sake makes all equal. There one sees princes sitting by the side of artisans, and young men enthusiastically descending into basements or climbing up to attics to visit the poor, listen to their needs and bring them gifts, while perhaps their friends pursue the pleasures of vice just round the corner." Thus his spiritual life, nourished on his reading and soon developing into regular meditation, was assisted by his charitable activities which brought him into contact with the misery of a large part of the population of the city long before social legislation was coping with the problems of the industrial proletariat.

In July 1863 Jerome left Berlin. The two and a half years he had spent there proved decisive for his interior life. Far from weakening his faith, the dangers of living in the diaspora had only strengthened him in the practice of his religion, which under the influence of his confessor and the associations he had joined became more conscious and vigorous than it had been in his Catholic home. He returned to Treves a mature Christian, secure in his beliefs and determined to continue his prayer life in the midst of his professional activites.

As soon as he had returned to his native city he obtained a post in a machine factory but had to relinquish it in October 1864 when he was called up to do a year's military service. In October 1865 he became an engineer for blast furnaces and mining equipment at the Friedrich-Wilhelm works near Cologne, but had to leave in May 1866, when war broke out between Prussia and Austria and he had to join his regiment. Immediately before, he went to pray in the Lady chapel of Cologne cathedral, when he suddenly seemed to hear a voice saying to him: "Go in peace; in all spiritual needs pray to the Saviour, in all physical needs ask Mary for help, both will assist you." This experience had a profound effect on him: he was full of joy and went into the war without any fears or misgivings: "The rifle slung over my shoulder, the well filled knapsack on my back, I carried my cross after the Saviour." Once, in the seven-hour battle of Königgrätz, he was in constant danger, and as the grapeshot were whizzing past he asked God to give him the grace either never again to commit a mortal sin or to grant that he might be killed at once.

Jerome remained unhurt, and he emerged from the war an officer wearing several decorations. He returned to Treves at the end of 1866 and once more joined the machine factory where he had been employed before, first as an engineer, later as a commercial administrator. As soon as he had set-

tled down—he was then living again with his parents—he
resumed his spiritual readings and meditations. In the next
year began what he calls his life of mystical graces. He himself describes it thus: for many years he had been longing
for a more intimate relationship with Christ. One night, as
he was praying in his bedroom, this longing became particularly strong. Suddenly he saw with his inner eye Mary standing before him, an interior illumination assuring him that it
was she. Then he rose from his knees "and saw the Saviour,
again in his imagination. He rushed into His arms, He received him, and suddenly all imaginative representations had
disappeared. No word was spoken, the soul retained its full
consciousness. The spiritual joy and the conviction at last to
have found the Saviour were so great that he could do no
more work for the rest of the evening."

While Jerome became thus more and more immersed in
the mystical life he did not forget the needs of others. About
the same time, towards the end of 1867, he founded an association for young businessmen, called "Harmonia," designed to strengthen their social as well as their religious
life; he remained its president for many years.

His peaceful existence was again interrupted by a war,
this time the Franco-Prussian War of 1870–71, during which,
however, he did not go to the front but remained mostly
at Coblenz. But the real fighting began for him after the
war, when Bismarck launched his *Kulturkampf*, which has
already been mentioned in the chapter on Isaac Hecker. Bismarck, who would not tolerate any independent action on
the part of the Church, particularly in the educational field,
had been inspired by Hegel's idea of the omnipotent Prussian
state. In his philosophy the divine "world-spirit" manifests
itself in different ages in different nations; its latest mani-
festation was Prussia, which therefore was all-powerful and
could do no wrong. The defeat of France in 1871 seemed
to have confirmed Hegel's idea of Prussia's divine status, and
Bismarck now began to attack the Church, because she
claimed an independent spiritual authority over its subjects.

He was helped in this campaign by certain circles of "liberal Catholics" who were working for a national Church independent of Rome.

The Prussian government used every means in its power to enforce its will, suppressing seminaries and religious orders, Catholic societies and newspapers, fining and imprisoning priests and bishops, so that by 1878 nine out of the twelve episcopal sees were without their bishops, over fourteen hundred parishes without their pastors and four hundred and eighty convents and monasteries dissolved. The archbishop of Cologne was gaoled as the "straw-worker Paul Melchers," and archbishop Count Ledochowski of Poznan had to share a cell with thieves. As a countermeasure the Church authorities founded the *Katholikenverein* (Association of Catholics). Its object was to "defend the freedom and the rights of the Catholic Church and to apply Christian principles to all spheres of public life by every morally and legally permitted means." Within a few weeks of its foundation the government forbade all members of the Prussian civil service to join the association, whilst army officers were told that it was incompatible with military honour to belong to it. The *Katholikenverein* replied by calling meetings in which speakers explained the Catholic position and asked for the right of freedom of conscience and religious practice for the Catholic citizens.

Such public speaking on behalf of the Church, of course, had its dangers. In Treves only two men came forward to defend the Church in this way; Jaegen was one of them. Indefatigably he addressed meetings which were only too frequently dissolved by the police, though this rather enhanced their popularity. In the next local elections the government suffered a resounding defeat, to which Jaegen, too, had contributed his share. His activities were resented by the liberals and the anti-Catholics, and he was promptly denounced to the military authorities. He was summoned before the district commander who ordered him to put a stop to his public opposition to the government. Jaegen flatly refused: it was in the interest of the nation that the anti-Catholic laws should be repealed, he was not prepared to obey the prohibition to speak, because he spoke not as an officer, but as a German citizen. As such he was not willing to obey military orders which diminished his rights. The mystic who spent long hours on his knees knew very well how to intervene in the great questions of the day and was not afraid, like so many of his countrymen, to defend his own rights as well as the rights of the Church.

The military authorities were not prepared to put up with such a flagrant case of insubordination. They reported to Berlin, and the case was laid before no less a personage than William I himself, the commander-in-chief of the German armies. In May 1873 Jaegen was deprived of his military rank and dismissed from the army, a punishment carrying a grievous social stigma, since in the Prussia of those days the military caste occupied the very top of the social ladder. The anti-Catholic press added to his ignominy by violent tirades against the "itinerant apostle of ultra-montanism." Jaegen bore the attacks with complete resignation and patience. Many years later he wrote about the relation between Church and State in terms that reflect his own experience in those days of battle: "God ordained the state as a secular power to take its place by the side of the spiritual power of the Church. While it is the task of the latter to guide man to eternal happiness by way of the spiritual struggle, the state is called by God to take care of the temporal peace and welfare of men so that they should be enabled to fulfill their eternal destiny without interference. Within their divinely appointed spheres both powers should act independently, living peacefully together and supporting each other. History proves that nations have flourished as long as such harmony persisted, which, however, did rarely last long; for the three enemies (the world, the flesh and the devil) which attack the individual in the spiritual sphere also attack the Church as a whole. In this fight they use first of all the spiritual weapons of the written and the spoken word to

attack the Church. As her members we are then obliged
to defend her with the same weapons. But her enemies also
use the even more effective material weapons, seeking to stir
up the secular against the spiritual power. Then begin those
struggles and persecutions which the Catholic Church has
endured throughout the centuries. . . . If you are fortunate
enough to live in such a time of combat, be not downcast
but fight bravely and endure, the victory will be yours."

Far from counselling Christians to withdraw from the
troubles of the world into the mystical sphere where no
earthly concerns would reach them, Jaegen tells them to
descend into the arena and fight, to defend the Church with
the weapons of the mind and to stand up for their faith in a
hostile world. At a time when no one was as yet speaking of
the lay apostolate he was already practising and recommend-
ing it as, in her own way and in different circumstances,
Elisabeth Leseur was doing at the same time.

When the excitements of the *Kulturkampf* had died down
Jaegen resumed his normal life, in which daily Mass and
Holy Communion had a prominent place. Long before Pope
Pius X's decree on Frequent Communion Jaegen communicated daily; but in order not to give scandal to those who
could not understand this, he would go to different churches
during the week to do so.

Towards the end of 1879 he had to give up his work in the
machine factory, because the eldest son of the proprietor had
finished his studies and took over Jaegen's duties. Another post
was immediately offered to him: he was asked to become the
managing director of the newly founded *Trierer Volksbank*,
a people's bank looking after the interests of the small in-
vestors and businessmen who were practically debarred from
the large bank of the city, which catered almost exclusively to
the wealthy. Jaegen, who had long been interested in social
questions, accepted the offer with alacrity, since it would give
him scope to put his ideals into practice. This, however, does
not mean that he would indulge in imprudent experiments
and idealistic ventures which could only lead to bankruptcy.

Neither his mystical life, which grew steadily, nor his keen sense of social justice prevented him from regarding business matters with the cool, calculating common sense without which a banker would necessarily make shipwreck. "In financial matters," he wrote, "one must always proceed quite soberly and objectively according to figures and facts and take account only of these."

As an engineer, bank manager, and an active member of the St. Vincent de Paul Society, Jaegen came into contact with men and women from all walks of life and was able to observe their needs at close quarters. In 1883 he published a book, *The Struggle for the Highest Good (Der Kampf um das höchste Gut)*, an ascetical manual, destined especially for the laity. For in Jaegen's view it was at that time particularly necessary that good Christians should remain in the world, in order to leaven it by their sound principles and actions. For Christ, too, had lived in the midst of the world; so they should do the same, striving for the most intimate union with God in their ordinary daily life. He tells the Christian in the world to do his utmost to gain influence in it; and as the world has a great regard for money, education, and power, he advises his readers to use even these means as far as is compatible with Christian principles. His battle cry is that, "One should not save oneself from the world but save the world." This does not mean, of course, that those who have the vocation to withdraw from the world ought not to. do so; it means that in our time there is also a very definite vocation to remain within the world, for the sake of the world—a vocation Jaegen anticipated almost a century before the Church herself set her seal on it by approving the secular institutes.

For this reason he treats in his ascetical manual subjects which until then had found no place in spiritual books, namely the problem of the industrial worker and of the relation between employer and employee in general. In his view the industrialists themselves can make the greatest contribution to the solution of the social question: "For them to do so it is necessary that they should see the situation from the point of view of genuine Christian charity and humility. They must not regard the worker merely as merchandise for which they pay a certain sum, and then think they have no more obligations towards him. They should rather love their workers as their neighbours both in and outside working hours." This, of course, is an ideal that is hardly possible in the case of the contemporary enormous combines, where employers and workers are no longer personally known to each other; and the unions as well as social services have done a great deal to improve the situation of the worker; it is no longer true that most of them live, as in Jaegen's time, in unwholesome dwellings and work in degrading conditions. But what is still missing is the personal element of Christian charity which he wanted to see introduced into the relationship between industrialists and their workers. Where this existed, no social legislation would be necessary, and at the same time both employer and employee would live much fuller lives. For Jaegen the Christian virtues must penetrate right into the economy of our time, a doctrine taught, eight years after the publication of *The Struggle for the Highest Good*, in Leo XIII's great encyclical *Rerum Novarum* (1891).

Jaegen himself lived up to his teaching. His personal life was as simple as possible for the director of a bank. Indeed, his friends were staggered when they realized that he was living in a two-room apartment furnished only with a bed, a sofa, a wardrobe, a writing desk, a table, a book shelf, and a few chairs. When they expressed surprise at this ascetical form of life he would reply that he really did not need more, as he used his home only at night and for a few hours in the day time. Thus he had always sufficient means to give away large sums of money, though never indiscriminately, according to his principle that "no one has ever become a beggar through generous and reasonable almsgiving." He preferred those poor who were ashamed to beg and knew how to help them without humiliating them. Apart from his money, he also put his spare time and his financial experience at the disposal of those who needed them; looking after the affairs of several convents and Catholic associations. One of his most highly prized activities was the organization of the great Corpus Christi procession at Treves. The bishop had become dissatisfied with the rather haphazard and not too reverent way in which this was conducted, and so Jaegen, used as he was to the most exact calculations, produced a very intricate plan, having himself walked through all the streets, watch in hand, calculating the number of steps and the time it would take to walk in procession from one stopping place to the other. The plan was so satisfactory that Jaegen was appointed leader of the procession and retained this office for thirty-three years until, at the age of seventy-four, he had to resign from it on account of his failing health.

Jaegen's life, however, was not only work and prayer. He realized quite well that man also needs recreation and he took part in many social activities with great gusto. Though he had taken a vow of chastity and remained unmarried, he was frequently invited to weddings, and when toasting the newly married couple he would often unobtrusively introduce a Christian thought in his speech. For, as he said himself, such festivities do not prevent the awareness of the divine presence. He had a great number of friends whose houses were always open to him; he liked a quiet game of cards and would play with the children, of whom he was extremely fond. In the summer he usually went to Switzerland for his holidays, most often to Engelberg. There he would enjoy the beauties of nature, which he appreciated as much as Contardo Ferrini, though he did not indulge in climbing expeditions but contented himself with more leisurely walks.

Despite his recreations, however, Jaegen's health deteriorated; he was subject to headaches and migraine, and so he decided to give up his post at the Trierer Volksbank at the end of 1898. A little over two months later, in March 1899, he was elected a member of the Prussian Parliament, the *Landtag*, representing the Catholic Centre Party. From that time he had to spend part of the year in Berlin, where he stayed at a guesthouse run by Dominican nuns. His quiet, deeply recollected manner made a great impression on the Sisters. Apart from Jaegen several other members of the *Landtag* were staying at the house, and among these sometimes rather excitable politicians he stood out as a man who lived his Catholic faith in a way different from his colleagues. This is not surprising, for soon after his election, in the year 1900, he received the grace of the mystical marriage, the highest stage of the spiritual life in which the soul is, as it were, "transformed" into God. This happened during one of his holidays at Engelberg. He at once consulted his spiritual director, who judged this grace to be genuine. As St. John of the Cross, St. Teresa of Avila, and many other mystics confirm, when a man has entered this stage his mystical life is carried on quite unnoticeably without at all hindering him in the accomplishment of his ordinary duties. The member of the Prussian Diet who had reached this high state one day heard Christ say to him: "I should like always to repose on your heart. When the soul objected that it would be impossible for Him always to repose on his heart, because he had so many external duties in the world, the Saviour replied: Just in the midst of the world I always want to rest on your heart, so that you might 'console' me for the many insults which the world constantly heaps on me. This repose will be so interior that it will not disturb you in your duties."

Perhaps even more interesting than this mystical experience is the explanation Jaegen gives, for it will throw light also on the terminology used by many other mystics. Jaegen comments: "This dialogue was an intellectual conversation which took place in full consciousness, by a mutual exchange of ideas. The Saviour did not use the term 'console.' The notion used in the colloquy comprised much more; but the soul did not know another German word which could express the idea communicated to it better than 'console' [German *trösten*]."

This interpretation is so interesting because most mystics,

especially those who have received visions of the Sacred Heart, use the term "console" without further comment, thus giving the impression that Christ is not in possession of perfect happiness and needs human comfort. Jaegen's remarks, on the other hand, make it clear that the idea expressed by the word "console" is really something much larger and more sublime than the human term implies, but that this is the nearest, even if inadequate, equivalent. This careful distinction is impressive evidence of what the well-known German Thomist scholar, Martin Grabmann, calls Jaegen's "high degree of theological perceptiveness."

This intimate life of union with Christ made its impact on Jaegen's attitude to his political opponents; for, as a member of the Catholic Centre party, he was frequently attacked by non-Catholic members of the *Landtag*. Wherever necessary he expressed his opinions freely and courageousiy, but he never indulged in personal invective. In fact, his serenity and calm were noticed by everyone, including the Sisters of his guesthouse, one of whom remembered an amusing incident, the only occasion on which she saw Jaegen lose his temper. One summer evening she was opening the door of his room, at the same time turning on the light, when he burst out: "But, Sister, how can you turn on the light before the window is closed. The gnats will come in, and then I shan't be able to sleep all night!" And though his anger lasted only a minute, the Sister comments that she was really glad to have seen Herr Jaegen lose his temper for once.

When he was not working, he could almost always be found in his room, deep in prayer. Sometimes he would tell the busy Sisters that they were too active, he was afraid that the constant rush in which they seemed to live would damage their spiritual life, and he asked the superior to give them more time for prayer.

Though he himself was very busy—he was a member of many financial commissions, and besides remained in constant contact with his constituency—he never curtailed his prayer time. His Catholic fellow politicians who were staying at the

same convent guesthouse were deeply impressed by his recollection. One of them tells how he saw him at Mass in the
morning or during the day in the chapel, kneeling for a long
time without moving, and then rising and carrying the
atmosphere of trust and peace with him into the world. Like
many mystics before him, he found it increasingly difficult to
say vocal prayers such as the rosary. "When I am saying the
rosary," he writes, "I am immediately immersed in God. I
cannot continue with the words."

In 1908, at the end of ten years as a member of the
Prussian Diet, Jaegen's health gave way; his headaches increased, and he did not seek re-election. During these last
years of retirement he felt impelled to write a book on the
mystical life—his first work, *The Struggle for the Highest
Good*, having been devoted to the ascetical life. And so, in
1911, appeared the first edition of *The Life of Mystical Grace*,
a unique work in that here an engineer and businessman does
not only present a treatise on the mystical life, but also
illustrates it with descriptions of his own experiences—without, of course, making known that he himself was the recipient of these favours; he indicates them, however, in an
autobiographical note which is printed in the posthumous
editions of his work.

This remarkable book is divided into three main sections,
dealing with the relations between asceticism and mysticism,
the distinction between the essence and the accidental phenomena of the mystical life, and the gradual ascent to its summit
that is to say to the "mystical unity" with God. In his
introduction Martin Grabmann stresses that the mystical life
as presented by Jaegen is no strange experience far removed
from our everyday life, but that it is, so to speak, "a gentle-
manly form of the most interior and elevated union with
God through prayer, in the midst of a practical profession."
In his own preface to the first edition of the book Jaegen
explains why he wrote it. The good, solid books on the
subject he says, are mostly in Latin and very complicated,
while those in the vernacular "do more harm than good,

because they increase the desire for extraordinary experiences and hence may easily lead to deception and illusion." Jaegen himself distinguishes very clearly between three groups of experiences; these are what he calls essential mystical graces, concomitants of these, and mystical phenomena. For Jaegen the most important part of the mystical life is God's own gradual giving of Himself to the soul, accompanied by the soul's increasing consciousness of the coming divine dominion over her, "all with the co-operation of the human freewill." This essence of the mystical life may be accompanied by experiences such as visions, ecstasies, and raptures. Besides these, there is a third group, the "mystical phenomena," to which belong extraordinary happenings such as ecstatic levitation, flight, luminosity, and stigmatization. Of these last mentioned phenomena Jaegen says that "they are quite unnecessary for union with God and full of dangers." The clear-sighted businessman and politician had read his St. John of the Cross and the other great mystic teachers of the Church and knew that such extraordinary physical phenomena occur not only within the Christian context and need not have a supernatural origin at all. He therefore would not discuss them in his book, which is devoted only to the growth of the authentic mystical life.

At the time when Jaegen wrote his study the question whether the mystical graces are given in the normal context of the pursuit of sanctity or are extraordinary gifts of God accorded only to a few privileged individuals was a much discussed problem. In his earlier days, under the influence of the well-known Italian mystical theologian Scaramelli, Jaegen had held the latter view, assuming that the normal way to sanctity is asceticism, that is to say, the practice of the Christian virtues with the normal assistance of grace, outside the sphere of the mystical union; while the latter was given only in a few very special cases and was quite unnecessary for reaching sanctity.

Under the influence of his own experience, however, as well as of his wider reading of the mystical authorities of the

Church, Jaegen gradually changed his views and came more and more to the conviction that the mystical union is generally given to those who strive with all their power to fulfil the commandments of Christ with ever increasing faithfulness. The former member of the *Landtag* uses an illustration from the political life to make his meaning clear: "Just as in a monarchy," he writes, "no official has a right to become a minister of state, since the monarch calls only men enjoying his special confidence to this office, so also has no man by himself a right to the most beautiful mystical union, since God, too, elects the souls for this privilege according to his own just choice. But as in every state there are very highly placed politicians who are justified to envisage the possibility of being called to join the government, so there are also souls which are so high up on the mountain of Christian perfection that they, too, may envisage the possibility that God will introduce them to the mystical sphere."

Jaegen does not hesitate to combine the classical image of the mount of perfection with the political realities of his own day; and the outcome is a much more vivid and universally intelligible presentation than can be found in the ordinary text books. Basing himself on this view that all those Christians who have reached a high degree of moral perfection are entitled to desire the mystical union, Jaegen's purpose is to "instil enthusiasm for this high goal in the reader and to examine whether and how we can gradually reach it." Living in the world in a highly respected position he has no time for conspicuous dress or behaviour: he follows St. Francis de Sales rather than St. Benedict Labre. The member of the *Landtag*, whose duties included receptions at the imperial palace and dinners in the smartest hotels wrote that the soul aspiring to the mystical union ought "always to act according to the principles of Christian prudence and to avoid all extraordinary behaviour and offences against good manners. Everything in its time: external activity according to one's station in life and interior converse with God must peacefully progress together, helping one another until both reach the heights. This will then be a sure sign of authentic Christian mysticism."

So Jaegen consciously teaches a mystical doctrine that will not only not prevent a normal professional and social life but actually assist it. The two lives, the spiritual and the worldly, though not encroaching on each other, are nevertheless constantly reacting on one another. Jaegen himself was an extremely conscientious worker. As we have seen, he had no use for unbusinesslike financial adventures, but neither for any selfish exploitation violating the rights of others. His mystical life certainly influenced his worldly existence, but this influence acted subterraneously, as it were, making him more and more sensitive to the feelings of others; whereas this delicacy of conscience again nourished his mystical life by making him more and more open to the influence of the divine Presence.

Jaegen describes this mystical life in strikingly simple, and at the same time very convincing language. Its essence is the "finding of God in our innermost being"—this is common to all stages of the mystical life. This "finding," "is not simply a particularly lively faith in the presence of God, but an absolutely certain fact of experience; it does not come to pass through 'man being transferred into the presence of God' but through 'God being transferred into the presence of man.'" This does not mean that the soul sees God in His actual being, which can only happen in the next life; it means that God makes Himself present to the soul in a degree corresponding to His good pleasure as well as to the capacity of the soul in its present state. This description of the mystical experience is not only clear—that is to say, as clear as this experience can be made to those who have not had it—it is so valuable also because it is a simple explanation embracing all the various stages of the mystical life, which Jaegen then goes on to discuss.

At first, he says, "the soul has only an indistinct knowledge and a pleasant spiritual feeling of the nearness of God," by which she is attracted to Him and filled with joy. The lower her state, the more she is dependent on the impressions of her senses; therefore God often gives apparitions, imaginary visions and so fourth especially in this lower state. Jaegen, like St. John of the Cross, does not esteem these very highly, rather the contrary; he writes: "As the great majority of men is deeply involved in the life of the senses it unfortunately esteems mystical happenings the higher, the more strikingly they affect these senses. The contrary should really be the case." Jaegen then discusses these mystical phenomena with great knowledge—after all, he had himself had profound mystical experiences—including ecstasies and mystical betrothal and marriage, always in very clear, intelligible language and taking account of the many possibilities of self-deception: "Natural vivid ideas are taken for divine inspirations, a natural ease in the practice of virtue is thought to be perfection. Dreams and dream-like notions in the waking state are easily regarded as divine visions . . . mental fatigue during a strenuous meditation easily produces a state of languor which one thinks is ecstasy, and similar things." Like St. Teresa and St. John of the Cross, Jaegen much prefers the so-called intellectual visions, which only occur in the highest stages of the mystical life, when the soul has already far advanced in the pure reflection of God's image in herself.

Jaegen insists that such intellectual visions or "locutions" are of a nature that can hardly be communicated to others, and again he uses a very telling image to make his meaning clear. If God wants a man to communicate these high experiences to his director He "causes the most essential of the received notions to overflow into the imagination of the recipient of the grace. . . . If the soul wants to communicate this notion to another, she must first translate it into her native language and be very careful when doing this, so that she may find the right words for the notions and not add anything of her own to what comes from God. For her own understanding the soul that is able to receive such intellectual communications does not need a translation into her native language. . . . She is in the same case as a person who knows another language perfectly. For example, if a German with perfect French reads a French treatise, he does not need to translate the individual French words into German words, because he thinks in French. But if he is to communicate his French thoughts to one who does not know French, he must translate them into German words." This simple illustration clears up this abstruse subject considerably, while also explaining the fact that even the most authentic mystics have sometimes given wrong interpretations of their experiences, either because they themselves misunderstood something "spoken" in the foreign, mystical language, or because they mistranslated it.

The third section of Jaegen's book describes man's ascent to the mystical union with God, and here he inserts from time to time his own mystical experiences. They have nothing flamboyant, nothing sensational about them. To give only two more examples. What is usually called the mystical betrothal, which some mystics, especially women, often describe with a great wealth of imaginative detail, Jaegen presents very soberly only by giving the words of Christ: "I wish to transform you into myself, gradually, step by step, until, in the hour of death, you will be able to celebrate the heavenly wedding feast with me." And of his "mystical marriage" he merely says that he was one day "instructed by the Saviour, how he was to pray, work, suffer, and hold interior converse with Him, that is to say how he was permanently to live together with Him in his heart. This visitation by the Saviour came in the form of an intellectual vision and allocution through ideas (i.e. not through human words), in full consciousness, hence without ecstasy. The heavenly Father and Mary, the heavenly Mother, were present as witnesses to this sort of contract for their Son, so that the soul was able to recognize their presence quite clearly and certainly in intellectual manner, not in human form."

Thus Jaegen, engineer, bank director, and politician had attained to the highest mystical union that is possible in this life, and when, old and incapable of any further activity, he asked God why he was still in this world he received the answer: "To pray with me, near my heart, to the Father." When the soul asked further: "And for what shall we pray, for what You have at heart or what we have at heart?" the Saviour told him: "For the former." And Jaegen concludes: "What earthly vocation can be compared with this: one's heart united to that of the Saviour to pray to the heavenly Father for His interests."

While Jaegen's health was deteriorating, he continued to improve his book, the third edition of which he finished at Whitsun, 1918, a few months before the end of the first World War. In July of the same year he was attacked by a painful intestinal disease aggravated by heart trouble and nervous depressions. When he felt that death was near he put his affairs in order, leaving his few possessions to those of his relatives who most needed them. As the war had overshadowed the last years of his life, so his last months were darkened by the defeat of his country, the revolution, and the ensuing famine and epidemics. He died on January 26, 1919, a man in outward appearance like millions of other conscientious businessmen, but inwardly a mystic called to the most intimate union with Christ.

CHAPTER EIGHT

Maximilian Kolbe

(1894–1941)

The time: August 1941. The place: Auschwitz concentration camp. Ten prisoners have been condemned to the "hunger bunker" where they are being slowly starved to death, deprived not only of any food but even of a drink of water. Usually horrible screams issue from these modern torture chambers, where innocent men, after months or even years of inhuman sufferings, are left to their gruesome fate. But this time the guards hear no cries. Only the sound of hymns and a murmur of prayer. It seems incredible. The man who was responsible for this transformation of a hunger bunker into a place of prayer was a Polish priest, whose life had been as extraordinary as his death.

Raymond Kolbe was born at Pabianice, near Lodz, the second son of a poor weaver. Both parents were devout Catholics and Raymond (to give him his baptismal name), an extremely lively boy, was brought up very strictly. Once —he was ten years old at the time—he annoyed his mother particularly, and she exclaimed with great emphasis: "My poor child, whatever will become of you?" These words made a profound impression on him, and he went into the church to ask the Blessed Virgin what was to become of him. Then, according to the story told by his mother, the Virgin appeared to him holding two crowns, one white, meaning that he would retain his purity unblemished, the other red, signifying martyrdom. When he was told to choose, he replied: "I choose both."

As Raymond's parents were very poor it was decided that they would send only their eldest son to school, while Raymond should stay at home and help in the grocery shop which his mother had opened to eke out the scanty wages of her husband. It was a great disappointment, for he, too, would have liked to become a priest like his elder brother. Then quite accidentally the local chemist discovered his intellectual gifts and himself undertook to prepare him for the examinations which would secure him a place in the school. He passed them with flying colours, and so his parents decided to make the additional sacrifices and give him, too, a proper education.

In 1907 he was sent to the minor Franciscan seminary at Lwow, which at that time belonged to Austria. He was a brilliant pupil; his favourite subjects were science and mathematics; indeed, he indulged in surprisingly modern dreams of what was then no more than science fiction: he would invent a machine to fly to the moon. He was also very military-minded; he was greatly interested in problems of strategy, modern fortifications, and many other subjects which did not seem to tally with a religious vocation at all. His early love for the Blessed Virgin had not diminished; he wanted to serve her like a medieval knight, fighting her battles, for was she not Queen of Poland? But priests could not be soldiers.

So one day, when he was sixteen, he decided to tell his superior that he would have to leave. But before he could do so his mother arrived at the monastery with an astonishing piece of news: their youngest son had also decided to become a priest, and now she and his father had resolved to realize an idea that had long been in their minds: they, too, would dedicate their lives to God; he would become a Franciscan brother, she a Benedictine nun. Raymond thought quickly. If he left the seminary now, this would mean that his parents would still be responsible for him and could not carry out their plan; was this not a sign from heaven that he was to stay? And so, instead of asking to leave, he went to his Provincial and begged to be clothed with the Franciscan habit.

At the ceremony he was fittingly given the name of the saint Maximilian, who suffered martyrdom in the third century for refusing to be a soldier. It is not surprising that, after the sudden reversal of his decision the time of Raymond's noviciate should have been a difficult period. He was tortured by scruples, for ever wondering whether he had done the right thing or committed a fault, and only strict obedience saved him from becoming a nervous wreck. But the storm blew over; in 1911, when he was seventeen, he made his first vows, and in the following year he was sent to Rome to study for the priesthood. Though it is a great honour for a young religious to be sent to Rome for his studies, Brother Maximilian at first was very upset about it. The reason? He had been told that in Rome young religious were constantly accosted and otherwise molested by women. But he soon found out that things were not as bad as all that and wrote to his mother, whom he had asked for special prayers, that the Italian women did not seem to be unduly interested in him and his brethren, quite apart from the fact that they never went out by themselves.

So Brother Maximilian was free to enjoy his studies and the beauties of Rome, the ceremonies at St. Peter's, the visits to the Colosseum, and all the other impressive experiences of a clerical student in the Eternal City. Besides, he prayed much and intensely. His fellow religious regarded him as a contemplative, and so he was, but a contemplative with a difference. For he was still a soldier at heart, a soldier and a scientist, besides, he was a great lover, like all true mystics, and his heart belonged to her whom he preferred to call simply "the Immaculate One." At first glance this combination of a very militant spirit with an intense devotion to Mary may seem strange. But it was, in fact, in accordance with a very old tradition. The breviary office for the Feast of the Assumption uses the verse from the Canticle: "Who is she that cometh forth as the morning rising . . . terrible as an army set in battle array" (6:9) as an antiphone. On several other feasts Mary is bidden to "Rejoice, for you alone have destroyed all the heresies in the world," and the pictures of the Immaculate Conception show her crushing the head of the serpent with her foot. So beside the image of the retiring Virgin of Nazareth we have that of the great conqueror of all evil. It was thus that Brother Maximilian saw her when in 1917 he first conceived the idea of founding an association which was to be called *Militia Immaculatae*.

That year—incidentally also the year of the apparitions at Fatima—was in many ways decisive for the young religious. The first World War had been raging for three years, during which he had faithfully followed his studies, receiving his doctorate of philosophy in 1915 and now preparing for ordination. In the spring he had begun to spit blood during a football match. The doctor ordered him to keep to his bed, and gradually the haemorrhages ceased. He made very little of his illness and hardly spoke about it; the times were too grave to be preoccupied with one's health. For, apart from the international catastrophe, Rome had just been the scene of outrages committed by the Freemasons who had assembled there to celebrate the bicentenary of their foundation. Brother Maximilian saw them waving their banners with pictures of the devil trampling on St. Michael right under the windows of the Vatican, and this gave him the idea conceived in his hours of prayer of founding his own spiritual army, the army of the Immaculate Virgin, to counteract the evils of the time. Convinced that the idea had been inspired by the Blessed Virgin herself, he sought and received the approval of his superiors and soon gathered six fellow students, with whom he hoped to "set large artillery engines in motion"—for he used the military imagery of his time for his spiritual aspirations, just as St. Ignatius of Loyola would speak of standards and armies spread out in the plains.

At first his Militia made only very little progress. Maximilian's health deteriorated, he was again coughing up blood and had to be temporarily dispensed from his studies. During this time he made a fair copy of his programme for the association, whose main activities in those days were prayer and the distribution of the "miraculous medal" of Our Lady. He sent the programme to the general of the order who gave it his full approval, and from that time the Militia began to grow rapidly.

In April 1918 Maximilian was ordained priest, and in the following year he took his doctorate in theology. Himself gravely ill, he returned to Poland in July 1919. The country was exhausted by the war, in the grip of inflation as well as epidemics. Despite his tuberculosis Father Maximilian was sent to Cracow as a professor. The six months he spent there were among the most difficult of his life. His fellow religious did not understand him at all but made fun of him. They did not guess his state of health, and his slow movements combined with his great zeal—he tried to make them give up smoking—made him ridiculous in their eyes. So they had little sympathy for his Militia; but he found followers outside, to whom he gave addresses and whom he sought to fire with his own enthusiasm to do and suffer great things for God. In one of these conferences, given in November 1919, he speaks of suffering as the purifying fire and refers especially to misunderstandings and persecutions by good people, as well as to interior purifications by trials in the spiritual life. But these sufferings, he continues, are really to be desired; for through them we can prove our real love for God and his Immaculate Mother. This is the language of the mystic, for whom the "dark night of the soul," as St. John of the Cross calls it, is greatly to be desired, because it purges him from all self-love and makes him a perfect instrument in the hands of God.

In the following weeks Father Maximilian's condition deteriorated so much that he was sent to a nursing home at Zakopane, where he spent nearly the whole of the year 1920. For the first time in his life he was surrounded almost entirely by unbelievers. He obediently followed the hospital régime, he spent long hours in prayer, but his apostolic drive was too strong to allow him the complete rest for which he had come. He was soon engaged in controversy with some of the freethinkers among the patients and asked to give conferences, which resulted in some spectacular conversions. For, well versed in modern philosophy no less than in science, he could meet his opponents on their own ground. Ever since his student days it had been his principle to keep abreast of modern developments; in his opinion Catholics should be in the vanguard of contemporary life, examining all things, as St. Paul had written, and retaining whatever was good. Thus, while his brethren were bewailing the cinema as an invention of the devil, Maximilian realized at once that it could be put to good use in the right hands. Small wonder that his young fellow patients were amazed at the keen intelligence and up-to-date information of this ardent young priest who combined a gentle persuasiveness that won their hearts with the cogent arguments that convinced their heads.

After his return to Cracow, in December 1920, Father Maximilian's Militia began to grow to such an extent that he felt the time had come to carry out a plan that had long been simmering in his mind: he wanted to have a kind of bulletin through which all the members could be kept in touch with him and with each other. His superiors consented; but he would have to find the necessary funds himself. So, in line with the old Franciscan tradition, he went begging, and in January 1922 the first number of *The Knight of the Immaculate Virgin* made its appearance. When the second number came out there was no money to pay the printer's bill—for the galloping inflation had eaten up all the funds. The superior told the unfortunate editor that he would have to meet his liabilities as best he could. Father Maximilian prayed hard— and, after Mass, found an envelope on the Lady altar con- taining the exact amount that was due to the printer, ac- companied by a slip of paper with the instruction: "For my beloved Immaculate Mother." The superior could not but allow Father Maximilian to pay his debt with this unexpected gift.

Nevertheless, he had to struggle with a good deal of opposition; for in the Poland of the early twenties many Franciscans had not yet realized that the press was going to be an essential instrument of the apostolate in the modern world. They clung to the old, well-tried method of preach- ing and hearing confessions—surely publishing was an occupa- tion only for laymen? Father Maximilian was not to be put off. Quite the contrary. He was fed up having to worry about printer's bills—why not buy a printing press himself and do his own printing? His superiors had no objection—again, on condition that he should find the money for it himself.

One day his idea came up at recreation. Maximilian's fellow religious thought it a good subject for entertaining them- selves at the ambitious editor's expense. A printing press, indeed! With no money to pay for it, and in a Franciscan house into the bargain! An American priest on a visit to Poland happened to be present at this discussion, and he was not amused. In the United States many religious orders were running their own printing presses very successfully—what was there to mock at in the young Father's idea? And then and there Maximilian was given a cheque for a hundred dollars.

With this money he bought a very ancient printing press and proceeded to produce his magazine himself. But this was too much for the good Fathers at Cracow, who suddenly found their peaceful, almost medieval existence invaded by the machine age. So from Cracow, in the south of Poland, quite near Silesia, Father Maximilian was sent to Grodno, right up in the north, near the border of Lithuania. The

Franciscan house there was more or less a place of retirement for old Fathers.

Three rooms were put at his disposal, but he could expect neither understanding nor support from his fellow priests, who found it quite impossible to take his literary work seriously. So he was dispensed from none of his normal duties; indeed, being younger than the rest, he was often sent to distant villages to hear confessions and visit the sick. He started with no more than two helpers, and the old printing press was extremely hard to operate. He was a born leader and soon collected a number of devoted assistants, but continued to write most of the articles himself. Though he was not a professional writer, his transparent sincerity and enthusiasm as well as his gift for simple exposition of the truths of the faith gained the small blue magazine an ever increasing number of readers.

Soon the printers were turned into Franciscan lay brothers and the monastery at Grodno was presented with the problem of housing only very few priests and a vast number of brothers. The old-established routine was completely upset; besides, Father Maximilian insisted on treating priests and brothers alike, there was no class distinction as far as he was concerned, they were all "working brothers in a working world." To show his readers what the religious life was really like he published photographs of the brothers at work before their machines. The effect of these pictures was astonishing, and many more aspirants presented themselves—but they insisted on working under the direction of Father Maximilian and nobody else. In 1925, the Jubilee year, he had the idea of publishing a special calendar of sixty pages in honour of the Blessed Virgin, with a printing of 12,000 copies. This undertaking, of course, involved an enormous amount of additional work for the already overworked editor and his staff. But they all thought it well worth the effort; for the calendar was a tremendous success, and in the course of the year both the number of copies issued and that of brothers working on the review had doubled.

The Franciscan superiors could not remain indifferent to this form of the apostolate which had proved so far more successful than even its supporters had ever dared to anticipate. So, on his next visitation, the Provincial ordered a whole wing of the Grodno monastery to be turned into a printing house. The old Fathers were aghast and planned to frustrate the scheme. But Father Maximilian was quicker. Immediately after the Provincial's departure the printers turned themselves into a demolition squad; they came by night and took down partitions, removed furniture, and generally turned the whole place upside down, so that next morning the wing, which had housed the old kitchen and refectory, could no longer be put to its original use.

As soon as Father Maximilian found himself in possession of sufficient space he began to improve his tools and bought a large saw machine as well as a Diesel engine. Where did the money come from? Of course, the review, which now sold over 40,000 copies, paid for much of the outlay, but Father Maximilian also had a knack of getting things far more cheaply than other people. The Diesel engine, for example, was acquired at 65 per cent of the original price demanded by its owner, whom Father Maximilian rewarded for this generosity by making him go to confession after living without the sacraments for twenty years.

However, early in 1926 the incessant work, combined with the lack of sufficient sleep and food, once more broke down Father Maximilian's always-delicate health, and this time the relapse was very serious indeed; so much so that at first the doctors despaired of his life. He was again sent to Zakopane, where he stayed for eighteen months. It was a terrible blow: just when his work had begun to flourish he had to leave it; for he was under strict injunctions not to occupy himself with his publishing and printing house at all, which was left in the care of his brother. So he tried to do all he could for it in another way, by suffering and prayer, abandoning himself completely to the Immaculate Virgin to whom he had dedicated his life. But his enforced inactivity was not his only affliction. As happens so often, his physical illness was accompanied by spiritual suffering; God and His Mother seemed far away; he was left alone, to all appearance a useless tool that had been thrown aside.

Towards the end of his stay at Zakopane his whole life-work seemed to be in danger of being destroyed. His brother, though very conscientious and devoted to him, was not the personality to cope with the difficulties that had arisen during Father Maximilian's absence. Once more the old Fathers at Grodno were on the warpath. They grudged the printing house the money that was fed into it—if this were properly invested instead of being spent on ever more up-to-date machinery, they could all live in greater comfort and security, while the review would continue to yield a certain amount of profit. Besides, all these horrible huge machines—what would St. Francis say if he saw all this? He who was such a lover of nature? But Father Maximilian had not the slightest doubt that St. Francis would have thoroughly approved of his work—he who was such a lover of souls. It was to lead souls to God and his Immaculate Mother that Maximilian wanted the most efficient printing presses, the Diesel engines and the rest: technical achievements were a gift of God as well as everything else, they should be consecrated to his service. He and his workmen led the most exemplary life of poverty in the spirit of St. Francis—but to spread the kingdom of God only the best was good enough. As in the Middle Ages dedicated architects and craftsmen used all their technical knowledge and artistic genius to build magnificent churches, so in the modern world he would use wonderful machines to spread the knowledge of the Christian faith that had declined so perilously—largely because of just these machines, which were used by unbelievers to make money while Christians were afraid of turning them to the service of God.

In the summer of 1927 matters at Grodno had reached boiling point. The old Fathers there complained that the printing establishment upset their religious life completely:

the worker-brothers, for their part, found it extremely difficult to continue in such an atmosphere of hostility. Not
cured by any means, but a great deal better, Father Maximilian returned to the scene. He realized at once that the
only thing to do was to remove everything from Grodno.
His Provincial gave him permission to set up a place of his
own, as the hubbub of a publishing-*cum*-printing house was
bound to disturb the regular observance of an ordinary
Franciscan friary. So Father Maximilian prayed more intensely
than ever while looking out for a suitable site,

At last he had found exactly what he wanted. The place
was near Warsaw, beautifully central; when he went to look
at it he was delighted. He immediately set up a statue of the
Immaculate Virgin on the site and went back to see his
Provincial to report on the terms under which the owner,
Prince Drucki-Lubecki, was prepared to sell. He was to be
bitterly disappointed, for the Provincial thought the price of
the land much too high and refused point-blank to give his
consent to the transaction. But even a firm *No* of his superior
could not daunt the indomitable knight of Mary. He went
back to the prince, himself a good Catholic Pole, to tell him
of the decision. The prince asked what, then, was to happen
to the statue, which was still in the place where Father
Maximilian had put it. The Franciscan saw his chance at
once. Quickly he replied: "Let it stay where it is." There was
a moment's silence, then the Prince told him he could have
the site—for nothing. Overjoyed Maximilian wrote to the
Provincial to tell him of this unexpected turn of events and
then travelled back to Grodno to wait for an answer.

Naturally, the Provincial could not very well refuse such
a generous offer. No sooner had the permission been received
than Father Maximilian began to organize the transfer both
of men and machines to the new site, which he called
Niepokalanow, city of the Immaculate One. But when he
arrived there in October 1927, the place was anything but
a city. The first consignment of brothers had managed to
build a few sheds with holes for windows, and there Father

Maximilian slept in the frosty October nights, after his frequent expeditions to Warsaw to buy more tools and machinery. Finally, at the end of November, the whole community of workers left Grodno to settle down in the as yet extremely primitive conditions at Niepokalanow. The enthusiasm of Father Maximilian was catching. The neighbouring peasants helped the hard-working community in their midst with gifts of food, and new members presented themselves in growing numbers. Father Maximilian's principles of admission were significant: he hated inefficiency, and his "little brothers," as they came to be popularly known had not only to be sincere Christians who knew the value and efficacy of prayer, but also highly trained and capable workers. In his view devotion to Christ and his Mother was no excuse for bungling, quite the contrary. The Immaculate Virgin had every right to expect from her servants that they would give her the very best not only of their prayer, but also of their natural capacities. But such an insistence on competent workmanship meant also that he encouraged responsibility and the development of special abilities.

In an earlier age the story of the religious who was sent by his superior to plant cabbages upside down and did so without question or murmur was held up for the admiration of readers as an example of perfect obedience. Father Maximilian belonged to a different generation—moreover, if you have to deal with machines it would be dangerous, indeed, to treat them in the way that religious was told to treat the cabbages. The Polish Franciscan, whose personal life was one of total reliance on the supernatural power of prayer, was at the same time convinced that in the carrying out of one's daily work all the natural means of invention, industry, and technical achievement should be used carefully and intelligently, to further the Kingdom of God. With this combination of spiritual and material elements Niepokalanow grew at an amazing rate. In 1927 the *Knight of the Immaculate One* had a circulation of 50,000 copies; three years later it had almost reached the 300,000 mark.

Father Maximilian belonged to the race of those who can never rest satisfied with their achievements; for he could say like St. Paul: "The love of Christ urges us on."

During a journey he had had to undertake in connection with his work he had met a group of Japanese students. He had presented them with some medals of Our Lady, and they had given him in exchange some elephant-shaped pagan amulets. Since then Japan had been constantly in his mind as a country to be converted to Christ and his Immaculate Mother, needing a Niepokalanow of its own. When he explained his idea of making a foundation in Japan to his Provincial he was naturally asked such awkward questions as whether he had any money, or friends in Japan, or at least knew the language of the country, all of which he had to answer in the negative. However, he seemed so sure that the Blessed Virgin herself wanted such a foundation that his superiors, remembering what he had already achieved contrary to all considerations of ordinary prudence, allowed him to choose four brothers and set out with them for the land of his apostolic dreams.

Early in 1930 he and his companions travelled to Marseilles via Lisieux and Lourdes, where they prayed fervently for the success of their undertaking. During the voyage the five Franciscans studied Japanese and used whatever opportunity came to them for making converts. On April 24, 1930, they landed at Nagasaki, where, in 1597, twenty-six Japanese Christians had been crucified for their faith, the most prominent among a number of other martyrs. Now Catholicism had made headway again; the hierarchy was established, and Father Maximilian went to see the bishop to ask him for permission to publish his review. He had to admit that he had hardly any funds for the purpose, so the proposal did not meet with much enthusiasm. But in the course of the conversation the bishop learned that Father Maximilian held doctorates both in philosophy and theology, so asked him to teach at his seminary. Again the Franciscan was quick to seize his opportunity. He was prepared to fall in with the bishop's wishes, if he would be allowed to publish his review. Within exactly one month he had achieved the incredible: on May 24 the first number of the Japanese *Knight of the Immaculate One* was issued from his own printing house.

It seemed a near miracle, and it had been achieved by very hard work in the most penitential circumstances. The religious had very little food—and that of a variety which did not at all agree with Father Maximilian—scarcely any shelter, and besides had to cope with a foreign alphabet of about two thousand signs. Father Maximilian could not write his articles in Polish but had to do them in Latin or Italian; they were then translated by a Japanese who was a Methodist but who, under the author's powerful influence, soon became a Catholic. While Father Maximilian was wearing himself out in Japan, suffering from fever and headaches, his superiors in Poland were not happy about this latest adventure and the expenses involved; so they recalled him, after barely three months, to give an account of his work to a chapter meeting at Lodz. But his irrepressible personality once more won the day. He was given permission to make a sister foundation of Niepokalanow in Nagasaki, with authority to open a noviciate for native postulants.

But when he returned to Japan he found his work in a deplorable state. The review had not come out, and everything was in confusion. So, armed with all the permissions given him at the chapter, he bought a site for his new foundation outside Nagasaki, on a height facing away from the town instead of towards it, as would have seemed much more reasonable. His decision appeared providential when, fifteen years later, an atom bomb was dropped on Nagasaki. For, protected by the hill, Father Maximilian's foundation suffered no casualties and hardly any damage beyond a few broken windows.

There is little we know about his mystical life, as he scarcely ever mentioned his spiritual experiences either in letters or in conversation, but it seems certain that he was given some extraordinary illuminations. Several years after his return to Poland he admitted, under the persistent questioning of his religious after an unguarded remark, that during his stay in Japan he had been promised heaven; but more than that he would not tell them. He added, however, as a safeguard, that they ought not to long for extraordinary experiences but do the will of their Immaculate Mother, which was the same as the will of God.

This simple, childlike devotion to Mary and the mystical graces Father Maximilian received in the course of his tremendously active life were combined with a penetrating insight into the requirements of the modern apostolate. In a letter written during his stay at Nagasaki he laid down the methods which alone could be effective in the struggle with militant atheism. The first need, he wrote, was to make a thorough study of these anti-religious movements in all their aspects, and this not only in a negative spirit. For they also contained something good, and it was the duty of the Christian apostle to find these good elements and incorporate them in his own teaching and action. Failure to do this had resulted in the catastrophic events in Mexico and Spain, then in the throes of persecution and civil war. Father Maximilian was well aware that many of the setbacks Christianity had suffered in the contemporary world were due to the failure of Christians to live up to the principles they professed in theory and to apply them to the needs of their time.

After two years of hard work at Nagasaki the Franciscan community which looked after the printing and publication of the Japanese *Knight of the Immaculate One* seemed sufficiently well established for Father Maximilian to go still further afield. He went to India to prepare the ground for yet another foundation, though he could not stay to see it actually carried out, and so, without his compelling presence, it came to nothing. The constant overwork had once more seriously impaired his health, and in 1936 he returned to Poland and became superior of Niepokalanow, which had continued to flourish in his absence. The *Knight of the Immaculate One* had reached three quarters of a million copies per issue;

there was a special magazine for children and an international
one, in Latin, *Miles Immaculatae* (*The Soldier of the Immaculate One*) had been added for the Catholic clergy everywhere; and the year before a Catholic periodical with a mass
appeal, the *Little Journal*, had made its first appearance,
launched after a novena of prayer and fasting.

For in all the beehive of activity that Niepokalanow had
become the spiritual values were always given first place. The
six priests and over seven hundred brothers who made up
the large community at the time of Father Maximilian's
return gave several hours to prayer and meditation each
day. Except on visiting days, they had their meals in silence,
because Father Maximilian held that God would not speak to
them in noise and excitement. To him, who spoke of Christ,
his Mother, and the saints in the familiar way of the genuine
mystic, it was self-evident that his worker brothers would
also be brought into close contact with the supernatural world
if they prepared themselves by prayer and silence; for to him
Niepokalanow was not only a religious publishing house but
also "a school for saints." He himself set the example, not
only by his simple life—the office from which he conducted
his operations contained no more than a table, two chairs,
book shelves, and a bed and washstand—but also by the
fatherly goodness with which he looked after all his "little
children," visiting the sick despite the crushing load of work
and receiving guests with never-failing hospitality. In a world
of machines he retained the authentic Franciscan spirit; more,
he integrated the machines themselves into this spirit, speaking of "brother engine" as St. Francis had done of brother
sun. For to him the machines, too, were servants of the
Immaculate Virgin to whom all his life was dedicated; they
worked to fulfil her commands, transmitted to them by
"brother engineer." So, while men like G. K. Chesterton and
Eric Gill hurled defiance at the machine age and all its works,
an attitude that could not but be futile in the long run, Father
Maximilian saw it as subject to God like all other ages; we

might almost say he gave "brother machine" a "soul" by making it do the will of God.

In these last years before the second World War he had great plans. He had already established a radio transmitter, he was planning a hangar to house aeroplanes so that he and his helpers should be able to get about more quickly, and he hoped to produce some good Catholic films. Nevertheless, he was well aware of the dangers that threatened from neighbouring Germany. Even before Munich he predicted that war was inevitable. And his main concern now was to prepare his religious for it, so that they would not fall into despair when it did come. He urged on them the sanctifying power of suffering, the glory of martyrdom that would open heaven to them. He was very precise in his forecast: a dreadful conflict was imminent, and it was Poland that would suffer the worst.

So when on September 1, 1939 the Nazi armies invaded his country, he was prepared. Niepokalanow, being so near Warsaw, was savagely bombarded. Father Maximilian sent back most of the working brothers to their families, who needed them, and where they might be safer than in the printing establishment, and retained only a small number of his most devoted helpers. On September 19 motorized SS men arrived and took them all to a prison camp. This was not yet a concentration camp; they suffered much from filth, cold, and hunger; but there was no torture. Indeed, the wife of the warden was so impressed by Father Maximilian's personality that she sent him a cake which, of course, he immediately distributed among his fellow prisoners. Together they prayed and offered their sufferings to win men for Christ. Father Maximilian even gave them conferences in the camp, in which he exhorted them to profit from all they had to endure; for had not the Immaculate Virgin herself urged Christians to pray and do penance when she appeared at Lourdes and Fatima?

Then, after almost three months, they were suddenly set free, on December 8, the feast of the Immaculate Conception.

They returned to Niepokalanow, which had been sacked but was otherwise intact. There could be no question of resuming any of their work at the moment; Father Maximilian therefore introduced the practice of perpetual adoration of the Blessed Sacrament, so that their apostolate might be carried on by prayer and suffering alone, as they could no longer serve God by work. However, when Poland had been completely occupied and the war moved to the Western front, Father Maximilian's helpers began to drift back; others had to hide from the Gestapo. To keep in touch with all of them, circular letters were secretly printed and distributed, in which the Father insisted on the value of suffering and tried to infuse into them his own boundless courage and love.

Incredible though it may seem, he had the ambition to revive his cherished review even in the face of the German occupation of his country. And, even more incredibly, after endless applications and negotiations with the Nazi authorities, he received the permission and published the one and only number exactly a year after he had returned from the prison camp, on the feast of the Immaculate Conception, 1940. In it he wrote words that read like his last will and testament: "No one in the world can change truth. What we can do and should do is to seek truth and serve it when we have found it." For Nazism was built on lies—the lie of the superiority of the "Nordic" race, the lie of the inferiority of the Jews, the lie of the ultimate victory of brute force. But no one, not even the most powerful propaganda machine in the world, can change truth. The real conflict, he went on to say, is an inner conflict: "Beyond armies of occupation, unrestrained passions and the hecatombs of extermination camps, there are two irreconcilable enemies in the depth of every soul: good and evil, sin and love. And what use are the victories on the battlefield, if we ourselves are defeated in our innermost personal selves?"

This was a defeat Father Maximilian himself was never to know. On February 17, 1941, a powerful black car arrived at the gates of his monastery, from which emerged five members of the Gestapo. They arrested him and four other Fathers, two of whom survived. We owe our knowledge of what happened inside the Warsaw prison of Pawiak to their testimony. Put in an overcrowded cell filled with men whose only crime was to be Poles, and many of whom had already been cruelly tortured, he at once exercised an apostolate of gentleness and compassion which brought light into the darkness of hate and despair. One day the cell was inspected by an SS officer who was a particularly enraged enemy of Catholicism. As soon as he saw Father Maximilian's religious habit he tore off the rosary the friar wore on his belt, scattering the beads on the floor, and holding up the crucifix, shouted: "Dirty idiot of a priest, do you believe in this?" "I do believe," came the calm answer. Two savage blows on his face rewarded this confession of faith. "Do you still believe?" "Indeed I do." There was an avalanche of blows, Father Maximilian's face turned from white to purple, he managed only with the greatest difficulty to keep on his feet. A third time: "And now, do you still believe?" And again, as firmly convinced as before: "Yes, I do believe."

The officer was beside himself with rage. Seized with a paroxysm of hate, he belaboured the slender, exhausted body of the priest with his fists, kicked him with his jackboots, and finally departed, leaving him laying unconscious on the floor. After this Father Maximilian was placed in the prison hospital, where he stayed until the middle of May. Then he was transferred to the concentration camp at Auschwitz where he had to put on secular clothes. In the letter he was allowed to send to Niepokalanow to ask for these, he wrote to the brothers, of whom many had offered themselves, without success, as hostages in his place: "Why are you troubled, my little ones, seeing no ill can come to us without the permission of God and his Immaculate Mother? Let us follow where she leads us with ever increasing docility, so that, having done our duty to the end, we may be able to save all souls through love."

At Auschwitz Father Maximilian was placed in a group

under the command of a monstrous individual called Krott who was devoid of all human feeling whatsoever. He persecuted the Franciscan with a hatred such as the very evil sometimes have for the very good. He forced him to carry heavy tree trunks running as quickly as he could and, when he fell, beat him mercilessly. When his companions tried to come to his aid Father Maximilian told them not to incur the wrath of the terrible Krott in their turn—the Immaculate Virgin was helping him, he would hold out. This kind of treatment continued for two weeks. Finally Krott ordered him to lie down on a pile of wood, and the most brutal of his minions showered fifty blows on him. At the end of this the priest was left for dead in a hole.

His fellow prisoners had watched in silence but had not dared interfere because that would only have made things worse for him. But at night, when they had finished work, they came to take him away. He was still alive, and next day he was taken to the camp hospital, a vile place where the "patients" hardly ever recovered. Despite strict prohibitions he used to hear their confessions at night, for, as he would frequently say: "I am willing to suffer much more for Jesus Christ. The Immaculate Virgin is with me. She is helping me. . . ." Indeed, it seems almost impossible that this always so delicate priest whose tuberculosis had never been completely cured should have survived all these sufferings without supernatural help.

But even allowing for that his spirit was truly indomitable. After a fortnight in the "hospital," Father Maximilian was transferred to a kind of "nursing home" where the patients were dispensed from work but had instead their starvation rations halved. Father Maximilian often gave away his own, telling the others that they were hungrier than he. He even gave spiritual conferences to them, one of them on the subject of the relations of the Immaculate Virgin with the three Persons of the Trinity.

When he had sufficiently recovered to be considered fit for going back to the normal concentration camp routine, he was transferred to another part, Block 14. There, towards the end of July, a prisoner was reported missing. Since despite all precautions, attempts at escapes were sometimes successful, the camp authorities had decided that for every man missing a certain number of the inmates of the camp were to die the dreaded death of starvation in the hunger bunker. On this particular day the alarm had been raised that there had been an escape from Block 14. About three o'clock in the afternoon the prisoners had been given their soup and then been ordered to stand to attention in the glaring sun to await orders. Towards evening the head officer of the camp went round for an inspection. Slowly, taking his time as if he were enjoying a particularly amusing situation, he went past the men of Block 14 and picked out here one, there another, telling them to stand out from their line. They stepped forward in silence, all but one. That one cried out: "O my poor wife! My poor children! Never shall I see them again!" Without taking any notice an underling of the head officer shouted at them to take off their shoes and turn left. The same prisoner started again to bewail his family in heart-rending tones. Suddenly to the consternation of all Father Maximilian stepped forward and asked the head officer to let him die in the place of this man. The Nazi was dumb-founded. Such a thing had never happened in all his ex-perience. In his astonishment he quite forgot to give his usual bark and asked in an ordinary voice: "But why?" Father Maximilian told him that he was old and good for nothing, that he had no family. "Who are you?" "A Catholic priest." And the incredible happened. The officer released the con-demned man and let Father Maximilian go to the hunger bunker in his stead. And from this bunker there sounded no screams, no curses, but prayers and the faint sound of hymns. When the nine others had died, comforted by their priest, Father Maximilian was still alive.

On the fourteenth of August, the vigil of the feast of the Assumption, the guards entered, accompanied by one of the prisoners who had been appointed corpse bearer. To him we owe the description of the priest's last moments. When they came into the hunger bunker they found Father Maximilian sitting on the ground. He held out his arm where there was hardly a place left, because he was so emaciated, to plunge the syringe with its lethal poison. Then he, too, disappeared in the furnaces of Auschwitz.

CHAPTER NINE

Edel Quinn

(1907–1944)

A very attractive Irish business girl, with large blue eyes, an irresistible smile, smartly dressed, fond of dancing, a good golfer and tennis player, bubbling over with mirth—could anyone correspond less to the popular idea of a "mystic?" Nevertheless, Edel Quinn, this extraordinary young woman, was all this.

Both her parents were Irish born and bred, the father a bank manager who was fairly frequently transferred from one place to another. Edel herself was born at Greenane, County Cork; but her parents moved to County Tipperary when she was still quite small. She was the eldest of a family of four girls and one boy and soon learned to assume responsibility for them when needed. Her primary education was entrusted to the Loreto nuns, who found her a very lively child, always full of fun and mischief despite her obedience. Later she was sent to a boarding school in England, where, among other things, she became captain of the cricket team. Her high spirits were noticed by all; yet she kept faithfully to the rule of the house; for example, she always tried to stop talking as soon as the sign for silence was given. However, before she had finished her education, her parents' financial situation deteriorated considerably and she had to leave school. She returned to Ireland, took a course in commercial subjects and, at the age of nineteen, became a shorthand typist at an import firm for building materials.

Her employer was a young Frenchman, Pierre L. He greatly appreciated the efficiency of his new typist, who soon became his personal secretary. She worked extremely hard, identifying herself completely with the firm, so much so that Pierre himself became worried about her health and proposed to engage an assistant for her. But she replied gaily that she had "never too much work to do." Nevertheless she sometimes regretted it that her business duties left her very little time for her favourite sports; soon she could no longer play golf, but she still enjoyed a game of tennis and an occasional private dance. For apart from her job she had to help in the house; holidays were almost non-existent, except for one journey back to England to visit her old school, where she had the misfortune "to share a cabin with a terribly loquacious woman. She talked and talked and talked, and when I did get to sleep, she woke me up again at about 5 A.M. to tell me she was thinking how lonely her little white cat must be without her! This beautiful creature she feeds on fish always and, as a result, it has a beautiful silken coat! You can imagine how nice it was to hear these interesting details at such an hour!"

This ability to see the funny side of things was characteristic of Edel, and, as we shall see, remained with her throughout her life. It was the other side of her deeply religious nature, of the seriousness of purpose she brought to her relations with God and with her neighbour. She already led a very mortified life, though no one would have suspected it who only knew her merry laughter, which hid her profound spirituality but was partly also its expression. She rose early every day to attend a seven o'clock Mass and from there went straight to work, breakfasting on not much more than an apple, if that. Her lunch hour would frequently be devoted to an errand of charity, her evenings either to her family or to Church activities. Meals were a very minor concern; she did not mind in the least going practically without food a whole day if her many activities left her no time for it. But if weekdays were overflowing with work of all kinds, Sundays were entirely given to God. She shared the tremendous devotion of her countrymen to the Mass, and would spend almost the entire Sunday in church. In the afternoon, and sometimes again in the evening, she would go to Benediction.

In the summer of 1927 Pierre, her employer, transferred his business to another French firm, and Edel was made manager. But, being separated from her, Pierre suddenly realized that he had fallen in love with her. Having to return once more to Dublin he took Edel out for lunch and then and there proposed to her. To his great surprise the girl looked distressed and then told him that she could not return his feelings, as her heart was no longer free. She had promised herself to God, and as soon as her family could spare her she would become a Poor Clare.

Pierre, like many Frenchmen, had been a very slack Catholic; under Edel's influence he had returned to the practice of his religion. She feared that the shock of her refusal might once more estrange him from the Church, and so she kept up a correspondence with him, in which she mingled personal feeling and compassion with very delicate spiritual instruction: "You see, Pierre," she writes in one of her letters when he had expressed his hope that she might still change her mind, "I have not changed my views, and if it is God's will, I do not believe I ever shall. I feel absolutely certain that I am doing what God wants of me. . . . I know this is difficult to understand, but perhaps one day God may be pleased to enlighten you. It is very, very difficult to explain my reason, and I would not attempt the task but that I would like you to see my point of view. . . . I feel that you could do great things for God and that He has work for you to do. . . . I believe that when we unite our sufferings with

His and offer them up for His Glory, those sufferings become sweet and bring us very close to Him, and will be a source of real happiness. Do you not feel, Pierre, that we are in His hands, and that whatever comes to us is for the best? So let us unite our wills with His Divine Will, and entrust the future to Him."

But she did not always write to him in this serious vein. She was a real woman and utterly natural even in this rather delicate relationship with a rejected suitor. After she had sent him a tie for his birthday she wrote: "I am glad you like the tie. I was on pins and needles trying to choose it, because nobody can choose a tie for a man except that man himself! It was the red stripes that gave me the spasms. I was afraid they would displease your majesty's taste. In fact, if I had not immediately posted it, you would never have got it, as I know my courage would have failed in the end. I spent from one until two choosing it, and the girl was nearly frantic at the end." It is a letter any girl might write to her lover—but she put the initials H.B.S. after her name, standing for "Hand-maid of the Blessed Sacrament," a eucharistic league, to remind him that, for all her teasing, she belonged to God.

In the same year, 1927, Edel took a step that was to change her whole life. She joined the Legion of Mary. This lay organization, which is wholly devoted to the spiritual apostolate, bringing lapsed Catholics back to the sacraments, teaching the catechism, rehabilitating fallen women, and the like, had been founded in Ireland six years before and was organized on military lines. Its basic unit is the praesidium of between about ten and thirty members which is run by a spiritual director, a president, vice-President, secretary and treasurer. The praesidium meets every week for prayer and reports on the work done as well as for discussing future work, which, if it involves visiting, is always undertaken in twos. Edel heard about the Legion from an acquaintance who had known her only for a very short time. When she expressed her desire to attend a meeting, the newly found friend warned the president of her group that the immaculately groomed Edel seemed so lively and gay that she would surely not be able to stand the exacting and regular work of the Legion for long. The friend had made the mistake of a lifetime. For, in the little spare time her job left her, Edel threw herself into the Legion activities with tremendous zest. She visited hospital wards and slums, lonely old people, and families of dubious religious practice, though she was shy by nature and disliked talking to people she had never seen before, risking indifference and even insult. She rarely spoke of her spiritual life, but her friends noticed that all her spare moments seemed to be given to prayer—after all, she wanted to be a Poor Clare, which is a purely contemplative vocation.

In 1929, after two years of Legion activity, Edel was made president of a group which had been given the task of rescuing prostitutes. When she, a slip of a girl barely of age, made her first appearance before the praesidium, the members thought the superiors of the Legion had taken leave of their senses. They sent their spiritual director to "headquarters" to protest against such a young president for this extremely delicate and dangerous work. The priest came back defeated: headquarters insisted that the young woman was just the right person for the job, and, to the surprise of the whole praesidium, she proved it in a very short time. She impressed them both by her extraordinary efficiency and by her intense recollection at prayer time, when she seemed completely absorbed in God. And, despite her intensive Legion work she still found time for social duties: one night she appeared at a meeting in evening dress, because immediately after she had to go to a dance that had been arranged for her brother's twenty-first birthday.

Her personal attractiveness and her natural gaiety made Edel very popular with the girls at the hostel Sancta Maria, which the Legion was running for the ex-prostitutes it had reclaimed. She organized entertainments for them and finally she went there every night after her day's work, stayed until midnight, and then travelled five miles back to her home for a

very short night's rest, only to be up again early next morning to go to Mass and from there to the office. The older
members of the Legion of Mary were alarmed—no girl of
her age could keep on at this rate without serious damage to
her health. But she laughed off all remonstrations. When
they warned her that they would soon have to have Mass
offered for another dead legionary if she was not careful,
she simply replied that "That would be fine."

After all, she was hoping soon to enter one of the austerest
orders of the Church; there seemed no sense in sparing herself. As her family no longer needed her, she was to enter
early in 1932. Then a blow fell which shattered all her hopes
of a religious life: she had a haemorrhage, and when the
doctor examined her he found she suffered from tuberculosis.
The disease was already far advanced; there could be no
question of her ever being accepted for the religious life;
instead she had to go to a sanatorium for a very long rest.
Though this development came as a great shock to her, it did
not surprise many of her friends, who had noticed that to her
tremendous load of work she had for many years added un-
reasonable mortifications, such as depriving herself almost
completely of milk, butter, and sugar and missing meals
whenever she found it inconvenient to make time for them.
Though sorely disappointed, Edel met her new circumstances
with the ready acceptance that was the mark both of her
exceptionally happy and balanced personality and her perfect
submission to the will of God, in accordance with one of her
retreat notes: "Rejoice to imitate Our Lord in joyful acceptance of suffering: difficulties of health, daily upsets are
His choicest gifts."

In the nursing home, which she entered in February, 1932,
she immediately put these principles into practice. She never
complained about her illness; if she was disappointed at not
being able to become a Poor Clare, she never showed it.
Instead she would consistently look at the bright side of
everything, often joking and laughing with her fellow patients
even till the tears ran down her cheeks. St. Teresa of Avila

once said that a recreation at which her nuns did not laugh had not fulfilled its purpose: Edel would have fully agreed with this, even though she fought shy of reading books like the saint's *Interior Castle*. This may at first sight seem strange. But Edel felt very strongly that such extraordinary things as visions and ecstasies were not for her, and that reading about them could not serve any useful purpose. For intense union with God can be vividly experienced also without such extraordinary phenomena—Edel herself is a very good example. Her Retreat notes often speak of resting peacefully in the presence of Christ, which she felt most strongly after receiving Holy Communion and which sometimes showed itself in a radiant expression on her face and a forgetfulness of time; but when a friend ventured to remark on it she would laugh it off; her reserve in this matter was extreme. Though she did not care for descriptions of extraordinary ecstatic experiences she liked to read other spiritual books: St. John of the Cross for example and St. Teresa of Lisieux, Blosius, and Grignion de Montfort, whose works play an essential part in the spirituality of the Legion of Mary, but also a more liturgically-minded writer like Dom Marmion.

At the nursing home she had plenty of time to read, besides exercising a silent apostolate among her fellow patients.

Despite the rest, however, her health did not appreciably improve. After eighteen months at the sanatorium Edel decided that it was useless to stay any longer, especially as the doctors had given her no hope of a final recovery. Besides, the treatment was very expensive for her family and she felt she could just as well rest at home. But Edel was the very last person to rest unless she was absolutely forced to; so she had not been home long before she found herself another job, this time in a place entirely unsuitable for someone suffering from tuberculosis. The office of the motor engineering firm in which she had decided to work was above a garage, penetrated by neither daylight nor fresh air, but instead by most unhealthy fumes. Her doctor told her to give up this almost suicidal work at once, but she simply laughed and said everything was "all right." Perhaps this complete unconcern for her health was due to a special object she had in accepting this particular job; but in any case it did her no harm, on the contrary, there was a slight improvement. She resumed her habitual penances, even slept on boards—a fact accidentally discovered by a friend, though she tried her best to cover it up—and took up her work for the Legion of Mary again.

Early in 1936 the Legion authorities in England asked for helpers. Edel at once volunteered for this new mission: she proposed to give up her much needed fortnight's holiday to go to North Wales. Despite the opposition of her superiors, who feared for her health, she had her way. So she spent her vacation trying to persuade priests of the usefulness of the Legion and laymen of the necessity of the apostolate, explaining at meetings the work of the Legion and endeavouring to establish it at least in a rudimentary form. Despite this strenuous work Edel came back to Dublin refreshed, ready to take up again her typing in the gloomy office. But the thought of Wales, where at that time Catholic life was almost non-existent, did not leave her. Slowly an idea matured in her mind: Why not return to England, take a job there and devote all her spare time to establish the Legion where it was most needed?

However, before this idea could be realized another plan took shape. Edel was called to the head office and asked whether, instead of going to Wales, she would be prepared to go out to Africa, as a full-time envoy of the Legion. It was a momentous decision to make—to go so far away from her beloved family and from her country. Yet she did not hesitate. This, surely, was God's call—and she accepted it wholeheartedly. After some doubts as to which part of the continent she was finally to go to, it was decided that Central Africa had the greatest need of a vigorous lay apostolate such as the Legion was designed to carry out.

But before the final decision could be made the project had to be approved by the highest authority of the Legion, the concilium. There ensued a fierce debate. Doing pioneer work for the Legion in Africa called for an experienced person of robust health, well able to sustain the rigours of travelling in the tropics—to send a girl suffering from tuberculosis of both lungs, who might collapse at any moment, seemed sheer madness. From the point of view of prudence and common sense the opponents of Edel's venture were certainly right. When the matter was debated a former General of the Calced Carmelites with great experience of Africa rose to his feet and told the assembly that it would be utter folly to send a delicate young woman on such a mission which was beset with dangers of all kinds—a deadly climate, perilous and exhausting journeys across vast distances, savages, wild beasts, disease.

Suddenly Edel chimed in. All these difficulties had been explained to her; she knew perfectly well what she was letting herself in for: "I am going with my eyes open. I don't want to go on any picnic." The Father could not resist the cue. "Picnic!" he roared. "You'll make a nice picnic for someone out there!" While the assembled officers of the Legion could not help laughing aloud the president quipped: "I call on all of you to witness that the picnic will not be a substantial one." Edel had won the day. When her appointment was put to the vote it was unanimously approved. Not even the Carmelite Father dared to resist the determined young woman.

On October 24, 1936, Edel left Ireland after a heartrending leavetaking from her family, and six days later she embarked for Africa at Tilbury, together with several nuns and priests who were also going out to the missions. In the intervals of seasickness—the Bay of Biscay fully lived up to its reputation—she lost no time in propagating the work of the Legion among her fellow travellers: "I find that I have all the instincts of a commercial traveller," she wrote jokingly about her efforts to "sell" the Legion to recalcitrant priests and laymen. Towards the end of November she landed at Mombasa and set out almost at once for Nairobi, which became her headquarters. The Catholics with whom she made contact, priests and laymen alike, did their level best to discourage her. "You do not know Nairobi," was the refrain that greeted her whenever she outlined her plans. The difficulties were formidable indeed. There was, first and foremost, the racial problem. Europeans, Indians from Goa, and Africans kept strictly apart. Thus, when one day she wanted to discuss something with a lady from Goa there was no hotel or restaurant in Nairobi where she could go without risking that the Indian might be asked to leave. She finally secured a private office at the top of a hotel whose manager was known to a friend of hers.

Edel herself would have liked to bring together all races in the same group, but this was impossible, not only because of racial prejudice but for linguistic reasons. But she hoped one day at least to secure this ideal at the higher organisatory level of the "curia," the governing body for a whole district. However, she realized that she had to advance very cautiously, step by step, and so she concentrated first on the Europeans and the Goans. There was the further difficulty that the Europeans in Nairobi had come to Africa chiefly to better themselves and were unashamedly materialistic. The idea of the lay apostolate was far removed from their thoughts, and when Edel announced that she was going to give addresses on the Legion both in the Goan and the European churches everyone was convinced the venture would end in complete failure. A number of people came to the opening talk, many out of sheer curiosity. At this talk Edel asked for volunteers to attend another meeting in which she would explain the details for joining the Legion. Of the twenty-five people who attended, six ladies declared themselves ready to join the Legion, and so Edel had the great joy to be able to form her first "praesidium" in Kenya. A few days later the first African group was founded, consisting of thirteen men and three women who undertook to teach the catechism, visit hospitals and prisons, and recruit catechumens. The pessimists had been defeated; the Legion had started in Nairobi, an elite of both black Catholics and white had responded to the call for lay apostles. Greatly encouraged, Edel spent her first Christmas in Africa at the Midnight Mass in the African Church: "The people sang, of course," she wrote home. "It was a treat to see the African boys as acolytes, perfect discipline and reverence, not a mistake. . . . I would not have missed it for anything."

Despite these initial successes the task before her was formidable. There were a number of Legion rules which she was told over and over again were inapplicable to Africa, such as the weekly meetings and visiting only in pairs. Edel had to be adamant and to resist criticisms from missionaries far more experienced in African affairs than she herself, who kept insisting on modifications. But she realized that any such changes would very soon lead to all-round relaxation and finally to the destruction of the work that had just begun. Her tact, her charm, and her manifest devotion to the apostolate, however, usually overcame prejudice and convinced even the more sceptical of her critics of the correctness of her views.

Her greatest successes were achieved with the Africans. At first they would be both incredulous and suspicious that a white lady should concern herself with them, more, that she should encourage their own women to work in the apostolate. Besides, they had always regarded such work as belonging exclusively to priests and catechists—it came as quite a shock to them to be told that it was their duty to spread Christianity and to concern themselves not only with their own but with the salvation of others. Nor was this kind of work devoid of danger. The hostility of witch doctors was not to be underestimated; recent events in Kenya have shown only too clearly what may simmer under the surface of apparent calm in these primitive pagan tribes. Besides, there were the sheer physical hardships. During the rainy season travelling—so essential to Edel's extension work—was extremely difficult and at times quite impossible; and in the dry season the heat and the dust were very hard to bear. Edel used her long hours in cars or lorries for intense prayer:

"To be with Him in union with Mary—just loving Him in my soul during the day, during travelling, uniting my actions with similar actions done by Him whilst on earth. 'Master, where dwellest Thou? And they abode with him.' My privilege is the same. Rest in His presence . . . Silence. Everything is His, through Mary. Delight to give oneself more and more in everything to Him through her." All Edel's intense activity of her African years was nourished on this unceasing union with Christ through Mary, who helped the frail envoy of her own "Legion" to unite herself ever more closely to her Son.

Breakdowns on the bad African roads were frequent. Before she had her own small car she often travelled in lorries and other none-too-comfortable conveyances for hundreds of miles. But far from complaining, she rather cheered up her fellow travellers who invariably commented on her unconquerable high spirits. Her success surpassed all expectations. As early as April 1937, exactly six months after she had landed at Mombasa, she could realize her dream and found the first curia, in which all the races were gathered irrespective of language or colour. Edel may not have known Nairobi when she first unfolded her plan to the Catholics she met there, but she knew what God wanted her to do and did it—conquering not only human opposition but also natural obstacles and her own physical weakness by her indomitable spirit.

After the founding of the first curia at Nairobi Edel went further afield, for she now had a well-established centre representing a variety of races and responsible for the growth of the Kenya Legion and its contact with the highest authority in Dublin. At the instigation of the Apostolic Delegate to Missionary Africa, the bishops gave the energetic young woman generous assistance, especially when they saw the effect of her work in an intensified Catholic life in their dioceses. In the course of 1937 Edel spread the Legion far and wide in East Africa. In August she was in Bura, on the road to the vicariate of Kilimanjaro, from where she wrote a letter that is typical of her sense of humour and her way of making light of her work: "The Mission is circled by trees, and one of the 'rigours' of my work in Africa consists in sitting in a deck-chair in a shady grove, a tree stump for footstool, and the Baby Empire (her typewriter) balanced on my knee. There is a tip for you, all the way from Africa, for dealing with correspondence in comfort. Of course the quality of my typing suffers, so for your peace of mind I had better explain that when I write to Bishops and such-like important people, I go indoors!"

By the latter half of September Edel had reached the mission of Kilema, quite near Mount Kilimanjaro. There she met great distrust of white men; the members of one tribe flatly refused to join the Legion because they would not give the necessary promises—though they had made their baptismal vows. Edel very sensibly suggested accepting them nevertheless and gradually leading them to an understanding of the promises they were asked to make. Nor were the priests always favourable; as one of the nuns at Kilema wrote: "She was not always or everywhere received with enthusiasm, and if she was able to start praesidia in almost all the Missions here and keep them running, it was due to her heroic efforts, her strength of mind and her perseverance." Sometimes it was more difficult to keep them running than to start them; for the visiting in pairs was frequently neglected, and one of Edel's most exacting tasks was to keep her praesidia up to mark by correspondence and, when necessary, repeat visits.

In February 1938 she was called to Zanzibar, peopled mostly by Swahilis, Indian merchants, and Africans from the mainland. After a lightning tour through the island she returned to the mainland. As her work spread she found transport an insuperable difficulty and asked "headquarters" at Dublin to be allowed to buy a car. The necessary permission arrived almost at once, and she took driving lessons and bought a small Ford two-seater which she called her "Rolls Royce." The Dublin authorities very sensibly forbade her to drive herself except for very short distances. It was not easy to find a chauffeur; but Edel at last engaged a Mohammedan called Ali, who soon came to be known as Ali Baba in the missions she visited.

The possession of the car stirred her to new ventures. In July 1938 she extended her apostolate to Uganda. After one of her introductory talks at a mission centre there she was asked the memorable question: "If I become a Legionary, may I pay someone else to do the work for me?" Indeed, the questions asked called for extraordinary patience; most of them were not so original as the one just quoted, and Edel wrote that answering them she often felt like a gramophone with only one record.

One of the greatest difficulties her Legionaries were up against in Uganda as elsewhere in Africa was the regularization of marriages; for often Christian couples were living together without marrying because the dowry had not been fully paid by the husband and the pagan father of the girl could take his daughter away and give her to someone else as long as this debt had not been settled. So Edel concluded that: "Life out here is not quite so simple as the Mission booklets would have us believe. Baptism is merely the start of a strenuous Catholic life. Between that beginning and a happy death lies a great deal of hard battling on the part of the individual, and on the part of the priest. The majority have many a lapse. But then, pagan customs and surroundings are all against them and we are only at the beginning of the foundation of the Church in Africa."

This was why many people thought that Africans were simply not ready to receive the Gospel. Edel was of a different opinion. If one waited till people were "ready," Christ would never be preached. What had to be done was to prepare converts carefully and then to keep up their zeal by setting them to work for Christ among their fellowmen.

At the end of 1938 Edel succumbed to a severe attack of malaria. Until then she had remained in good health despite the superhuman load of work she imposed on her frail body. She reported to Dublin that only if she thought her work suffered from her ill-health would she give up, "much as I enjoy doing it." She ends her letter: "Christmas time and all; I would not willingly change places with anyone at home this minute. One gets great happiness in the work." In the accounts of many, we might say of most, saints and mystics great stress is laid on their sufferings, on the cross that was never absent from their lives. "To suffer or to die," said Teresa of Avila. Nevertheless, we are told that Teresa, too, loved laughter and fun. But she did not say so much about it in her spiritual writings, nor did St. Teresa of Lisieux, for example, who in her autobiography spoke much of her sufferings. Edel Quinn simply never mentions suffering in connection with herself. Everything is "all right," misfortunes on her travels are usually "great fun." Her descriptions do not sound "mystical" at all, she refuses to take her illness or her setbacks seriously. Indeed, she sounds a most unlikely mystic, compared with most others known to us, so much does she hide her inner life under a cover of fun and jokes.

The reason for this difference is very simple. Edel is a modern Irish girl, and neither the Irish nor the English like to hold forth about either their inner life or their sufferings. Where a Frenchwoman would exclaim: "*Oh, j'ai tant souffert* [Oh, I have suffered so much]," an Irish (or English) girl will say: "Never mind, it doesn't matter." In Edel Quinn this national characteristic was deliberately developed for a supernatural purpose: it served her as a veil both for her inner experience and for her heroism. Once, when she had been in fits of laughter over a joke, a friend asked her: "Are you naturally so lighthearted or do you practise it as a virtue?" She answered: "It is about three quarters natural." Edel's sense of humour and her lightheartedness were certainly natural—but she also cultivated them. If people thought her over-gay they would not think her holy—and that was exactly what she wanted. As to making nothing of her sufferings, she once said: "To suffer for love of Our Lord is my very greatest joy"—and she hid her physical weakness, even her exhaustion, so well that those who did not know about her illness never suspected anything. After all, if it was a joy, she would show it was this also outwardly and let her Irish sense of humour brighten up life both for herself and for others.

And so Edel became a living proof, as it were, that the life of the Christian apostle is a life of joy, that the work, however hard, however full also of disappointments, is nevertheless a joyful life: "I am enjoying myself thoroughly," she writes in the letter which has just been quoted. So, as soon as she could get about again after her attack of malaria, in January 1939, she resumed her travels in what one of the Legion's correspondents dared to call her "dilapidated Ford." When this derogatory remark was repeated to Edel she was up in arms, and in her wrath she gave a most graphic description of her "Rolls Royce": "If it is the same correspondent that called the Legion car 'a dilapidated Ford' we will not remain long on a peace footing. . . . I will certainly send you a snap of the car. It looks well; there are a few patches on the mud-guards, put on with nails. . . . The paint work is a unique shade of purple . . . and comes in now and then for comment. The original set of tyres were new when the car was bought, but have worn out since. Two new tyres were bought last May; but two of the original ones were still on in September last, when on safari they let me in for a hurricane series of seven punctures, after which it was obvious that their day was done. The engine is good. . . . The car has weathered hills and roads you could have no conception of, has been embedded in mud; it has had petrol troubles and parts required renewal, of course. But because of those few things to call it dilapidated—no, Sir! It has also the advantage, being a coupé, that if one ever has a breakdown in the bush, one could spend the night inside it in safety, because unlike other cars it would be lion-proof. . . . It is very much a case of "the country cousin comes to town" when we, i.e. driver, car and myself, arrive back in civilization." This passage from one of her letters home shows, for all its offhandedness, the hardships and dangers she braved when she drove through mud and lion-infested country from one mission to the other, only too frequently with breakdowns thrown in for good measure.

Early in 1939 the authorities in Dublin suggested a holiday in Ireland to recuperate. Edel would not hear of it. She had been in Africa only two and a half years—not nearly long enough to deserve a holiday; besides, it would be easier for her family if she did not come home till she had finished her work in Africa, because "it only means another heart-break for them if I go home and leave again." So she stayed on, but she promised to take a full week's rest at the end of every three months; for otherwise "it is impossible for the Envoys, when at work, to get any rest. Sundays and weekdays are all the same, and there is always correspondence in any spare hour. There is never a question of being longer than a night or two at a time in a Mission post." Of course, the week of complete rest every three months never became a reality. Edel's work went on without any interruption, and always, travelling, travelling, travelling, attending meetings, giving talks, answering questions, writing letters: "We must do what we can for Him," Edel wrote, "and rely on Him to give us each day the strength for the work He expects from us. The weakness which He leaves in us must not hold us back from our desires." She certainly did not allow her own weakness to hold her back; and it is scarcely possible to explain the sick young woman's resistance to the tremendous strains she imposed on herself other than by supernatural assistance.

In September 1939 war broke out in Europe. There was every chance that Africa would soon be drawn into the world-wide conflict: surely, Edel was told by many of her friends, this was not the time for her to carry on her work, as no one knew how long any missionaries would be safe anywhere. Far better to return to Ireland while there was still time.

But Edel was obstinate. As long as there remained any opportunities for her to carry on the work she had under-

taken she would do so. There was no question of her going
home. For now she saw even greater chances for the Legion
than before, as Europe could send no more priests to the
missions. Now lay apostles would be more necessary than
ever. So Edel continued her work as before, willingly responding to every call. The next one came from Mauritius.

She went there in January 1940 and was received with
great honour by the Holy Ghost Fathers, the sons of Francis
Libermann. As Libermann, not quite a century before, had
been led to his missionary foundation by two Creoles, so
now Edel interested herself particularly in the problem of the
Creoles of Mauritius who, though Catholics, had an atavistic
fear of marriage and preferred to live in concubinage. Within
a week of her arrival Edel had established the first praesidium
in the face of many difficulties, the chief of which was the
fact that the Legion had not originated in France. Nevertheless, at the end of April the work had proceeded sufficiently
to organize the curia, and after that she allowed herself the
"luxury" of a three-day retreat.

As the war was making movement more and more difficult,
Edel was given a completely free hand and decided to return
to the mainland in September, when the Legion had been
securely established. She had made many friends again, and
when she said good-bye to them she could not restrain her
tears. "My life is always thus," she said, "as soon as my work
becomes really interesting and I have made real friends, I
must break away and face again the unknown." It is one of
the few glimpses she allows us into the sacrifices her work
demanded from her; for her natural gaiety was matched by a
very sensitive heart which felt deeply the constant partings
her vocation demanded.

The voyage back from Mauritius was rough, and Edel's
strength began to fail. She had decided to go to Nyasaland,
where she had not worked yet. En route she attended a series
of Legion meetings at Durban and from there proceeded to
Nyasaland, where she set to work immediately. Despite her
increasing weakness she did not slow down the tempo of her

work. Nor did she mention her health in her letters to Ireland, apart from telling them that she had decided to take sometimes a weekend off but had not yet managed to do so. Then, suddenly, in March 1941, she broke down completely. She had an attack of pleurisy; her weight had gone down to seventy-five pounds—the poor exhausted body refused to let itself be governed any more by the indomitable spirit animating it. She had carried on even after severe attacks of malaria and dysentery until a priest, in the middle of a conversation, asked her whether she realized she was going to die and had prepared herself. Then at last she had to admit to herself that she was gravely ill.

The doctor ordered an immediate change of climate and suggested Johannesburg, where she entered a sanatorium at the end of April. It was not a Catholic institution, and she could receive Holy Communion only once a week, a privation she felt very deeply. She herself hoped to be able to resume her work after a sufficient rest, but the doctors were less sanguine. In November she moved to a Dominican hospital in the Cape Province, where she had the joy of being able to receive daily Communion. The nuns were greatly impressed by her personality, most of all by her joyful acceptance of her suffering, which she had not allowed to dim her high spirits, nor did she abandon her enormous correspondence which she tried to keep up as best she could. Contrary to all expectations, slowly her health continued to improve. In April 1942 she could write home that the medical verdict was that in the not too distant future she might be allowed to go home and even undertake some light Legion work, though long journeys and other strenuous activities would be out of the question. So, for the time being, she continued to give up her days to prayer and suffering.

Five months later, in September 1942, she felt strong enough to travel back to Nairobi. But, owing to the war, the ship in which she had booked a berth was deflected from its original destination, and, greatly fatigued, she finally arrived in Zululand instead, where she entered a hospital run by

Benedictine nuns. In January 1943 she returned at last to Nairobi after three days of air travel, during which she had been violently airsick. Her friends who welcomed her were profoundly shocked by the ravages the disease had worked in her always frail body, though not in her spirit. She was as cheerful and full of plans as ever, far more interested in the progress of the Legion than in the deterioration of her health. Soon she was fully back at work, attending meetings by car and carrying on her enormous correspondence. Not that she would not often have rather remained at the feet of Christ in silent contemplation. But, as she wrote in her private notes: "My vocation is a Legionary one, Envoy and Praetorian (a special grade of Legionaries), consecrated to work for the Father by the Holy Spirit of Jesus and by Mary. Daily review, to see how far I have lived the day for Jesus and the Father with Mary. I must be a channel of grace to every soul—or rather, Mary through me. . . . Our duty to work when we would sometimes rather be with Him. His will alone counts. If at times work is our duty, then rejoice in His will while doing it." This complete surrender to the will of God and the conviction of being a "channel of grace" bear eloquent testimony to the intense life of prayer sustaining Edel's apostolate.

As if she had not been at death's door a very short while ago, she quickly found herself immersed in a constant round of visiting and instructing, both by letter and by word of mouth. About three months after her return to Nairobi she had already started three new groups and put new life into the old ones. In May she felt strong enough to make her first "trial extensions trip," to a distance of eighty miles from Nairobi, visiting fifteen praesidia and attending curia meetings. Since this journey had not brought about a relapse, she intensified her activities. Though unable to walk much she travelled around a good deal, convinced that sparing herself would not improve her state of health any more than taking risks would harm it. Thus, in September 1943, she made a six-week tour in order to strengthen the Legion spirit in the various groups, for it would to a great extent depend on them whether Africans would remain only nominal Christians or become true Catholics. She returned exhausted —only to set out almost immediately again for Kilimanjaro, a trip that involved endless train journeys: "It was on the lines of the old days," she writes, "quick travelling: one night here, another at the next mission—a meeting or two, and then off again. I am just halfway through; have rested at every chance; but I do not feel so fresh when starting off each day." She complained that she was tired after a day full of meetings and talks, though never at the meetings themselves. She was told that, except for her voice, she had changed almost beyond recognition. Edel herself was the only person who did not realize that she was at the point of death, utterly exhausted, but carrying on a work that would have taxed the strength even of a woman in the best of health. Towards the end of the year Edel went on another tiring tour, this time to Tanganyika.

After that, however, she caught a severe cold which she called "a bit of a chill," and before she had been able to shake it off again she did over a week's intense travelling. This time she had to allow herself some rest, which she took in a convent of Irish nuns. She realized that she would not be able to do her work much longer, and she began to train a successor. Nevertheless, in March 1944 she started on yet another expedition, though her friends and herself, too, were wondering whether she would be able to go through with it. But this time her body would no longer obey her spirit. After a month of travelling, meetings, and inspections she broke down. She had to rush back to Nairobi, where she entered a nursing home run by nuns. She knew that the end was near. She spent her days partly in bed, partly in a little summerhouse to have some fresh air. In addition to the cough that had been her companion for so many years she was now also suffering from severe heart attacks. Nevertheless, her gaiety remained unchanged. On the morning of May 12 she still made notes about affairs to be seen to; she even made arrangements to start a holiday at the Irish convent next day. In the evening she had one more attack, the last. Her work was done; the Legion of Mary was firmly established in Africa; the time had come for her to rest.

CHAPTER TEN

Pierre Teilhard de Chardin

(1881–1955)

"Neither in its impetus nor in its achievements can science go to its limits without becoming tinged with mysticism and charged with faith." Thus wrote Pierre Teilhard de Chardin in his famous book, *The Phenomenon of Man*, in which he expounded what we may well call a mystical view of evolution.

This remarkable man, one of the first to attempt a synthesis between modern science and integral Christianity, was the fourth of the eleven children of a small landowner of Auvergne. Monsieur Teilhard de Chardin was at the same time an archivist with an interest in natural history which Pierre inherited from him. The boy gave early evidence of a quite remarkable affinity with the earth and its treasures. Though brought up in the normal atmosphere of a good French Catholic home and taught to love "the little Lord Jesus" he felt early drawn by matter, or, as he expresses it himself, "rather more exactly by something that 'shone' at the heart of Matter." As other pious children might retire to a quiet corner to pray to their favourite saint or their guardian angel, six-year-old Pierre would withdraw and repeat the words: "God, Iron." Instead of collecting holy pictures, he hoarded plough keys, metal staples, and shell splinters which he contemplated lovingly. As he wrote more than sixty years later: "In this instinctive movement which made me truly worship a small piece of metal, there was a strong sense of self-giving mixed up with a whole train of obligations, and my whole spiritual life has merely been the development of this." A new type of Christian mystic was making its appearance: the mystic who did not despise creation, but rather found in the ever more profound study of the world that God had made, and above all in its summit, man, the food that nourished his own most interior life.

At the age of ten Pierre was sent to the Jesuit college at Mongré, near Viellefranche-sur-Saône. He was a gifted pupil who obtained high marks in most subjects, but was particularly attracted to geology and mineralogy, which is not surprising considering his early interest in scraps of metal. His masters also found him "dreamy"—evidently he was even then given to silent thought and the thorough consideration of problems presenting themselves to his young mind. When he was eighteen he decided to become a Jesuit and entered the noviciate at Aix-en-Provence. Here he made contact with the famous philosopher Maurice Blondel, who had published his great work, *L'Action*, in 1893, in which among other things he examined the relations between science and belief, though from the philosophical rather than, like later Teilhard, from the strictly scientific point of view. As a result of the anti-religious French laws of 1901, the Jesuit noviciate was moved to Jersey, where Pierre spent the next four years of his training studying philosophy. There his overpowering interest in nature came into conflict with his religious vocation. Could he combine the two, or should he give up his scientific studies in order to devote himself wholly to his "supernatural" activities?

The good sense of his novice master saved him from such a course, which would certainly have ended in disaster. The Father "limited himself to assuring me that the God of the

Cross expected the 'natural' expansion of my being just as much as its sanctification, without explaining to me how or why." To work out the exact manner in which this integration of his scientific with his spiritual aspirations was to be achieved was left to the young religious himself. It was the task to which his whole life may be said to have been devoted, for, as he himself expresses it: "The cosmic sense and the Christly sense definitely coexisted in my heart and attracted each other irresistibly."

In 1905 Pierre was sent to Cairo to teach physics at the Jesuit college there. It was a time of further quiet development; the Egyptian landscape provided him with the experience of an entirely new scenery as well as with new material for geological research. "All round it was . . . the growing appeal of vegetable and animal nature; and deeper down . . . I was initiated into the less palpable but no less tempting greatness revealed by the research of physics. On either side of matter was life and energy, the three pillars of my inner vision and happiness." These words, written much later in his autobiography, *The Heart of Matter* (*Le Coeur de la Matière*), show quite clearly that Teilhard was no "mere" scientist. For him matter, life and energy were not simply natural data but the elements of his most satisfying vision of the universe, fulfilling not only his scientific aspirations but actually giving him "happiness." At this time his thought was further stimulated by Bergson's *Creative Evolution* (1906), though his own view of evolution, as he was to develop it in later years, was quite different from that of Bergson.

After three years in Cairo Pierre returned to Europe in order to finish his theological studies at the Jesuit scholasticate at Hastings, in Sussex. There he grew increasingly conscious of a mysterious "presence," a "total drift" of the universe around him, once more blending mystical intuition with his scientific interests. In 1908, after his return from Cairo, he wrote his first article, published in the Jesuit periodical *Études* (January 1909), on the miracles of Lourdes and their

canonical investigation, defending the reality of the supernatural against the scepticism of contemporary scientists who
would not accept miraculous facts even when they were
proved beyond all doubt, merely because they did not fit in
with their theories.

In 1912 he was ordained priest and returned to Paris,
where he began his prehistorical studies in earnest. He
worked in the Institute of Human Palaeontology which was
attached to the Museum of Natural History; there he met
Abbé Breuil, the famous prehistorian who became his lifelong
friend. He now found the central object of his interests; the
evolution of man. In 1912 he wrote another important article,
this time on his own particular subject, "Prehistory and Its
Development." It appeared again in *Études* in January 1913;
here he suggests that religion and the findings of prehistorical
research are by no means opposed to each other. In the
same year he took part in Charles Dawson's excavations which
resulted in the sensational find of the "Piltdown Man,"
discovered to be a fraud only forty years later.

Teilhard's work was interrupted by the outbreak of the
first World War, in which he served as a stretcher-bearer.
His courage and *sang-froid* were admired by his fellow
soldiers, not least by the North African sharpshooters who
attributed it to his being protected by his "baraka," a term
signifying inherent spiritual power. When a friend once asked
him how it was that he did not seem to fear death he replied:
"If I am killed I shall only change my state, that is all." The
friend, Max Bégouën, was deeply impressed by the faith
expressed in these words, for he himself had lost his own,
largely because the findings of prehistoric research seemed
to contradict so obviously the Biblical teaching on creation.
Teilhard explained to him his ideas, especially the meaning of
evolution and the supreme part played in it by Christ. "That
evening," writes Bégouën, "I came to life, staggering like
Lazarus coming forth from the tomb at our Lord's command
'Come forth.' It was an extraordinary experience which was
soon to change my life completely." This conversion was

only one of a considerable number that were to follow; in fact, Teilhard's apostolate broke new ground; for he could speak to his fellow scientists in their own language, showing them that a Christian could accept the findings of contemporary research and especially the discovery of the evolutionary principle without having to give up his faith; indeed, that both faith and science had only to gain from such encounters.

As soon as the war was over Père Teilhard resumed his studies and prepared his thesis, a study of the first mammals, for a doctorate in science, in which he accepted the theory of evolution without any reservations. The work made quite a stir in French scientific circles, and in 1922 he was appointed professor of geology at the Institut Catholique in Paris. Already in the following year he was released from his duties for a year in order to take part in a palaeontological mission in China. His experiences during the voyage and in China itself are of paramount importance; for they not only greatly enlarged his outlook but also inspired his first *Lettres de Voyage* and *The Mass upon the World* (*La Messe sur le Monde*). Both the *Letters* and the *Mass* allow us a profound insight into his own spiritual life and into the way he had learned to resolve the early conflict between his scientific interest and his religious faith.

The combination of scientist and mystic becomes very apparent in his musings on Mount Sinai, the slopes of which he would have liked to visit "not only to test them with my hammer, but also to listen and see if I could hear the voice from the burning bush. But has not the time passed when God speaks in the desert . . . for the summits where He dwells are not in inaccessible mountains, but in a profounder sphere of things? The secret of the world is wherever we can see the universe as something transparent." The darkness into which Moses entered on Mount Sinai has ever been the image of the mystical darkness in which God meets man. For Teilhard the whole universe becomes the meeting place between God and man—but this does not mean that he subscribes to pantheism, a view of the world which he explicitly rejects and which is, indeed, quite incompatible with Christianity. What he does mean is that he sees the mysterious hand of the Creator in all that is; in the geological layers he tests with his hammer as well as in the Biblical revelation. Therefore he can write in *The Mass upon the World* that "the science of Christ in all things is the true science of mysticism," that his scientific research, however important for the fulfillment of his earthly vocation, is yet not the ultimate goal of his life. He finds the essence of it all in what he calls his "Mass upon things," which he works out not in his research but in his prayer: "It seems to me," he writes, "that in a sense the true elements that have to be consecrated every day are the growth of the world that day: the bread suitably symbolizing what creation produces, the wine (blood) what it loses, through exhaustion and suffering in its labour."

It is a bold conception; yet whoever has penetrated even a little into the thought of the Greek Fathers of the Church will see a certain affinity between the interpretation of the modern scientist and the allegorical explanations of the Alexandrian and Cappadocian schools of the third to the fifth centuries of our era. It may, however, be objected that in the thought of Christ Himself both, His Flesh and His Blood, are nourishment, both mean increase, neither signifies a loss. Nevertheless, the linking up of the Eucharist with the whole world, the vision of its cosmic significance is of high importance, especially in our time, when there is such an abyss between the world as seen by Christians and all non-Christian thought. During his journey to China Teilhard became increasingly aware of this cleavage. He felt that theologians would gain a great deal from experiences such as he had at that time: "I begin to think," he wrote, "that there is a particular view of the real world which is just as closed to some believers as the world of the faith is to those who do not believe." To make an impact on this other world, Christians have to know it and to find a synthesis between it and their faith—the task to which Teilhard's whole life was to be devoted, and his audacities must be seen and understood in this wider context.

His voyage to China was, however, a profound disappointment. For there he met a fossilized civilization which offered no nourishment to his spiritual life. "For week after week," he writes, "I was immersed in the masses of Asia. . . . Nowhere among the men I met or about whom I was told did I see the smallest grain which might be destined to grow for the future life of mankind. Either absence of thought, or senile thought, or infantile thought. . . . I am a pilgrim of the future, but I have come back from a voyage which was all in the past. . . . I believe that the only real science is the discovery of the growth of the universe, so I was distressed to have seen nothing during this voyage but traces of a vanished world." The "mystic of evolution," as we may well call Teilhard, was impatient of stagnation, of lack of progress. It would be interesting to know what he would say to China as it is now, trying to make up for centuries of backwardness by joining the materialistic camp and trying to absorb the science of the West as fast as it can, systematically destroying all those "traces of a vanished world."

Yet his disappointment was not final. For Teilhard was fundamentally an optimist, both as a Christian and as an evolutionist. He was firmly convinced that "through the civilizations which replace each other, something is being formed, no doubt something heavenly, but first something earthly. Nothing here below, none of man's travail, is lost to him." There is no place in all his work and thought for the existentialist pessimism of our time to which, indeed, he answers: Look at the universe: everything moves forward, and even what has had its day can never be lost.

After research expeditions to Mongolia and the Gobi desert Père Teilhard returned to France at the end of 1924. He resumed his teaching at the Institut Catholique. But his thought, far in advance of his time, was so profoundly influenced by his scientific research that his theology, especially as regards original sin and the fall of man, became suspect to his superiors. In the end he was forbidden to teach and it was decided that he should return to China to continue his archaeological research. He accepted the decision in the spirit of obedience, though one can perceive an echo of his disappointment in a letter to his sister to whom he writes that though he has not changed fundamentally during the last years, he is looking towards the future "with less warmth and almost without enthusiasm."

His twofold contact with the opposition of the French theologians and the congenial thought of his fellow scientists brought him face to face with the question of how the two could meet. In June 1926, shortly after his second arrival in China, he wrote: "I thought of the abyss which separates the intellectual world to which I belong and whose language I understand, from the theological and Roman world whose idiom I also know." He realized that there was no hope for the healthy future development of both unless they were brought together, and this could only be done by explaining the teaching of the theologians in a language that could be understood by the rest of the world, above all by the scientists. But for such a synthesis a "mystical" perspective was needed, which alone could lead to a true communication between souls.

The outcome of this preoccupation was *The Divine Milieu*, written at Tientsin between November 1926 and March 1927. As he writes in his preface, "this book is not specifically addressed to Christians who are firmly established in their faith and have nothing more to learn about its beliefs. It is written for the waverers, both inside and outside." It is nevertheless a work which will open quite new perspectives also to many well-instructed Christians even though they will at times have to make certain adaptations, for example as regards his views on the soul. This, "however independently created our philosophy represents it as being," he considers as "inseparable, in its birth and its growth, from the universe into which it is born." Here one has to ask whether Teilhard does not perhaps confuse the "psyche" of the psychologists, that is to say our whole psychological make-up, with the "soul" directly created in the image of God, which cannot be said to be inseparable from the universe. It is equally questionable whether "Jesus on the Cross is both the symbol and the reality of the immense labour of the centuries which has, little by little, raised up the created spirit and brought it back to the depths of the divine *milieu*." This statement, however poetic, cannot possibly give any sound idea of the Incarnation and Passion of Christ, which have nothing to do with the "labour of centuries" but are the irruption of a divine Person into his creation for the purpose of redeeming it from sin. Even the avowed purpose of the book of expressing Christian dogma in a language acceptable to modern unbelievers does not wholly justify such a departure from the traditional Christian teaching.

But apart from such flaws *Le Milieu Divin* is a book of great spiritual beauty and wisdom; especially in the prayers into which the author breaks forth from time to time. The first part deals with the "divinisation of our activities"—a concept which again reminds one of the Church Fathers who spoke freely of the deification of man. Here Teilhard obviously speaks from his own experience when he discusses the question how a man who believes in heaven and the Cross can nevertheless continue to believe also in the value of worldly occupations. It is a problem of particular importance for our own time, when so many, indeed most, of our occupations seem to have not the slightest connexion with the religious sphere. After giving three faulty solutions and one incomplete one to the problem Père Teilhard presents his own. He begins with a syllogism: "At the heart of our universe, each soul exists for God, in our Lord. But all reality, even material reality, around each one of us, exists for our souls. Hence, all sensible reality, around each one of us, exists, through our souls, for God in our Lord." As this is so, Teilhard concludes that it is the duty of every man to "make his own soul" by collaborating in the great work of completing the world, in whatever place he may be. "Owing to the interrelation between matter, soul and Christ, we bring part of the being which He desires back to God in whatever we do. With each one of our works we labour . . . to build the Pleroma"—that is to say the fullness of Christ of which St. Paul speaks in his letter to the Ephesians. After the divinisation of our activities Père Teilhard speaks of the divinisation of our "passivities," by which he means all those things that are outside our own decisions, for, as he so rightly says (in contrast with the view of existentialists such as Sartre): "My self is given to me far more than it is formed by me." He ends with a long prayer of thanksgiving for being allowed to "encounter, and kiss, Your two marvellous hands—the one which holds us so firmly that it is merged, in us, with the sources of life, and the other whose embrace is so wide that, at its slightest pressure, all the springs of the universe respond harmoniously together." Here the scientist makes way for the poet and the mystic; indeed, the image of the springs of the universe responding harmoniously to the marvellous hand of God is not so very far removed from St. John of the Cross's vision of his "Beloved . . . scattering a thousand graces."

Père Teilhard gives also a very balanced teaching on Christian asceticism. He firmly holds that "it is a truly Christian duty to grow . . . and to make one's talents bear fruit, even though they be natural." In this context he very rightly says that: "Far too often the Cross is presented for our adoration . . . as a symbol of sadness, of limitation and repression"— a degeneration of the true Christian conception of the Cross as the Tree of life. We must, in our own lives, preserve the proper rhythm between development and renunciation, attachment and detachment, which "are not mutually exclusive."

The most original thought developed in this book is the spiritual value of matter. For Teilhard, as we shall see even more clearly when discussing his principal work, *The Phenomenon of Man*, there is no fundamental opposition between matter and spirit. Here he defines matter as "the common, universal, tangible setting, infinitely shifting and varied, in which we live," containing all creatures around us. And this setting may carry us either upward or downward, according to the direction we take; for according to him, there are two zones in matter, one "material" and carnal, the other "taken in the spiritual sense"; each soul must find its own path through matter that will finally lead it to God; for matter contains "a certain quantity of spiritual power" which, if properly used, will lead us to Christ. This "spiritual power" of matter is a thought dear to Teilhard, as we shall see later, but one that cannot be accepted without some reservations. It should, however, be seen in the whole context of his spiritual teaching, which centres unmistakably in Christ Himself. Just as Teilhard emphasizes the life-giving element in the doctrine of the Cross, so for him Christ is not only the Redeemer who died on it for our salvation, though, of course, He is that, too, for as Teilhard emphatically states, "The mystical Christ, the universal Christ of St. Paul, has neither meaning nor value in our eyes except as an expansion of the Christ who was born of Mary and who dies on the Cross." But he is also the Creative Word, the All-Ruler, *Pantokrator,* as the Greeks called Him and loved to represent Him, and as such He must once more be contemplated especially today, when the universe is beginning to show all its grandeur and mystery, unsuspected by former generations. And so Teilhard prays, in words imbued with all the fervour of the mystic exploring the wonders of creation: "Disperse, O Jesus, the clouds with Your lightning! Show Yourself to us as the Mighty, the Radiant, the Risen! Come to us once again as the Pantokrator who filled the solitude of the cupolas in the ancient basilicas! Nothing less than his advent (*parousia*) is needed to counter-balance and dominate in our hearts the glory of the world that is coming into view. And so that we should triumph over the world with You, come to us clothed in the glory of the world."

The work was never published during Teilhard's lifetime, no doubt owing to the sometimes questionable views expressed in its pages. It was, however, circulated in stencil copies and made a deep impression in the circle of his friends, as the testimony of someone who was both a scientist in the forefront of contemporary research and a mystic for whom Christ in His universal kingship and His eucharistic nearness is the very center of his existence; for, as he writes, "At every moment the Eucharistic Christ controls . . . the whole movement of the universe."

Even before the book was finished, in February 1927, Père Teilhard accepted the supervision of research on vertebrates and on man conducted under the auspices of the Carnegie Foundation in China. The organization to which his department belonged had its headquarters in Peking, and there he met scientists from all over the world with whom he not only exchanged views on professional subjects, but whom he regarded as a testing ground for his own views and influence. For he was a priest even before he was a scientist, and so he could write that the most active part of his day was "still the one when I say my 'Mass upon the World,' to divinize the beginning day." In August of the same year he went once more to France, and on his return to China, in November 1928, he broke his voyage to visit Ethiopia. His remarks on the rather backward native population of the country show how irrevocably he was vowed to the cause of progress. For though admitting that they were a fine type of humanity, he was nevertheless convinced that they were doomed to extinction, "like zebras and elephants": for "the more I look and the more I think, the more I can see no other way out for thought and action than an obscure faith in the march of thought, which is an insatiable power and destroys everything that has had its time."

Back in China he was at once fully occupied with excavation work, which was producing important finds of bones belonging to what is called the *Sinanthropus* (Chinese man), though he was very chary about any positive assertion that this type really was already fully human; all he would admit was that these finds enlightened scientists on the suc-

cessive stages by which the human type evolved among all
the other living things.

In 1930 Père Teilhard returned to France to prepare yet
another research expedition, the so-called *Croisière Jaune*.
In the course of these activities he had to visit the United
States, where he had many friends and, among other celebrities, met the great Christian poet Paul Claudel. It was a meeting between two opposite poles within Catholic oneness; for
though Claudel, too, saw the world as a unity, he made a
far sharper distinction between matter and spirit, the natural
and the supernatural, and had little interest in scientific dis-
coveries, least of all in those that seemed to upset the Biblical
view of the world. It was an attitude which was more
closely related to that of most American Catholics with whom
Père Teilhard came into contact, who, to his dismay, still
rejected evolution in any form out of hand. "In Paris they
see things more subtly," he remarked.

The expedition, full of all kinds of inconveniences, me-
chanical breakdowns, political difficulties, and the rest, was
nevertheless a precious experience to Père Teilhard, for in
the end he had "almost doubled" his knowledge of Asia and
of the tremendous gap between Christian men and those
who had never been under any Christian influence at all.
Scarcely two months after his return from this expedition in
March 1932, he undertook another journey, despite the intense
fatigue from which he was suffering. He felt that it was the
last of this kind "by mule, dirty inns, flies," for it seemed to
him that now, at fifty-one, he had reached a turning point
of his life. From now on he was to make the experiences he
had gathered bear fruit in his writings as well as in the
capacity of adviser and expert on all that concerned prehistory. And so, during the following years, he wrote a
great number of treatises, among them "How I Believe"
(1934), "Sketch of a Personal Universe" (1936), and "The
Spiritual Phenomenon" (1937)—none of them published,
because of the objection of his superiors. We can only guess
how much it must have cost him to accept this prohibition

which prevented his works, through which he hoped to bring Christ nearer to his unbelieving contemporaries, from reaching a wider public. He could only see in this decision of his superiors one of those "diminishments," as he calls them in *Le Milieu Divin,* which are "the way which most surely makes us holy," and he submitted to them in silence.

Though he had felt the expedition of the summer 1932 to be the last of its kind his journeying continued, though now in different, less exhausting style in his capacity as an expert rather than an explorer. After a stay in France from September 1932 to January 1933 to recover from his fatigue he was back in Peking in March. The next few months there were troubled by war between China and Japan, then he was called to New York to examine a collection of fossils for the City Museum. He next attended a Congress of Prehistory at Washington, at which he presented his book, *Fossil Man in China* and read a communication, took part in a geological excursion in Sierra Nevada during which he enjoyed the unconventional American life so different from his native France, and finally went back to Peking late in 1933. There he took part in yet more excavations during which human skulls, bones, and tools were discovered under the leadership of the famous Davidson Black. Black's sudden death, in March 1934, was a profound shock for Teilhard; and "the oppressive atmosphere of 'agnostic' condolences which surrounded it" shocked him even more, for he realized that his fellow scientists' refusal to believe in life after death could only lead to despair and the abandonment of all human effort. Therefore he took an oath, on the body of his dead friend, "to struggle harder than ever to give hope to man's labour and research." But, being a scientist himself, he did not content himself with the supernatural hope of the Christian. He felt that no human effort could be of any avail "unless there is some natural, as well as supernatural, future for the universe in the direction of some kind of immortal consciousness." We shall find this thought further developed in his principal work; it is important to note that it was given a decisive impetus by the severe emotional shock of the death of his friend.

In the summer of 1935 he was back in France for three months, where his spiritual influence continued to grow together with his scientific reputation. In September he set out once more for the East, this time for India, to accompany an American expedition to Kashmir. During his voyage he noted down his ideas about the goal of his research into prehistory. He was no longer interested in the past for its own sake, but because it showed him the shape of things to come; the scientist and the mystic in him combined to produce the prophet, the seer into the future of the world and of humanity. He became increasingly convinced that not all races would take part in shaping it; for, as we have seen before, he felt that some of them were condemned to sterility and extinction: indeed, he wrote in January 1936 that, in his opinion, the missionaries made a great mistake in admitting, "contrary to all biology," the equality of all races —which, of course, is a different thing from believing in the equality of all men before God. Teilhard speaks of the psychological and mental equipment of various races, not of their supernatural destiny. The condition of the Indian women, "poor things, prematurely wrinkled, wrapped in veils, always in fear," moved him particularly. Creatures so different from ourselves, he felt, could not be converted "unless one first transforms them on the human plane." On the other hand, he realized that their religion had a great deal to do with their condition, for he wrote of Hinduism that "one has got to go to India to assess how engulfing and lethal a religion can be which concerns itself only with material things and rituals."

At the same time he felt that he was only now finding his true vocation, which was not scientific knowledge in itself, but only in so far as it helped him "more fully to find God in the world." This, he continued, ". . . is a more tricky subject, but it is the only vocation I can admit, and nothing will make me turn away from it." He knew quite well that, in view of the modern conception of the world, the relationship between it and God was by no means so clear-cut as it had appeared in the Middle Ages; more, it was decidedly "tricky"—but he saw equally clearly that its reshaping in modern times was one of the most urgent tasks of our age and that, both by his training and his own inclination, he was called to produce such a fresh interpretation. He gave his thought a provisional form in the essay called "Sketch of a Personal Universe," written in 1936, where he outlines his idea of a "supra-humanity" following the trend of "personalization" in the universe, conceptions that were soon to be more fully elaborated in the great synthesis of his thought he·was already contemplating.

In the meantime conditions in Europe, by now largely in the grip of the two dictatorships of fascism and communism, became more and more harrying. Teilhard, whose vision of the ultimate unity of mankind was the mainspring of his world view, was inclined to disregard the political realities of his time which disturbed this vision. "Fascism, communism, democracy," he wrote in the summer of 1936, "no longer have any meaning. I dream of seeing the best of humanity regrouping itself round a precise mode of thinking," which he described as "universalism, futurism, personalism," meaning by this the development of a unified earth deliberately shaping the future by developing higher forms of "personality." The evolutionist and the mystic in him, both vowed to a unified vision of the world, would not allow for contrary forces disrupting this vision. If for him fascism, communism, and democracy had no meaning, history, moved not only by biological forces but by human wills, proved him wrong, at least for the time being; for, being above all an expert on geology and prehistory, Teilhard habitually thought in much larger periods of time than the rest of us. And so an observer situated several hundred or perhaps thousand years later might perhaps view the disruptive factors of our own age as no more than slight disturbances in the general movement towards a unified mankind.

The years between 1936 and the outbreak of the second World War were filled with more travels and literary work. In the early summer of 1937 he was back in Paris to prepare an expedition to Burma scheduled for January 1938. Later in the same year he was appointed Director of the Laboratory of Advanced Studies in Geology and Palaeontology in Paris. Before he took up his new post he went to America in June 1939, and from there to China, intending to return to France later in the year. But before he could get back to Europe the second World War broke out, and for six years he was immobilized in Peking. There, in his enforced external inactivity, he completed his great work which he had already begun, *The Phenomenon of Man.*

In the context of this brief study there can, of course, be no question of discussing more than a few main points bearing on the spiritual content of this remarkable book. In one sweeping survey, which takes us from the first beginnings of our earth as a fragment of matter, detached from the sun some thousands of millions of years ago, not only to our own age, but to the end of our planet, Teilhard traces the history of evolution from the first hydrogen atom to the human person and his final destiny. It is the work of the scientist, mystic, and prophet that he was, and it is only natural that in the attempt of such an incredibly vast synthesis there should be flaws and errors; indeed, the book has caused a storm of controversy, as was almost inevitable.

The work is divided into three main sections, headed "Before Life Came," "Life," and "Thought," and it is the purpose of the author to show that Life evolved from Prelife, and Thought from Life. One of his crucial concepts in this vast evolutionary vision is his idea that all things have not only a without, but a "within"—atoms no less than man. Indeed, he formulates as a principle that "in every region of time and space . . . co-extensive with their Without, there is a Within of things." Teilhard's first biographer, Nicolas

Corte, says, as it seems to us quite rightly, that this idea "comes neither from science nor from philosophy nor theology, but simply, one might say, from a poetic imagination." We should like to corroborate this by pointing out that it is a concept similar to that which the German poet Rainer Maria Rilke, a near-contemporary of Teilhard, called the *Weltinnenraum*, the inner space of the world. This mysterious poetic "within" of all things enables Teilhard to find one great line leading from the atom to the human mind without any essential break. He himself says that "the consequent picture of the world daunts our imagination, but it is in fact the only one acceptable to our reason"—to most of us it would rather seem that it appeals to our imagination while daunting our reason.

However this may be, there is one idea which Teilhard brings to the theory of evolution which is of the utmost importance, and this is that the universe culminates in man; that evolution is not a blind force leading no one knows where, but a force directed to a definite goal. "I believe," he writes, "I can see a direction and a line of progress for life, a line and a direction which are in fact so well marked that I am convinced their reality will be universally admitted by the science of tomorrow." This line he sees in this, that "there exists in living organisms a selective mechanism for the play of consciousness." From minerals to plants to animals and finally to man, consciousness becomes ever more explicit: "On the surface, we find the nerve fibres and ganglions; deep down, consciousness"—this again is a hypothesis unacceptable to most scientists as well as theologians, because it endows with a "soul" beings which neither of them can admit to have one. Indeed this poetic concept seems to resemble a kind of "panpsychism" which was formerly rejected by St. Thomas Aquinas; in modern times it was once more advocated by G. T. Fechner (1801–87) and other nineteenth-century German thinkers. It is Père Teilhard's originality to have incorporated it into his theory of evolution, but whether it can be modified further so as to be acceptable to science as well as to theology only the future can show; in the exact form in which it appears in *The Phenomenon of Man* it can probably not be retained.

Nevertheless, this theory does not lead Père Teilhard to underestimate the uniqueness of man. On the contrary, for him man is not just a superior variety of ape, as the representatives of evolution in its crudest form maintained, but the rational being to which the whole development of the universe is directed. For with man a new sphere appears on the earth; above the "geosphere," that is to say, the "earth" sphere of so-called inanimate matter, and the "biosphere," the sphere of plant and animal life, there now has come into existence the "noosphere," the region of mind, which is exclusively the sphere of man, for "can we seriously doubt that intelligence is the evolutionary lot proper to man and to man *only?*"

But evolution does not end with man. Teilhard's mystical vision foresees a long future for the race, in which man will even grow above himself and reach a final point of development which Teilhard calls Omega on which the "noosphere" is centred. This Omega is seen as a "distinct centre radiating at the core of a system of centres," as a "focus of union" in which the "grains of consciousness," that is to say, the spirits of men, "do not tend to lose their outlines and blend, but, on the contrary, to accentuate the depth and incommunicability of their egos." For as we have already seen, Teilhard emphatically rejects pantheism, and what he here describes is rather the mystical union of man with God in which both retain their identity while nevertheless in closest communion with each other. But why, it may be asked, did Teilhard use such esoteric language? Precisely because he was writing for scientists, not for theologians. His object was to show that evolution not only can make room for, but actually demands a supreme centre, itself not subject to evolution but directing it; for "while being the last term of its series, it is also outside all series"; transcendence, one of the essential attributes of God, is also an attribute of Omega.

The book ends with an Epilogue on "The Christian Phenomenon." "Christ, principle of universal vitality because sprung up as man among men, put himself in the position . . . to subdue under himself, to purify, to direct and super-animate the general ascent of consciousness into which he inserted himself. . . . he aggregates to himself the total psychism of the earth. And when he has gathered every-thing together and transformed everything, he will close in upon himself and his conquests, thereby rejoining, in a final gesture, the divine focus he has never left. Then, as St. Paul tells us, God shall be all in all."

It is a truly grandiose concept, the vision, once more, of a scientist and a mystic, which has already captured the imagination of a large part of our reading public. It shows the possibilities of integrating Christian theology with con-temporary science; but it is not yet a complete synthesis. It does not seem to distinguish sufficiently between the natural and the supernatural spheres; and though the description of the evolution of the human mind from its lower equivalent in the animal sphere is not entirely unconvincing, there seems no room left for the direct creation of the immortal soul "in the image of God," which is at the root of the Christian doctrine of man, and hence of all mystical theology. On the other hand, it should never be forgotten that *The Phenom-enon of Man* was written above all for Teilhard's fellow scientists, and that the introduction of such concepts as sancti-fying grace, sin, and redemption would have been out of place in a work of this kind. What gives the book its para-mount importance is that it builds a bridge between science and Christianity, that it shows that even the theory of evolu-tion, for long regarded as diametrically opposed to Catholic theology, can be integrated into the Faith. As has been pointed out, Père Teilhard has not been completely success-ful in this task which he set himself; indeed, it could hardly be expected that he would be, seeing that the theory of evolu-tion itself is still in flux and there is no scientific consensus on its extent. He was a pioneer, and those who come after him will no doubt correct or discard many of his ideas. But that a man who could write those mystical prayers of *Le Milieu Divin*, more, who, through truly heroic (in the ordinary sense of the word) obedience deprived himself of ever seeing his works in print, could also be a distinguished scientist acclaimed by his peers is, indeed, a new phenomenon of a Christian man and mystic.

After the end of the war Teilhard could at last return to Paris. In 1947 he was prevented by a serious heart attack from taking part in an expedition to South Africa with his friend Abbé Breuil. Instead, he had to rest for several months in the country. After his return to Paris he suffered many disappointments which must have affected him very deeply. First he was forbidden to write any more on philosophical subjects; and in 1948 his superiors vetoed his candidature for a professorship at the Collège de France as successor of Abbé Breuil. In 1950 he submitted a completely recast version of *The Phenomenon of Man*, *The Human Zoological Group* (*Le Groupe Zoologique Humain*) to Rome, but was refused the Imprimatur.

He accepted the rebuffs, which were offset, however, by growing recognition in the world of science. He had already been made a corresponding Member of the Academy of Science and was now made a Membre de l'Institut, an officer of the Légion d'Honneur and a director of research of the National Centre of Scientific Research. In 1951 he went to New York, where he was attached to the Wenner-Gren Foundation, which sponsored his two trips to South Africa, in 1951 and 1953. The archeological finds he was able to examine there suggested the idea that man might have originated in Africa, in the region of Lake Victoria or Lake Tanganyika; though, of course, as Teilhard himself admitted, there was not yet sufficient proof of this theory. Indeed, the evolution of man remained his main preoccupation till the end. In one of his last articles he wrote: "It is only a general view of evolution—and not an ever more solitary introspection of the individual by the individual—that can . . . save man of the twentieth century from his anxieties in face of life." For science and religion, though still regarded as strangers to each other, will in the end come together and give new hope to mankind.

Père Teilhard had long wanted to die on Easter Day, and he said so once more a fortnight before his death, at a dinner held at the French Consulate in New York. On Easter Day, April 10th, 1955, he said Mass in the morning, then attended Pontifical Mass at St. Patrick's Cathedral. In the afternoon he was at a religious meeting and finished the day in the company of some friends, telling them that he had never had such a wonderful Easter. Then, suddenly, as he was moving about the room he fell down. When his friends ran to help him he was already dead. His wish had been granted; the mystic of the evolution died on the day of the resurrection.

Bibliography

Francis Libermann

Works: *Écrits spirituels*, Paris, 1891.
Biographies: L. Grunenwald, *The Venerable Father F. M. Libermann*, Detroit, 1902.
G. Lee, *The Life of the Venerable Francis Libermann*, London, 1937.
E. Leen, *The Voice of a Priest*, London, 1947.
H. Walker Homan, *Star of Jacob*, New York, 1953.
Pierre Blanchard, *Le Vénérable Libermann*, Études Carmélitaines, 1960.

Hermann Cohen

C. Sylvain, *Life of Father Hermann*, New York, 1925.
Letters in the possession of Dom J. M. Beaurin.

Isaac Thomas Hecker

Biographies: Walter Elliott, *The Life of Father Hecker*, New York, 1891.
Katherine Burton, *Celestial Homespun*, New York, 1943. (Fictionalized).
Joseph McSorley, *Father Hecker and His Friends*, New York, 1952.
Vincent F. Holden, *The Yankee Paul*, Vol. 1, Milwaukee, 1958.

Contardo Ferrini

Bede Jarrett, *Contardo Ferrini*, St. Louis, 1933.

Elisabeth Leseur

F. Leseur, *Vie d'Elisabeth Leseur*, new ed. Paris, 1954.
A Wife's Story: The Journal of Elisabeth Leseur, translated by V.M., London, 1921.

Charles de Foucauld

Meditations of a Hermit, ed. by R. Bazin, New York, 1930.
R. Bazin, *Charles de Foucauld*, New York, 1923.
T. Lloyd, *Desert Call*, London, 1948.
A. Fremantle, *Desert Calling*, New York, 1949.

Hieronymus Jaegen

F. Delvaux, *Banquier Mystique*, Paris, 1939.
E. Mossmaier, *Hieronymus Jaegen*, Paderborn, 1959.

Maximilian Kolbe

M. Winowska, *Our Lady's Fool*, Westminster, Md., 1951.

Edel Quinn

L. J. Suenens, *Edel Quinn*, Dublin, 1954.

Pierre Teilhard de Chardin

The Phenomenon of Man, New York, 1959.
The Divine Milieu, New York, 1960.
Nicolas Corte, *Pierre Teilhard de Chardin*, New York, 1960.